The Springer Series on Death and Suicide

ROBERT KASTENBAUM, Ph.D., Series Editor

Arthur Freeman, EdD, ABPP, is professor in the Department of Psychology at LaSalle University in Philadelphia, and clinical professor of psychiatry in the Department of Psychiatry of the University of Medicine and Dentistry of New Jersey-School of Osteopathic Medicine. He is also senior consultant and supervisor at the Center for Cognitive Therapy at the University of Pennsylvania. He has published many books on psychotherapy. Dr. Freeman's works have been translated into Chinese, Dutch, German, Italian, Japanese, Spanish, and Swedish.

Dr. Freeman completed his undergraduate and early graduate work at New York University, and his later graduate and doctoral work at Teachers College, Columbia University.

He is a diplomate in clinical psychology of the American Board of Professional Psychology, a diplomate in cognitive behavior therapy of the American Board of Behavioral Psychology, a Fellow of the American Psychological Association, divisions 12 (Clinical Psychology), 29 (Psychotherapy), and 43 (Family Psychology) and of the Pennsylvania Psychological Association. He was awarded the Rudolf Dreikurs Distinguished Lectureship for 1990 by the Adler School of Professional Psychology, Chicago.

He has been a visiting professor at the Universities of Gothenburg and Umeå in Sweden and at Shanghai Second Medical University in the People's Republic of China. He has lectured internationally and presented seminars and workshops in 15 countries over the past 12 years.

Mark A. Reinecke, Ph.D., is assistant professor of clinical psychiatry and director of the Center for Cognitive Therapy at the University of Chicago School of Medicine. He is also a licensed psychologist and is on the faculty of the School of Social Service Administration and the Program in Mental Health Research at the University of Chicago. His areas of interest center on childhood depression and suicide, anxiety disorders, and cognitive mediation of adjustment to chronic illness. Dr. Reinecke has lectured internationally on cognitive therapy, and recently served as visiting assistant professor at the Graduate School of Psychology of National Chengchi University, Taipei, Taiwan.

COGNITIVE THERAPY OF SUICIDAL BEHAVIOR

A MANUAL FOR TREATMENT

ARTHUR FREEMAN, EdD, ABPP
MARK A. REINECKE, PhD

 Springer Publishing Company • New York

Springer Publishing Company, Inc.
536 Broadway
New York, NY   10012-3955

93 94 95 96 97 / 5 4 3 2 1

Library of Congress Cataloging-in-Publication Data
Freeman, Arthur M.
    Cognitive therapy of suicidal behavior : A manual for treatment /
Arthur Freeman and Mark Reinecke.
        p.   cm.—(The Springer series on death and suicide ; v. 12)
    Includes bibliographical references and index.
    ISBN 0-8261-6500-1
    1. Suicidal behavior—Treatment.   2. Cognitive therapy.
I. Reinecke, Mark.   II. Title.   III. Series.
    [DNLM: 1. Cognitive Therapy—methods.   2. Suicide—prevention &
control.   W1 SP685P v. 12 1993 / HV 6546 F855c 1993]
RC569.F72   1993
616.85'84450651—dc20
DNLM/DLC
for Library of Congress   92-48342
                                                               CIP

Printed in the United States of America

Contents

Preface

The willful act of self-destruction has implications not only for the individual who has made the attempt (whether complete or not), but for the significant others who are the survivors. These include parents, children, spouses, extended family, friends, neighbors, co-workers and colleagues, students, fellow patients, therapists, physicians, police, and clergy (Dunne, McIntosh, & Dunne-Maxim, 1987).

By its very nature, suicide is a crisis situation inasmuch as it presents a situation of life-threatening proportions. Slaiku (1990) offers a four-part definition of crisis as "a temporary state of upset and disorganization, characterized chiefly by an individual's inability to cope with a particular situation using customary methods of problem solving, and by the potential for a radically positive or negative outcome" (p. 15). The first part of the definition addresses the transient nature of crises. For some individuals, the suicidal crisis is immediate, transient, and temporary, and when the crisis is resolved the individual becomes less suicidal. For others, however, the crisis may become chronic and involve years of upset, life crises, and suicidal thinking. These actions may, in fact, become a way of life.

The individual's ability to cope, the focus of the second and third parts of Slaiku's definition, revolves around the issue of problem-solving ability. By using their common or traditional techniques for personal coping, suicidal individuals find themselves overwhelmed. Their traditional techniques are simply not adequate to the present task requirements. They then see suicide as a point of relief, surcease, or, at least, a reasonable option. The final part of the definition involves the potential for rather weighty consequences. We would certainly deem death to be well within the definition of weighty consequences.

Normally, when individuals are in a crisis situation and their present resources are not adequate to the task, they may call on little-used reserves of personal fortitude and spirit or on the resources of their social network. In addition, they may search for or create systems of support to assist them through the crisis. Depressed and hopeless individuals may perceive few resources (internal or external) that they can call on to assist them in dealing with their hopelessness. Whether the perceptions of hopelessness are consensually validated is a moot point. If one has a supportive family system, good friends, or a therapist to call on, various life crises can be more easily weathered. If not, then death may seem to be the only option of will, or the option that results from a loss of control.

Although crisis may be a response to a specific and identifiable event or circumstance (Slaiku, 1990), we must also include the personal perceptions of the event and beliefs of the individual in the attempt to understand the crisis situation. Research on life stress suggests that death of a spouse is rated as the most powerful stressor, and can be a standard against which other life stressors are measured. The death of a close family member is rated as 5 on the scale and the death of a friend as 7. In the case of an embittered estranged couple, the death of a terminally ill spouse, death may be a solution to long-term stress, bringing with it relief and financial security. Or, in the case of a terminally ill spouse, death may be prayed for out of love and caring, and may be seen as a great relief because of the peace it will bring to the terminally ill partner.

Slaiku (1990, p. 98) concludes, "Short-term, time-limited therapy is the treatment of choice in crisis situations." In this respect, the active, directive, goal-oriented, structured, collaborative, and problem-solving nature of cognitive therapy make it the ideal treatment model.

In this book we have tried to distill several decades of research and personal experience into a readable and useful clinical text. We have tried to structure it as a treatment manual that will, we hope, offer a goal, a direction, and the techniques for reaching that goal. Some writings never seem to end; this has been one of them. We have finally brought it to an end and into the hands of our publisher so that you, the reader, can, it is hoped, profit from our work. It was difficult to end this project for many of the reasons that we will be presenting and exploring in this book. First and foremost was the need to try to say everything that there was to say about the topic and the concern that if we left something out, it might be the very point that could mean life or death to a patient. We have not said it all. We have not ended up by including all of the material about suicide that we had included in earlier drafts of this book. We have tried to offer a cognitive therapy treatment model, not a review of all extant treatments of suicide. Nor do we suggest that the cognitive approach is the only approach that one should use. To the contrary, we hope that this book will add to the readers' therapeutic repertoire. For this reason, we apologize in advance for the omission of theories and techniques that have been omitted. This was not done to slight any theory, theorist, school of therapy, or individual.

The book is divided into two parts. The first part, composed of chapters 1 to 5, deals with the theoretical, historical, empirical, and conceptual model of the cognitive therapy of suicidal behavior. Chapters 6 to 8 focus on the clinical applications of the model with various populations. Chapter 1 offers an introduction to suicidal behavior in general. It will serve to conceptualize the act of suicide within a framework that will be addressed in the following chapters. In chapter 2 the cognitive therapy model is introduced. The basic theory underlying the model and the research supporting the model is described. Various other theoretical views of suicide are discussed and reconceptualized within the cognitive model. Chapter 3 deals with the important issue of assessment. As a data-oriented model, the cognitive therapy strategy is based on the collection of as much relevant data as possible. Because of the connection of suicidal behavior with depression, the assessment of the ideation and behavior of the suicidal patient cannot be easily separated from the hopelessness of the depressive. Chapter 4 offers a description and discussion of the cognitive techniques. Starting with a conceptual focus, the reader is taken from the point of developing a conceptualization to the development of a treatment strategy to the implementation of that strategy through specific interventions. The material in chapter 5 expands the repertoire of interventions by introducing the predominantly behavioral techniques. The problems of resistance, termination, and relapse prevention, all essential issues, are addressed here. Chapter 6 begins the clinical application material. The treatment of children, adolescents, families, and the significant others of suicidal patients is dealt with here. Chapters 7 and 8 focus on the treatment of high-risk individuals and on factors that may serve to exacerbate the suicidal risk.

Many people have been instrumental in the development and completion of this book. The primary person is Barbara Watkins, former vice-president of Springer Publishing Company. Barbara has had the patience of a saint. Her careful reading of the manuscript in its various incarnations has been extremely helpful. Her encouragement was very important. Robert J. Kastenbaum, Series Editor, has made many helpful and important suggestions for both the content and format of this book. We are proud to be part of the Springer Series on Death and Suicide.

Aaron T. Beck, MD, has been a supporter and inspiration for both of us. His early pioneering work in the cognitive therapy treatment of depression and suicide has been of incalculable importance to psychotherapists. It is on this solid foundation that our work is based. His more recent work in the treatments of anxiety, personality disorders, and substance abuse are further examples of his theoretical and clinical brilliance.

Our students have over the years asked the difficult questions that forced us to push the limits of our therapy model, which helped us to develop the strategies and techniques described in this book. Finally, our patients have come to us for help, burdened with their hopelessness, emotional or physical pain, depression, and anxiety. We hope that our concern for their well-being and our clinical interventions have helped them to be less burdened and less pained and to develop the skills needed to cope more effectively with their lives so that death by their own hand is, at most, a distant option.

Foreword by Albert Ellis

My first reading of this book led me to conclude rapidly that it is amazingly comprehensive and complete and omits practically nothing of importance in regard to its title, *Cognitive Therapy of Suicidal Behavior*. Well, I was wrong. As Drs. Freeman and Reinecke aptly note in their Epilogue, in no way could they have included all the important material in the field of suicidology and its treatment without producing a vast and probably unreadable volume. So, guided by an astute editor, they have cut this book down to practical proportions.

Still, they have done a remarkable job. They cover their chosen subject almost from A to Z, including the theory and practice of cognitive-behavioral therapy, the main causes of suicide, the application of cognitive and behavioral methods to suicidal individuals, and therapy with high-risk populations. In each of these areas they cite many research studies and come up with a number of specific therapy techniques that are original or unusual. All this is done in a relatively brief, yet thorough manner. Their material is well selected, and major omissions are hard to note.

Cognitive therapy, as used in this book, however, does omit some of the important elements of rational-emotive therapy (RET), so let me briefly add some of its emotive-cognitive aspects of treating suicidal individuals by summarizing a single-session case that I reported in *Individual Psychology* (1989, 45, 75–80).

Helen G. was an attractive, 27-year-old woman who was referred to me for consultation after she had seen one of our trainees at the Institute for Rational-Emotive Therapy in New York and was seriously threatening to kill herself. She was a resident in obstetrics and gynecology at a leading New York hospital, but was so chronically depressed that she was failing at her residency. She also had lost her last three lovers, all of whom she really liked, because they all felt that she was "too nutty" and would not make a good wife. She was very confused and found herself "all over the place." She had extreme panic states, several phobias, and a dire need to be approved of and loved by significant others. She thought that she was "radically different" from all other people. She was still very upset about the suicide, two years ago, of her younger sister—who was also bright, talented, and very attractive but had suddenly, "without any good reason," deliberately taken an overdose of sleeping pills. Like her sister, Helen considered herself a "hopeless failure," threatened to commit suicide, and could easily do so because she had access to several lethal drugs and knew how to use them.

A real rough case! I didn't exactly look forward with great joy to seeing Helen and (possibly) heading her off at the pass. But I kept my trepidation within normal bounds by using RET on myself and convincing myself that even if, at the very worst, I did not deter this client from suicide, I could still accept myself as person. According to RET, such a failure would not make me a rotten therapist; but one who had merely failed this time. Even if I generally failed at therapy (which, of course, I generally didn't), I would still not be a Failure with a capital F—nor would I be an incompetent person.

So, knowing in advance that I was to see Helen in a suicidal state and using RET vigorously on myself, I saw that consulting with her would not be like battling the Devil to a fatal "fare-thee-well." Indeed, I began to see my forthcoming encounter with Helen as a fascinating challenge and as a session (or two or three) to look forward to. My acute worry actually turned to, first, due concern for Helen's life and, second, excited anticipation about seeing her.

Probably because of my new challenge-filled attitude, I enjoyed my session with Helen from its first new minute onward. I decided—yes, decided—to see her as an individual with great potential rather than as a grim (and "dangerous") basket case. I focused on her possibly competent and enjoyable future rather than on her gory present and past. I imagined the good she might, with my help, do well for herself and others; and I saw her life-style, up to the date of our encounter, as benighted and invalid but definitely changeable. I was (probabilistically, not dogmatically) sure that she could restructure her disordered thinking (what Alfred Adler called her "private sense" rather than her "common sense") and come to see herself as a helpful, self-striving, and socially interested individual rather than as an incompetent who hardly deserved to continue her existence.

From the start I took an RET-oriented, highly *encouraging* attitude toward Helen. I tried to show her that she fortunately (partly because of her heredity) had most of the attributes for a good life—intelligence, ability to work toward a long-term goal, desire to relate intimately, and good looks. I joked about the discrepancy between her having all these assets and her paradoxical tendency to ignore these traits and (because of her perfectionism) put herself down. She easily laughed at my saying that the Martians, if they came to visit us on earth (and were sane!) would die laughing at her saying that she was no good when, by objective standards, she was really so good. When she responded with genuine mirth to my humorous sallies, I immediately congratulated her on her humor and remarked, "Anyone who can laugh as easily as you can at the same time she is plotting and scheming to kill herself really has a sense of humor! Too bad that you won't let yourself be around very long to keep enjoying it!"

As soon as Helen indicated that "life hardly seems worth it and I might just as well end it all"—which she said right at the start of our session—I just showed her that I wasn't personally intimidated by her suicidal tendencies. I respected her *right* to kill herself, while showing her that I thought she was damned foolish if she exerted that right. I told her—half humorously and half seriously—that death, nonexistence, would be for a long, long time, while accepting herself with her failings could be done swiftly and would leave her 50 or so more enjoyable years.

Although I only saw Helen once, I used several common techniques of rational-emotive therapy with her. Cognitively, I actively disputed her ideas that she had to be perfect and wasn't ever permitted to fail at important tasks and love affairs. I showed her, very strongly, the disadvantages of prematurely ending her life and the advantages of continuing it. I quickly outlined and combatted her demand for certainty—her irrational conviction that she *must* under all conditions do well and be loved. I pointed out that, logically, she was opting for just about the only certainty that exists for humans—death. But what a negative certainty. What a Pyrrhic victory! How silly to choose *that* certainty when she could choose, with a high degree of probability, to succeed if she persistently *worked* at doing so. I appealed to her native intelligence to act *wisely* in her own interest and to preserve her life so that she could thereby help herself and contribute to the social good. I highlighted her low frustration tolerance: The crazy idea that just because she *now* was in emotional pain, she thought that she was forced to end her life and all *future* happiness, forever.

Emotionally, I used encouragement and humor; and perhaps

best of all, accepted Helen *with* her foolish behavior and thereby gave her what RET calls "unconditional acceptance." But I also taught her, briefly but forcefully, that she could always accept herself *if* she stopped giving a global rating to herself or her "essence" and only rated her traits and performance in relation to the values she *preferred* to actualize. I also showed her that no human—not even Hitler—is subhuman or damnable; and that she never had to denigrate her *self* or her *personhood*, no matter how bad her behavior was. Humorously again, I convinced her that even if she killed herself she would not be a fool or a worm but only a *person* who was acting foolishly and wormily (that is, against her own interest).

Behaviorally, though I knew I would probably not see Helen again—because I referred her back to my associate who was her regular therapist—I gave her three homework assignments: (1) To agree that she would call her therapist or call me before she actually tried any real suicide attempt; (2) to look for and write down all absolutistic and perfectionistic musts and shoulds that led her to become depressed and suicidal; (3) and to sing to herself, at least three times a day during the next few weeks, some of my rational humorous songs, such as:

Whine, Whine, Whine!
(Tune: *Yale Whiffenpoof Song* by Guy Scull)
I cannot have all of my wishes filled—
Whine, whine, whine!
I cannot have every frustration stilled—
Whine, whine, whine!
Life really owes me the things that I miss,
Fate has to grant me the things that I miss,
Since I must settle for less than this—
Whine, whine, whine!

(Lyrics by Albert Ellis. Copyright 1977 by Institute for Rational-Emotive Therapy)

I only saw Helen this one time, sent her out of the session laughing, and was delighted to hear her say, at the end, "It was a pleasure talking to you. I really enjoyed it!" She returned to the Institute therapist who referred her to me for consultation and I received, a few weeks later, a note from this therapist thanking me for my intervention, stating that Helen had completely given up her suicidal ideas after talking with me and indicating that she and the therapist were now working satisfactorily on her long-standing problems of depression.

Back to Drs. Freeman and Reinecke's *Cognitive Therapy for Suicidal Behavior*. It is not exactly perfectly comprehensive and inclusive, but it goes a long way toward achieving this ideal. Perhaps there is an even better book than this on the cause and treatment of suicidal behavior—but I doubt it.

ALBERT ELLIS, PhD
President, *Institute for Rational-Emotive Therapy*

1

Introduction to Suicidal Behavior

Suicide may be a light matter, the recourse of anyone who has suffered some slight rebuff, an act that occurs constantly in tribes. It may be the highest and noblest act a wise man can perform. The very tale of it, on the other hand, may be a matter of incredible mirth, and the act itself impossible to conceive as a human possibility. Or it may be a crime punishable by law, or regarded as a sin against the gods.

—Ruth Benedict, Patterns of Culture

Suicide, whether it involves an active act of self-destruction or a passive act of allowing or hastening one's demise, has meaning not only for the patient and the patient's significant others, but for the therapist as well. Even the most experienced therapist reacts with an adrenaline surge when it becomes clear that a patient has placed a time limit on life, "If things don't change by the end of this week, I cannot go on," or when the patient has great difficulty in controlling impulses, "I can't stop myself. I sit at the table with the knife pressed to my belly and start pressing in," or when the patient wishes to punish someone, "I'm waiting until he graduates, and then, on the night of his party, I'll kill myself," or when the patient perceives an anniversary date as an auspicious moment to die, "It was a year ago that my husband died, it has been too long without him." Given the severity of the consequence, it is essential for the therapist to have an understanding of the causes, assessment, process, and treatment of suicidal ideation and action so that effective problem solving can be initiated immediately.

The literature on suicide has grown rather quickly over the past

1

several years. Part of the impetus for the growth of epidemiological and treatment studies has been the reported increase in suicide among children and adolescents. The *Journal of Suicide and Life Threatening Behaviors* and the newsletter of the American Association of Suicidology have been developed to offer continuing information for mental health professionals. The suicidal act has been the focus of several television shows, both dramatic and documentary, and has been written about in the popular press. Clearly, suicide is a topic of great importance. Despite decades of intensive research and clinical effort, suicide continues to be one of the most troubling problems of our society and represents an intransigent difficulty for mental health professionals.

Often, suicide and depression are seen as synonymous terms, or, at least, problems that are inextricably bound. Several studies have documented an association between suicide and depression. Although estimates of the percentage of suicidal persons who are depressed varies, there is a general consensus of opinion that a relationship exists between depression and suicide attempt or completion. The disparity between these research findings appears to stem from differences in sample selection, and the manner in which "depression" and "suicidality" were assessed. One major factor contributing to the confusion in the literature is that "depression" is a conceptually vague term. It can refer to the experiencing of a sad affect, a pervasive mood, a clinical syndrome, or a disorder. The study by Silver, Bohnert, Beck, & Marcus (1971) is exemplary in this regard. They examined the relationship between suicide and depression in a sample of 45 adults who had been hospitalized after a suicide attempt. Briefly, they found that 80% of their sample reported feeling moderately or severely depressed as indicated by their scores on the Beck Depression Inventory (BDI, Beck, Ward, Mendelson, Mock, & Erbaugh, 1961). As only 40% of the patients in their sample received a primary diagnosis of affective disorder, they concluded that suicidal patients, regardless of their primary diagnosis, are likely to be dysphoric at the time of their suicide attempt. Moreover, the severity of patients' depression was correlated with the intensity of their wish to die. As such, the authors concluded that the "primary diagnosis may be misleading in assessing the presence of depression in the suicide attempter." Although this study did not address the issue of the means by which depression contributes to an increased risk of suicide, it highlighted the importance of the relationship between depression and suicidal thoughts and action. The practicing clinician is well aware of the relationship between depression and suicide without resorting to the literature. The experience of working with depressed patients will quickly yield thoughts of self–recrimination for deeds done or not done, thoughts of personal worthlessness in the abstract and in relation to others, and negative views of the changeability of one's personal plight.

Suicidal behavior occurs within a sociocultural milieu, and is no doubt influenced by a range of physical and biochemical factors. It is, nonetheless, primarily a state of mind. That is, each suicidal act begins in the mind of the individual. It is there we must go if we are to understand and resolve this problem. Moreover, suicidal thoughts and acts are highly personal. Although commonalities can be identified among suicidal persons, it has become increasingly clear that there is no single "suicidal personality" nor one type of suicidal person. As such, it is necessary in attempting to conceptualize suicidality to use both idiographic and nomothetic approaches. Cognitive therapy speaks to the issue of specific differences between suicidal and nonsuicidal patients, and allows us to develop treatment programs tailored to the needs of individual patients.

As noted earlier, suicidal thinking or actions do not accompany every case of depression. Clinical observation and study from any theoretical perspective would show that clinically depressed persons systematically tend to view themselves, their world, and their future in an unrealistically negative manner. The individual's cognitive and perceptual processes are characterized by a sensitivity to several reactions including feelings of loss or feelings of abandonment. Suicidality, in turn, is believed to stem from consequent feelings of hopelessness, in conjunction with a belief that current difficulties are unendurable, or from a desire to manipulate or rapidly gain control of a frustrating or threatening situation. These difficulties are compounded by a lack of alternative supports or coping mechanisms. As such, the purpose of suicide is to seek a solution from what is felt to be intolerable psychological pain. Most often, suicidal patients feel hopeless and helpless. That is, they feel incapable of resolving their dilemma, and do not believe that others will be capable of assisting them. Suicidal patients typically view their world in a "constricted" manner, in that they are relatively incapable of identifying alternative courses of action, or of rationally examining the validity of their belief that their problems are serious and unendurable. Cognitive theories, then, incorporate both intrapsychic and interpersonal factors in describing and explaining suicidal thoughts and behavior. Like the parable of the Indian blind man and the elephant, diverse perspectives often yield significantly different perspectives on the suicidal act.[1]

General studies of suicide cover many areas from epidemiology to the psychoanalysis of individual cases. The current research focuses on the various sources of suicidal wishes and behavior (e.g., biochemical, psychological, and sociological), the definition and nomenclature of suicidal behavior, and the prediction of suicide. In this introductory chapter, we briefly present some of the diverse theoretical or ideological approaches. In chapter 2 we present a cognitive therapy conceptualization and the theoretical basis for cognitive therapy treatment.

Genetic and Biochemical Perspective

Pedigree studies have been used since the 19th century to demonstrate the heritability of suicidal behavior. Recent studies attempt to control for the relative contributions of family and environment including learned behavior, life-stress events, and psychiatric diagnoses (Roy, 1986; Tsuang, 1977). Two such studies, of Amish families and Danish adoptees and their relatives, have received attention for their contributions to the theory of a genetic predisposition to suicide.

Egeland and Sussex (1985) studied affective disorders and suicide among families of the Older Order Amish. This group is culturally isolated and buffered from many of the stressors of modern life associated with suicide risk. There are almost no incidences of drug or alcohol abuse, unemployment, or reported loneliness in the community. Suicide is also a taboo among the Amish.

Information gathered through structured interviews (Schedule for Affective Disorders and Schizophrenia, Endicott & Spitzer, 1978) with relatives of the 26 suicides verified between 1880 and 1980 yielded diagnoses. Ninety-two percent of the suicides were diagnosed as having incidence of depression, bipolar affective disorder, and other affective disorders. Although suicides were overrepresented in families with histories of major affective disorders, families with the severest cases of depression were not necessarily those with the highest incidence of suicide. There was, however, a clustering of suicides in family pedigrees (Egeland & Hostetter, 1983; Egeland & Sussex, 1985). Four Amish pedigrees accounted for 73% of the suicides. These four family groups comprised only 16% of the community's total population. The pattern of suicide in kinship lines in this closed community suggests a genetic component to suicide. It also underscores the importance of separating out the inheritance of depression from the inheritance of suicidal behavior.

Strong evidence of a genetic contribution to suicidal behavior comes from the Danish adoption studies of Kety (1986). This study of 5483 Danish adoptees found 15 suicides among 381 biologic relatives of depressed adoptees but only 1 among the 168 adoptive relatives. Only three suicides occurred among the adoptive and biologic relatives of the matched, nondepressed adoptee control group. Another Danish study found 12 cases of suicide among 269 biologic relatives of 57 adoptees who committed suicide. No case of suicide was found among the adoptees' 148 adopted relatives. It is hypothesized that the genetic component in suicide might involve a tendency toward impulsive behavior, not just depression. Brain biochemistry would, presumably, reflect a genetic predisposition for suicide, and several biochemical abnormalities have been noted in suicidal patients.

Serotonin, for example, has received much publicity as a neurotransmitter associated with suicide, aggression, and impulsive behavior. It is hypothesized that serotonin deficiency occurs in people prone to impulsive behavior and when they become depressed, they are likely to attempt suicide. Research on serotonin and its precursors and products was triggered by the findings of Asberg, Traskman, and Thosen (1976) that 40% of a group of depressed patients with lower than normal levels of a metabolic product of serotonin (5-hydroxyindoleacetic acid, or 5-HIAA) had attempted suicide. Only 15% of depressed patients with normal levels of 5-HIAA had attempted suicide, suggesting that monoamine neurotransmitters may play a role in suicidal behavior. Regardless of the diagnosis they had received, suicide attempters appear to have lower cerebrospinal levels of 5-HIAA than normal controls (Van Praag, 1982). Our ability to interpret this observation is complicated, however, by the fact that reduced cerebrospinal and plasma levels of 5-HIAA have also been found among aggressive patients, suggesting that this may not be a specific marker for suicide. Rather, as Depue and Spoont (1986) argue (p. 48), "perhaps suicidal and aggressive behavior are merely different endpoint indicators of a more central trait such as impulsivity, which becomes more evident under states of strong affect (e.g., depression or anger)."

This interpretation of the research literature is consistent with observations by Asberg, Schalling, Rydin, and Traskman-Bendz (1981) suggesting that low 5-HIAA concentrations are not associated with suicidal behavior in general but with violent suicide attempts. Serotonin, then, might be viewed as mediating a "behavioral dimension of constraint" or impulsivity (Depue & Spoont, 1986; Nordstrom & Asberg, 1992).

Sociological Perspective

Durkheim's seminal work, *Suicide* (1897), posits a sociological explanation of suicide and classifies it in terms of the individual's relationship to the social group. Altruistic suicide is self-sacrifice for the sake of the group, such as suicide missions completed by the Islamic Jihad. In egoistic suicide, society requires that the individual assume responsibility for his or her actions. It is a way out of a personal predicament, and may reflect feelings of separation from society and social supports. Adolescent suicide may best represent this category. Anomic suicide results from sudden shifts in the individual's relationship to the group, as occurs with life events such as the birth of a child, job loss, or death of a spouse and may be ascribed to an "identity loss." Finally there is fatalistic suicide, which derives from "excessive regulation" (Shneidman, 1968). The legacy of Durkheim's work lies in contemporary correlations between suicide rates and the social condition (Maris, 1975).

Psychoanalytic Perspective

Psychological explanations of depression and suicide have been dominated for years by Freud's theory of melancholia (1917), and his writings on thanatos and the death instinct (Litman & Tabachnik, 1968; Sandler & Joffe, 1965). According to these early formulations, a mourner suffers the conscious loss of a loved object. The melancholic individual, however, suffers the unconscious loss, which impoverishes the ego. The anger and aggression felt toward the lost loved object is then directed at the self and is manifested as self-reproach, self-hatred, and possibly self-destruction. Psychoanalytic explanations of suicide derived from this paradigm of introverted hostility ascribe meanings to suicidal acts such as rebirth or reunion with a lost object (Dorpat, 1973; Fenichel, 1945), revenge (Gabbard, 1990), or anxiety avoidance (Fromm-Reichmann, 1959). Fromm-Reichmann (1959) states, "On the one hand, they (the suicidal thoughts) are the final conscious expression of his ambivalence against himself; on the other hand, they unconsciously mean, at the same time, murdering impulses against the incorporated person, who, being identical with him, is supposed to be killed with him if he commits suicide" (p. 281).

Menninger (1933) believed that suicide involved three wishes: the wish to kill, the wish to be killed, and the wish to die. Suicide was for Menninger an act of murder, both of self and of the internalized object.

Religious Perspective

The traditional interpretation of the sixth commandment states "Thou shalt not kill." Another definition of the commandment has been translated as "thou shalt not murder." Western Judeo-Christian tradition considers self-murder a direct violation of that law though the Bible does not directly proscribe suicide (Maris, 1981). The Old Testament reports four cases of suicide (Samson, Saul, Abimelech, and Ahitophel). Ahitophel was, in fact, ceremonially buried in the family vault (II Samuel, xvii, 23). Samson dramatically ended his life, along with the lives of his captors. In the New Testament there is no condemnation of suicide (Williams, 1957). The suicide of Judas is a matter of great shame fitting justice (Maris, 1981). The first Christian prohibition of suicide is sometimes attributed to the Council of Arles, A.D. 452. By the second Council of Orleans, A.D. 533, suicide was considered worse than any other crime (Williams, 1957, p. 247). The teachings of various churches have, over the years, continued to develop according to their interpretation of the sixth commandment.

In general, suicide in predominantly Catholic countries is lower than the rate of suicide in predominantly Protestant countries. The available data suggests that Jewish rates of suicide fluctuate, but are generally lower than that of either Catholics or Protestants (Maris, 1981).

The Bhagavad-Gita identifies the auspicious moment for the individual to die, ". . . either accidentally or by arrangement." The Hindu view of the continuing cycle of life and death means that when one suicides, the body dies, but the soul ". . . accepts new material bodies, giving up the old and useless ones" (p. 104). The exact nature of the new body will, of course, depend on how one has lived one's life. There is, however, "considerable contradiction regarding the morality of suicide in the sacred writings" (Dublin, 1963, p. 110).

Many were horrified at the self-immolations of Buddhist monks who utilized suicide as a part of a powerful protest against the government policies in South Vietnam. In sharp contrast, is the Islamic prohibition against self-destruction under any conditions. Giving up one's life in a religious battle is acceptable, however, One may die with respect as a warrior in battle but not a suicide.

As with the ethnological view, an understanding of religious rules about life, death, and suicide are essential for understanding a client's behavior (Goss & Reed, 1971; Brandt, 1975).

Behavioral Perspective

Researchers employing learned helplessness models of depression (Abramson, Seligman, & Teasdale, 1978) have viewed depressed patients' feelings of hopelessness as stemming from beliefs in the uncontrollability of both positive and negative outcomes. They proposed that when individuals are confronted with uncontrollable events, they make attributions as to the cause of their predicament. These attributions, in turn, mediate their expectations of future noncontingency and their consequent feelings of depression.

Abramson and her colleagues (1978) postulate that these attributions are made along three orthogonal dimensions: internal versus external, chronic or stable versus time limited, and global versus specific. Individuals who tend to make internal, stable, and global attributions for events are believed to be at greater risk for developing depression. In short, to be depressed, one must anticipate that one will not be able to effect important outcomes in the future.

Research bearing on the attributional style of depressed and nondepressed persons has generally been consistent with this model. When individuals make "internal" attributions for failures or undesired events (i.e., it is "because of me or something I did" rather than something in the environment) there is a decrease in self-esteem and an associated increase in dysphoria. This is most common when the attributions are also chronic and general—as when the person believes that the aversive events were due to some intrinsic, unchangeable character flaws on their part. In contrast, depression is less likely when the attributions are unstable and specific—as when a person believes the aversive event occurred because of something they did (or did not do) that might be changed in the future. An example would be of two students, each of whom received an F on an exam. The one who believed it was because they "were stupid . . . and really didn't have what it takes to be in college" would, presumably, become more depressed than the student who believed it was "because I didn't study. . . . I'll just have to study before the next exam." Janoff-Bulman and Hecker (1988) have labeled these "characterological" and "behavioral" self-blame, respectively. Characterological self-blame is characterized by attributions that are internal, chronic, and general, and is frequently accompanied by an increased sense of vulnerability (as there is nothing one can do to change one's lack of an essential character trait) and a belief that "I got what I deserved." Behavioral self-blame, in contrast, is associated with attributions that are internal, unstable, and specific. Hence, there is an implicit possibility that there may be something one can do, behaviorally, to change the aversive situation. There is, in short, a sense of control and hope that serves to reduce feelings of vulnerability and helplessness.

Vulnerability to Suicidal Thoughts

For most individuals, in most situations, there is a high degree of control of thoughts and actions. Certain impulsive acts or reactions are moderated by the need for avoidance of pain or punishment, or the need for positive response. There are, however, certain situations or circumstances that have the effect of increasing vulnerability to both external and internal stimuli or, conversely, lowering the threshold of control. This is true of a broad range of psychological disorders including but not limited to stress, suicidal behavior, marital discord, eating disorders, substance abuse, and depression. Each individual has a threshold for control. If we picture this as a scale from 0 to 100, an individual may have a threshold of 20, indicating a fairly low threshold of control. The individual is able to cope with stressors that are between 0 and 30. When the threshold is exceeded, the organism goes on "automatic," that is, voluntary control is overridden by the autonomic system trying to help the organism to survive. For many individuals, the threshold is adequate to take into account most life stressors. The vulnerability factors serve to decrease the threshold so that a life event that was coped with quite successfully in the past now represents an overwhelming circumstance. Patients are often unaware of the situations and circumstances that appear to make them more vulnerable to stimuli to which at other times they would not respond. For some individuals the threshold-reducing stressor may be limited and transient. Given a brief period, the stressor is removed (or ends), and the individual may once again be in control. We hear this from the patient who comes to therapy and tells the therapist that, "I had some bad moments this week. There were four times that the idea of killing myself seemed to be the only way out. I (took a nap/ate dinner/called my friend/took an aspirin) and later it seemed to be better." For other individuals the lowered threshold is a surprise, and they come to therapy quite frightened by the proximity of the suicidal option. For yet other patients who enter therapy because of the suicidal ideation, the therapeutic relationship, the regularity of the therapy, and the warmth and positive regard of the therapist are often adequate to increase or restore the threshold to a higher point. When the therapist is unavailable or on vacation, the threshold may drop precipitously, and the patient becomes suicidal once again.

For other patients, the lowered threshold involves the individual effecting a response that is outside of normal limits or evidences a loss of control. A tenet of Alcoholics Anonymous is to make members aware of the acronym HALT—hungry, angry, lonely, and tired. These are stressed as conditions under which the individual may lose control and be more prone to drink. We see these conditions as only four of several vulnerability factors. By identifying the vulnerability situation patients can be helped to both take control of their response and respond differently from the way they generally do, or to limit their negative response and maintain control. If the period of vulnerability is brief and transient the increased vulnerability makes individuals easy prey for a variety of cognitive distortions that they might otherwise ignore. After some recovery period, the threshold returns to its previous level. Individuals with high thresholds for coping (or those who are less vulnerable) are often perceived by others as the "Rock of Gibraltar" on which a family may depend for support. If situations arise that increase vulnerability (or lower threshold), this individual may succumb to stressors that they previously weathered with equanimity. At some point in life the automatic thought, "I'd be better off dead" may flash briefly through the individual's mind. At certain points it is ignored, unrecognized, or responded to with a vigorous, "That's crazy. I'm much better off alive." Yet at other times, the same thought is entertained as reasonable and worthy of serious consideration. We are at these latter times more vulnerable to the thoughts, The various vulnerability factors include the following:

1. *Acute illness*—Any illness, no matter how objectively mild, may evoke vulnerability. Dormant schema regarding dependence, helplessness, or general inability to cope can be activated by any illness ranging from a headache to a severe flu to a broken limb. Even though the illness may be transient, the effect on the individual at the point of the illness is to increase their sensitivity to thoughts of suicide.

2. *Chronic illness*—Much like the acute illness discussed previously, chronic illness has the same effect of reducing the individual's threshold for effective coping. A degenerative illness or an ongoing medical problem makes the individual more vulnerable.

3. *Aging*—With aging there also comes a tendency toward increased illness, decreased physical strength, increased vulnerability to infection, decreased activity, and the loss of peers and family through death. The individual is thus rendered more vulnerable.

4. *Personal loss*—The loss through death of a family member, friend, neighbor, or pet can render the individual more vulnerable to suicidal thinking. The loss of a limb or body part can have a similar effect. The loss of a job or home are other factors that lower the threshold for coping.

5. *Hunger*—Consumer studies have demonstrated that the worst time to shop for food is when we are hungry as we are more prone to impulse buying of food. The same is true for hunger as a vulnerability factor. There is a greater likelihood of impulsive behavior, or loss of control, which might mean acting on suicidal thoughts, wishes, or impulses.

6. *Loneliness*—The perception of being alone, whether one is isolated in a tower or in the middle of a crowd, increases vulnerability. For many suicidal individuals loneliness may predispose them to more seriously entertain the suicidal thoughts that they may, at other times, reject or ignore.

7. *Fatigue*—Being tired and having low energy may be the result of a disordered sleep pattern or a concomitant of depression. Whatever the source of the fatigue, it renders the individual less able to cope effectively with life stressors or with suicidogenic or depressogenic thoughts.

8. *New circumstances*—Moving to a new home, a new job, or a new relationship increases vulnerability. The factors of stress, fear of the unknown, loss of the familiar, and expectations for self and others all converge to lower the coping threshold.

9. *Chronic pain*—Like acute and chronic illness, the experience of chronic pain can predispose the individual toward poorer coping. This impaired coping may result in the inability to deal effectively with life stress.

10. *Limited problem-solving ability*—For some individuals, having limited or poor problem-solving ability may go unnoticed in the course of life events. If their lives are uncomplicated and straightforward, complex problem-solving skills may be unnecessary. If life becomes complicated because of personal or natural disaster, however, the limited problem-solving skills that allowed relative life comfort

may be inadequate for managing the increased stress. In these situations the individual may see suicide as an option in that their limited problem-solving ability is inadequate to generate other more appropriate solutions.

11. *Substance abuse*—The abuse of alcohol, prescription drugs, street drugs, or nicotine may be, in and of themselves, self-destructive. In addition, substance abuse may be disinhibiting so that one's good sense or problem-solving ability is impaired, and individuals once again see the suicidal option as the most easily available and appropriate for them.

12. *Anger*—Generating anger in response to real or imagined circumstance makes the individual more vulnerable. We do not see anger as being stored as in a "well of anger," but rather being constantly generated by particular cognitions or images. When beset by anger, impulse control, or reasonable function, often leaves the individual.

13. *Poor impulse control*—The individual with poor impulse control may respond to any and all stimuli without discriminating the appropriate response. The impulse control difficulty may be part of many of the previously noted factors, or be a factor separate and apart from them. For this individual, any movement in a particular direction is followed without the self-monitoring that is part of prosocial behavior.

14. *Posttraumatic stress reactions*—any major stress experience may have as a sequela a lingering reduction in the individual's normal threshold. The stressor and the subsequent reaction do not have to be of a severity that they meet the *Diagnostic and Statistic Manual* (3rd ed. rev.) (DSM III-R) criteria for posttraumatic stress disorder. As the stressor recedes into the background of experience, there will be a return of the vulnerability threshold to its previous level.

15. *Psychological vulnerability*—The individual who is depressed or anxious is more vulnerable to interpret events or reactions of others as negative. This cognitive vulnerability toward seeing events as sad or hopeless (depression), or dangerous and threatening (anxiety) causes a further spiraling of the individual into the depression or anxiety.

16. *Neurological vulnerability*—Neurological trauma or disease may render the individual unable to deal with abstractions, and to therefore see the world, experience, and the future in very concrete terms. This will negatively affect problem solving and limit the generation of options necessary for effective coping.

Types of Suicidal Behavior

There are several variations on the hoplessness theme that need to be emphasized so that the therapist can better understand and treat suicidal thinking and behavior. We would divide suicidal behavior into four broad types: hopeless suiciders, histrionic or impulsive suiciders, psychotic suiciders, and rational suiciders. None of these types is mutually exclusive with any of the others.

In the hopeless type, the patient maintains the belief that there is no hope of things improving and therefore no longer any reason for continuing life. If, for example, a patient is depressed and considers suicide but feels that before exercising the suicidal option he has 27 other options, he might be upset and periodically think of suicide, but may perceive some measure of safety in the 27 options. A second patient, also depressed, sees herself as having 91 other options before suicide. She may never think of killing herself. A third patient has eight possible options before suicide. He thinks about suicide all of the time.

If all three patients, because of world economics, personal tragedy, or cognitive distortion, have seven options vanish, the first patient would become more upset. The second patient may still be unaware of any suicidal thoughts, whereas the last patient, having exhausted all possible options, would see himself as having no choice but to commit suicide. All people have their own option list of the things that they might do in any one of a number of circumstances. For most individuals, the option of suicide never gets exercised. For others it is an infrequent and annoying presence; for still others it is a constant, persistent, though unwanted companion. For a small group, it is an option that not only becomes exercised, but may dominate their thoughts and actions for years before or subsequent to a suicide attempt. Because suicide is at the bottom of everyone's list of options, it only becomes an issue as the individual gets closer to the bottom of that list. For many patients, available options objectively appear to remain the same. The patient's perception of the available options, however, may cause them to feel very hopeless. Throughout history there have been individuals who, although suicide was directly against their religious beliefs, have chosen death by their own hand as preferable to the other alternatives that they have faced (e.g., the defenders of Masada). Even though options may be limited, most individuals continually add to their option lists so that they never reach the nadir. By seeing a small victory as a reason to continue life,

an additional option is generated. The following case will serve to illustrate the hopelessness suicider:

Les, a 35-year-old man, self-referred because of severe depression. Early in
the course of treatment, Les discussed his general hopelessness. He saw his
marriage as over, his children lost to him, his job being lost, his income lost,
debts being overwhelming, and his health failing. Although there was some
reality to each of his concerns (i.e., he was having marital problems, and his
wife threatened to return, with the children, to her parents in Oregon), his
wife wanted to maintain the relationship.

The second type of suicider is what we would label the histrionic suicider. In any group, different individuals would manifest different stimulus needs. Conceptually, this type of individual has a
high need for excitement. To understand the need, we might see
some people as perfectly content and happy to spend 2 weeks of
their vacation on a beach doing absolutely nothing. They would not
read, listen to music, walk, swim, or play. Their idea of a good time
would be to do nothing except lay in the sun and tan, or to relax by
sitting in a rowboat all day with a fishing pole. On the other end of
the scale would be those individuals for whom that type of vacation
would be anathema. Their idea of a vacation would be to travel, be
active, sight-see, or play. There would be, of course, many points between these two positions. Given the need for activity on the part of
many individuals, the therapist may see patients for whom activity
and excitement are necessary parts of their lives. When these patients
feel anxious, nervous, itchy, or bored, they will often act to self-stim-
ulate in a variety of ways such as taking drugs or alcohol in quantity,
or speeding in cars or motorcycles. These would all add to the excitement of life. The net result may very well be physical damage or even
loss of life. This individual may even use the suicide attempt as a
source of stimulation and excitement. Three case examples serve to illustrate this type of attempter.

A 27-year-old man recounted several severe suicide attempts—as labeled by a
previous therapist. He reported feeling itchy or nervous. His manner of coping with this nervousness was to do one of two things. First, he would drive
his car at great speeds, often exceeding 100 miles per hour. He reported a
great relief after these driving episodes. His second strategy for relieving his
nervousness was to drive along back roads to small highway bridges over
streams or creeks and to jump from the bridges. He would get wet and
muddy, but was never injured. If a tree trunk, large rock, or other debris
were in the stream he might be injured or killed. This excitement was
enough to take the edge off of his nervousness.

A 35-year-old women was diagnosed as having a borderline personality disorder. When she became "bored" she would sit at her kitchen table and slowly draw a knife, razor, or piece of broken glass across her forearms. She reported that the blood welling up in the cuts would ease her boredom and anxiety. She would wrap her arms in kitchen towels after the cutting, and go to the emergency department of her local hospital. On entering the emergency department with her arms wrapped in bloody towels, a major furor would ensue. The triage nurse and medical-surgical resident would quickly try to stanch the bleeding (which had often clotted), and would then contact the psychiatry resident for her admission to the psychiatry unit. After several attempts, they became used to her behavior, and would stop the bleeding and send her home. After the attempts, her "urges" and "nervousness" were lessened, and she was able to go home and not make another attempt for a while.

There are times when the hopeless patient reports a suicide attempt that leaves the therapist both extremely concerned and in wonderment. These attempts may appear so naive that the hopeless and, in these cases, hapless individuals fail to kill themselves only because they have some "guardian angel" watching over them. The next example demonstrates this type of patient.

A young women was despondent over a lost love. She made all the plans to die of asphyxiation. She closed the kitchen window tightly and stuffed kitchen towels around the door to make it airtight. She then turned on the oven and put her head in it so that she could breathe deeply of the gas. Her oven, however, was electric, and all she did was singe her hair. Her intent, however, was most serious.

Part of the overall symptom picture of the histrionic attempter is that the suicide attempts are flamboyant and may be repetitive. These attempts may be questioned as actual suicide attempts and be classified by the clinician as manipulative or motivated by needs for attention. Even when this is true, the possibility of a histrionic attempt being lethal exists, so that the ideation and attempts still need to be taken seriously.

A third group of individuals attempt suicide as a direct result of command hallucinations, or voices from within (Roy, Mazonson, & Pickar, 1984; Gardner & Cowdry, 1985). It is very important to assess whether the attempt is psychotic or not, for in psychotic individuals it is not the hopelessness per se that must be addressed but rather the voices that are prompting them to consider or act on suicide. The primary intervention with patients experiencing command hallucinations would be pharmacological (i.e., the use of antipsychotic medication that would have as its function a reduction in the delusional system and hallucinatory phenomena). In addition, however, individuals having command hallucinations can be helped to address two basic issues: the power to respond and the nature of the voices.

1. *The power to respond*—As a general therapeutic strategy, the patient with command hallucinations needs to be helped to gain power over the internal stimuli. This may take the form of helping the patient build new self-statements. For example, when the voices say, "Cut your wrists, cut your wrists," the patient can refuse and say, "I don't have to. I won't, I won't, I won't." When the voices state, "You are not worthy to live, you need to die," it would be important to help the patient to respond, "I want to live, I want to live" in an almost disputational way. In addition, the therapist needs to use self-statements and self-instructional strategies to gain more control. The therapist working with psychotic patients having command hallucinations to suicide needs to know as quickly and precisely as possible the nature of the commands. Questioning the patient very directly about the content, nature, press, and power of the thought is essential. The therapist must know who and what he or she is dealing with so that the interventions can be as direct as possible.

2. *The nature of the voices*—The therapist needs to determine the nature of the voices and, if possible, to help the patient identify them as not all-powerful so that the patient does not need to respond immediately. Pharmacological intervention is essential with the psychotic suicider. The proper medication, carefully controlled, is a vital part of the treatment plan. The danger with the medication is that unless it is carefully controlled and dispensed, the patient can hoard the medication to use it as part of a suicide attempt.

The fourth type is the rational suicider. These are the individuals who have chosen to die based on some rational consideration. These individuals rarely seek therapy to discuss their rational decision, so that therapists generally see these individuals after a failed attempt. The type of situation generally offered as the model for rational suicide is that of the terminally ill cancer patient in intractable pain. These patients come under the broad heading of "right to die." Whenever a patient demands that life-support systems be withdrawn and that extraordinary means of life-support be terminated, the intended result is that death would follow shortly. One manifestation of the right to die comes with the patient's decision to ask the medical staff to agree to affix the label DNR (do not resuscitate) on the patient's medical chart. The patient has made the choice, often in conjunction with family and significant others, that should the patient's condition deteriorate, and they need resuscitation, none would be given. No ambulance would be called to a convalescent home or care facility, and no "code" would be called to work to keep the patient alive.

Forty-one percent of the respondents to a 1975 Gallup poll said that they believed that a patient with no hope of improvement in their medical condition *and* in great pain had the moral right to commit suicide. By 1990, that figure had risen to 66%. Associations such as the Hemlock Society were founded to offer responsible alternatives to the hopeless, pain-filled life by espousing euthanasia as an alternative in such cases. *Final Exit* (Humphry, 1991) offers information for patients and their families of what he calls "self-deliverance" and "assisted suicide." The issue of an individual's right to die is a biomedical-ethical-legal issue that is still hotly debated by ethicists, physicians, legislators, theologians, hospital administrators, attorneys, and hospital risk managers. It is being actively discussed and, in many cases, tested in the courts.

We have found, however, that many suicidal individuals who think that their suicidal thoughts and actions are the most rational, reasonable, and intelligent course of action can, with therapy, see other options. We are not, however, ruling out the possibility of an individual making a rational choice and the need for the therapist possibly to aid and assist the patient in making that choice. The need for the therapist to be prepared for sensitive discussions, and for a testing of the therapist's own schema regarding death and dying is quite powerful.

Summary

Even the most experienced therapist reacts with an adrenaline surge when it becomes clear that a patient has placed a time limit on life. Several studies have documented an association between suicide and depression. Although estimates of the percentage of suicidal persons who are depressed varies, there is a general consensus of opinion that a relationship exists between depression and suicide attempt or completion.

Suicidal behavior occurs within a sociocultural milieu, and is no doubt influenced by a range of physical and biochemical factors. It is, nonetheless, primarily a state of mind. That is, each suicidal act begins in the mind of the individual. Suicide can be viewed from sociological, psychoanalytic, biological, and religious perspectives.

The relationship between early negative experiences and current symptomatology is not through the invocation of a descriptive personality structure, but is mediated by the activity of specific assumptions and schema. These beliefs are understandable within each individual's personal meaning system, and although highly personal and idiosyncratic, are available to conscious awareness. The cognitive therapy model postulates that depression may be seen as a manifestation of these enduring belief systems, assumptions, and schema.

Studies suggest that the early environment of suicidal individuals is often chaotic, and that they may be characterized by early losses. The consequent lack of continuity in parental care, emotional support, and modeling of effective coping strategies renders the child vulnerable to feelings of helplessness, and sensitive to the loss of social attachments and supports. There are certain situations that have the effect of increasing vulnerability or, conversely, lowering the threshold of response. This is true of a broad range of psychological disorders including but not limited to stress, suicidal behavior, marital discord, eating disorders, substance abuse, depression, and problem solving. Patients are often unaware of the situations that appear to make them more vulnerable to stimuli to which at other times they would not respond. For other patients, the lowered threshold involves the individual effecting a response that is outside of normal limits or evidences a loss of control.

We would divide suicidal behavior into four broad types: hopeless suiciders, histrionic or impulsive suiciders, psychotic suiciders, and rational suiciders. None of these types is mutually exclusive of the others.

The issues and problems of working with the suicidal patient are described, and the general conceptual framework for the treatment model is discussed.

Endnote

1. Each man touching a different part of the elephant "saw" the elephant from his own perspective (e.g., the man touching the ear reported that an elephant was like a broad leaf). The man touching the trunk reported the elephant to be like a great snake.

2

Theory, Research, and Practice of Cognitive Therapy

> For there is nothing either good or bad, but thinking makes it so.
>
> —*William Shakespeare,* Hamlet *(Act II, Scene 2)*

Recognizing the difficulty and potential consequences of working with the suicidal patient, it is essential to use an effective, short-term treatment model. In this regard, cognitive therapy has become an increasingly important model for our understanding of emotional and behavioral disorders. Although initially developed as a means of understanding and treating depressive disorders, it has been applied to an increasing range of problems (Beck, Emery, & Greenberg 1985; Beck, Freeman, et al., 1990; Dobson, 1988; Epstein, Schlesinger, & Dryden, 1988; Freeman & Greenwood, 1987; Freeman, Pretzer, Fleming, & Simon, 1990; Freeman, Simon, Beutler, & Arkowitz, 1989). The theory has been refined during recent years such that it has become an articulated model for the development of depressive disorders, and as a consequence, cognitive therapy is also an effective approach for the conceptualization and treatment of suicide.

Cognitive therapy is a short-term, active, directive, structured, collaborative, psychoeducational and dynamic model of psychotherapy. Developed by Aaron T. Beck (1967, 1973, 1976; Beck Rush, Shaw, & Emery, 1979), it is one of several cognitive-behavioral models of therapy. These include the works of Ellis (1958, 1962, 1979, 1984, 1985), Lazarus (1966, 1982, 1984a, 1984b), and Meichenbaum (1977).

The major therapeutic focus in the cognitive-behavioral models is to help the patient examine the manner in which he or she construes and understands the world (cognitions), and to experiment with new ways of responding (behavioral). By learning to understand the idiosyncratic way in which he or she perceives the self, the world, and experience, and the prospects for the future, the patient can be helped to both alter negative affect and to behave more adaptively. Cognitive therapy is both a psychoeducational or coping model of therapy and a mastery model. The major goal of cognitive therapy is to increase the patient's skills so that he or she can more effectively deal with the exigencies of life, and thereby have a greater sense of control and self-efficacy in their lives. The directive nature of the model involves the therapist being actively involved with the patient in the therapeutic collaboration. The therapist works, through a Socratic questioning, to develop greater awareness in the patient. Further, the therapist can offer hypotheses for consideration, act as a resource person, or directly point out areas of difficulty. By developing an understanding of the patient's problems, the therapist can begin to develop hypotheses about the patient's life issues, and thereby begin to develop a conceptualization of their problems within the cognitive-behavioral framework. The cognitive therapy model has been applied with both outpatient and inpatient populations, and may be the psychotherapeutic treatment of choice, along with appropriate pharmacotherapy, for depressed or suicidal patients needing inpatient or day hospital treatment (Wright & Schrodt, 1989). A significant literature has emerged addressing the applications of cognitive therapy with inpatients (Bowers, 1989; Freeman & Greenwood, 1987; Greenwood, 1983; Wright, Thase, Beck, & Ludgate, 1993).

A central premise of cognitive psychotherapy is that there is an essential interaction between how individuals perceive themselves, their world, and their future, and how they feel and behave. Depressed individuals tend to view themselves, their world, and their future in a negative manner. They may, for example, view themselves as incapable and unlovable, believe that others are rejecting and critical, and view their future as bleak and hopeless. Given this belief system, it is not surprising that depressed individuals demonstrate apathy and lowered energy. As they believe their efforts will be fruitless, it makes sense to "conserve one's energy" (Beck, personal communication, 1986) and to "spare effort" that would result in failure (Guidano, 1987). This pattern of thinking has been labeled a "cognitive triad" by Beck (1967), and has been observed among depressed adults, children, and adolescents.

Although an emphasis is placed on examining the manner in which individuals perceive their lives and their circumstances, the cognitive therapist does not avoid or dismiss emotional and behavioral issues that arise in therapy. Rather, explicit attempts are made to elicit and clarify patients' feelings, as well as both adaptive and maladaptive behavior patterns. As these emotions and behavior patterns are revealed, efforts are made to identify the thoughts and beliefs that typically maintain them. As such, the cognitive emphasis serves in assisting patients to change their behavior actively, to adapt more functionally to their world, and to feel better generally. Within the cognitive model, affect, behavior, physiological processes, environmental events, and cognitions are seen as interacting components that reciprocally influence one another. These relationships among the components are transactional, in that they occur across time and mutually affect each other. Interventions, then, might reasonably be directed at each component, and would be expected to influence the other components over time. Regarding vulnerability to depression, Beck (1985) observed, however, that "the cognitive habits of the depressive are prepotent factors in the development and maintenance of the depressed state. It follows from this proposition that treatment of depression would be most effective if attempts were made to directly modify these cognitive habits."

Similar reasoning applies in our understanding of the etiology of suicidality. The ultimate "causes" of this behavior may or may not be found in the cognitive structures and beliefs of the individual. Moreover, the very nature of the "cause" depends on the level of analysis employed. A discussion of the nature of causation in psychopathology and psychotherapy is beyond the scope of our discussion. For our purposes, suicidality, like depression, might best be understood as a "final common pathway" of interacting physiological, developmental, environmental, and cognitive factors (Akiskal & McKinney, 1975).

The basic premises of the cognitive therapy model include the following:

1. The way individuals construe or interpret events and situations mediate how they subsequently feel and behave. Cognitions are postulated, then, to exist in a transactional relationship with affect and behavior, and with their consequent effect on events in the individual's environment.

2. This process of interpretation is active and ongoing. The construing of events allows the individual to derive or abstract a sense of meaning from their experiences, and permits them to understand events with the goal of developing an adaptive approach to establishing their "personal environment" and to responding to events. Behavior is seen as goal directed and adaptive.

3. Individuals develop idiosyncratic belief systems that guide behavior. These beliefs and assumptions influence an individual's perceptions and memories, and lead the memories to be activated by specific stimuli or events. The individual is rendered sensitive to specific "stressors," which include both external events and internal affective experiences. They contribute to a tendency to attend to and recall information selectively that is consistent with the content of the belief system, and to "overlook" information selectively that is inconsistent with those beliefs.

4. These stressors consequently contribute to a functional impairment of the individual's cognitive processing and activate maladaptive, overlearned coping responses. A feed-forward system is established in which the activation of maladaptive coping behaviors contribute to the maintenance of aversive environmental events and the consolidation of the maladaptive belief system.

5. According to the cognitive specificity hypothesis, clinical syndromes can be distinguished by the specific content of the belief system and the cognitive processes that are activated.

Individuals actively seek and create meanings for their experiences. It is through this process that they adapt to their environment, and organize information about themselves, their relationships, and their world into increasingly coherent and differentiated systems. Intention, agency, and will are aspects of the individual rather than the environment. As such, the mechanisms of psychological development and psychotherapeutic change reside with the individual.

Based on these assumptions, Beck (1976) and Beck et al. (1979) made several postulates regarding the nature and organization of emotions. He proposed the existence of three factors in depression: (1) the cognitive triad, (2) cognitive distortions, and (3) schema and assumptions.

Cognitive Triad

Depressed individuals tend to view themselves, their current experiences, the world, and their future in an unduly negative manner. The first component of the triad is a negative view of the self. Depressed individuals, as a group, tend to view themselves as incapable, unlovable, and inadequate. They typically attribute these shortcomings to enduring, irreparable defects in personal capacities they value. As such, they perceive themselves as lacking the requisite abilities for gaining a sense of happiness or satisfaction in life. This is consistent with Freud's belief that melancholic individuals demonstrate a "fundamental lack of self-regard."

Suicidal patients typically adopt a negativistic view of their world and of their relationships with others in it. They view their lives as an unending struggle against recurring obstacles, and tend to see others as critical, unsupportive, or rejecting. Although they view themselves as inept, and their difficulties as insurmountable, they feel unworthy of the support of others and anticipate rejection. Theirs is a bleak world with few rewards. These beliefs, however, are not entirely unfounded. As recent research suggests, the behavior of suicidal individuals does, after a time, become wearing, and precipitates rejection and the loss of the support from others.

The final component of the cognitive triad centers on suicidal patients' pessimistic outlook for their future. They anticipate continued hardships and, as they see themselves as lacking the necessary capacities to overcome these difficulties, see little chance of resolving their predicament. Although there is some controversy about the presence of this component among depressed latency-aged children, it has been observed among depressed adolescents and adults. Within this perspective, suicidal ideations are seen as reflecting a desire to escape what the individual perceives as an unbearable, unresolvable situation.

Evidence of the presence of a cognitive triad in depression has come from a range of sources including the development of structured measures of depressive cognitions. The Automatic Thoughts Questionnaire (Hollon & Kendall, 1980), for example, is an empirically derived self-report measure of depressive thoughts. Researchers employing the scale have reported significant differences between the responses of depressed and nondepressed college students (Hollon & Kendall, 1980; Dobson & Breiter, 1983), as well as depressed and nondepressed psychiatric outpatients (Eaves & Rush, 1984; Harrell & Ryon, 1983) and inpatients (Hollon, Kendall, & Lumry, 1986). Moreover, correlations between levels of depressive thoughts and the severity of depressive symptoms are typically moderate to high.

These findings are in accord with work by Missel and Sommer (1983), who reported that depressed inpatients make "significantly less positive and significantly more negative self-verbalizations in both success and failure situations" than nondepressed psychiatric inpatients. Attempts to document the occurrence of negative beliefs about the self, the world, and the future among depressed individuals, then, have generally supported the cognitive model.

Cognitive Distortions

An individual can distort in a variety of ways. These distortions can be positive or negative. The patient who distorts in a positive direction may be the "fool that rushes in where angels fear to tread." The positive distorter may view life in an unrealistically positive way. He or she may take chances that most people would avoid (e.g., starting a new business, investing in a stock). If successful, the positive distorter is vindicated. If unsuccessful, the positive distorter may see their failure as a consequence of taking a low-yield chance. The positive distorter can, however, take chances that may eventuate in their being in situations of great danger (i.e., experiencing massive chest pains and not consulting a physician. The positive distortion in this case might be, "I'm too young and healthy for a heart attack").

As there is a potentially infinite amount of information about "stimuli" surrounding us on a given day, we must selectively attend to the specific information that is most valuable for our survival and successful adaptation. As such, our capacity for selective attention, perception, and memory of events serves a highly adaptive function. As these cognitive processes are selective, however, there is an inherent potential for distorting reality in a range of significant ways. If the distortion is severe enough, the individual may lose touch with reality and be labeled psychotic. The depressed individual also distorts reality in several specific, albeit less severe, highly dysfunctional ways.

Beck (1976), Beck et al. (1979), Burns, (1980), and Freeman, Pretzer, Fleming, and Simon (1990) have classified particular types of cognitive distortions that are most commonly seen among depressed-suicidal individuals. These include the following:

1. *All or nothing thinking*—This refers to the tendency of many individuals to evaluate their performance, experience, or personal qualities in a dichotomized, black-or-white manner.

2. *Catastrophizing*—Many depressed and suicidal individuals tend to systematically exaggerate their difficulties. Although such an approach to evaluating situations may, presumably, serve an adaptive function (it

may, for example, elicit the support of others, lead the person to "always be prepared," or avert a sense of failure or inadequacy by leading the individual to avoid challenging or difficult tasks), it more often causes the individual to live in a rather constant state of fear.

3. *Overgeneralization*—Suicidal individuals often have a tendency to draw general conclusions on the basis of isolated events, and to apply these conclusions to both related and unrelated situations. They will arbitrarily conclude that a single negative event will happen repeatedly. Therefore, suicide becomes a reasonable option.

4. *Selective abstraction*—This refers to a tendency to attend to information or experiences selectively that validate or support hopeless beliefs, and to overlook other available data that may be more helpful. In effect, these individuals attend to the negative details in any situation and dwell on them exclusively. They consequently conclude that the current predicament is entirely negative. For example, if we add $3 + 6$ we get 9. However, $5 + 4 = 9$, $7 + 2 = 9$, $8 + 1 = 9$. It suggests that the reasonable method for ascertaining an answer is to evaluate the available data. It also suggests that there are many ways to get the same answer. The individual who selectively abstracts will observe that $3 + 6 + 50 = 9$. When questioned they insist that their answer is correct despite the data. The depressed and suicidal patient who selectively abstracts may insist, for example, that "I will be rejected" despite all evidence to the contrary. They strenuously maintain that their standard or typical conclusion is correct. Were such an individual asked to "re-add" the example of $3 + 6 + 50 = 9$, they would tend to ignore the 50 by saying, "Oh that! It really doesn't count". We are reminded of Paul Simon's observation in his song, *The Boxer*, "All lies and jest. Still a man hears what he wants to hear and disregards the rest"—so it is with the individual who selectively abstracts from their experiences.

5. *Arbitrary inference*—This is a related distortion, and refers to a tendency to draw arbitrary and negative conclusions in the absence of evidence, or in direct contradiction to the available evidence. Two common forms of arbitrary inference are "mind reading" and "negative prediction." Mind reading involves the idea that others should be able to read one's mind and know what one would like. It might also involve the idea that a person has the skill to "know" what others think about him or her, and that it is therefore not necessary to verify their opinions. Negative prediction is reflected in individuals' tendencies to imagine, and in fact predict, that bad things are about to happen. They then take this prediction as fact, even though it may not be realistic or true. The danger in these predictions is that they frequently become self-fulfilling prophecies. The manner in which this occurs is relatively straightforward. The anxious driver, for exam-

ple, may be so fearful of becoming involved in an accident, and may consequently drive with such timidity, that they provoke an accident. As is so often the case, we often get what we fear the most.

6. *Magnification and minimization*—This reflects a tendency to overestimate the significance of negative events, and to underestimate the magnitude or significance of desirable events systematically. These might, then, be called the "binocular distortions," as the individual is either exaggerating things as out of proportion, or shrinking them. For example, when looking at one's mistakes or flaws, or at what one sees to be the skills or talents of others, there is a tendency to make things seem bigger than they really are. In contrast, when looking at one's own attributes and skills, or at the problems or flaws of others, the minimizer will look through the opposite end of the telescope, which makes things seem small and distant. When individuals magnify their imperfections and minimize their attributes in this manner, the net result is that they ultimately feel inadequate and inferior.

7. *Emotional reasoning*—This distortion involves taking one's emotions as evidence for the way things really are. The logic is, "I feel; therefore, I am." Examples of emotional reasoning include "I feel guilty; therefore, I must be a bad person and should die." Similarly the depressed person may state that "I feel overwhelmed and hopeless; therefore, my problems must be impossible to solve."

8. *Should, must, ought to, statements*—Should statements are among the most pervasive and dysfunctional of beliefs commonly seen among depressed individuals. These statements seem to have the nature of a finger wagging under the nose. Their adaptive value typically centers on motivating the individual to act in an appropriate manner. By saying "I should or ought to do this," or "I must do that," the imperative seems clear. As a consequence of their imperative nature, however, these statements frequently engender feelings of guilt, anxiety, resentment, and anger. Interestingly, the result of this type of distortion may not be to motivate, but rather to demotivate individuals, and to leave them feeling helpless and apathetic. This is because the depressed individual does not feel that they are capable of meeting the standards that they have set for themselves. They are not, in short, capable of accomplishing what they "ought to." When one directs should statements toward others, a likely reaction is to become frustrated, angry, or indignant.

9. *Labeling and mislabeling*—Labeling involves creating a negative identity that is based on one's errors and imperfections, as if these revealed one's true self. Labeling, then, can be seen as an extreme form of overgeneralization. The philosophy behind this tendency is "the

measure of a man is the mistakes he makes." This distortion is frequently encountered among depressed individuals who regularly describe themselves beginning with "I am. . . ."

10. *Personalization*—This involves taking events that have nothing to do with oneself and making them personally meaningful. We see this in its extreme form in the paranoid patient.

11. *Control fallacies*—This distortion, related to dichotomous thinking, involves the idea that if I give up control for the smallest moment, I will be totally out of control. This leaves the individual always on guard for the smallest slippage in control of self or of life experience.

12. *Comparative thinking*—As one patient phrased it, "I think; therefore, I am." People who use this type of thinking only exist in their view as they compare themselves with others. The essence of self-esteem or confidence was lacking unless it was measured against others. Too often, the comparison was a negative one, with the patients seeing themselves as far less attractive, bright, competent, successful etc. Their conclusion, therefore, was why continue to live, given their inability to compete or compare.

13. *Disqualifying the positive*—The classic statement that accompanies this type of distortion is, "Yes, but. . . ." Our clinical experience has taught us that this type of distortion is cross-cultural. Whether the patient says "Oui, mais. . .," "Si, pero," or "Ja, über. . . ," the message is the same: "This success experience was only a fluke. Now let me explain why it cannot be trusted."

14. *Fallacy of fairness*—The belief that life should be fair, or that good things come to those who wait (or suffer) becomes, for many individuals, the basis of their difficulty. Given that they have experienced an unfair situation or expect the "world" to be unfair, they often conclude that suicide is the most reasonable alternative. The double bind is that if they receive or achieve what they want, they conclude that their belief is correct and that it should always be that way. When they hear or experience any unfairness, they become despondent in that they demand that the world be fair.

Although the preceding distortions are negative and can lead to dysfunctional behavior, it should be noted that each of them can, under some circumstances, and in some degree, serve an adaptive function for the individual (e.g., working toward perfection may be adaptive if you were defusing bombs or doing microsurgery as an occupation). Therapeutically, it is important for depressed or suicidal individuals to learn to monitor these cognitive processes, and decide

on where and how to modify any of these distortions. As they become aware of their occurrence and negative consequences, steps can
be taken to alleviate them.

Cognitive distortions, then, are not always detrimental to an individual. There is, for example, a large body of research regarding
"depressive realism" that suggests that the perceptions, attributions,
and inferences drawn by depressed individuals may actually be more
accurate or realistic than those of nondepressed persons (Abramson
& Alloy, 1981; Alloy & Abramson, 1979, 1988; Lewinsohn, Mischel,
Chaplin, & Barton, 1980). Concomitantly, it would seem to indicate
that nondepressed individuals tend to overestimate their abilities systematically, as well as their capacity to influence outcomes. It is the
nondepressed individual who may, in actuality, be misperceiving
events in the environment. As such, cognitive distortions and a self-
serving attributional bias may serve a protective function in that they
insulate persons from the depressogenic effects of uncontrollable or
aversive situations (Alloy, 1988; Miller & Moretti, 1988). People tend,
for the most part, to be optimistic regarding their future and their
ability to meet the challenges of life (Janoff-Bulman, Madden, &
Timko, 1983; Weinstein, 1980; Perloff, 1983). Although this may, in
some ways, be seen as unrealistic, this illusory sense of invulnerabil-
ity may serve an adaptive function (Tiger, 1979), and highlights the
significance of depressed persons' feelings of hopelessness and dysphoria. As Janoff-Bulman and Hecker (1988) stated, "For one who is
depressed, the assumptions of protection and safety no longer oper-
ate, and he or she is overwhelmed by feelings of pessimism and despair" (p. 178).

When unchecked, cognitive distortions can have a pernicious,
negative effect. As in the case of suicidal individuals, cognitive distortions can contribute to significant emotional difficulties and become a
legitimate focus for psychotherapy. Moreover, cognitive distortions
do not typically appear in isolation, but occur in a range of combinations and permutations. There is a certain overlap in the nature of the
specific distortions, such that they are given different names by different authors. Their specific titles are less important, however, than
the fact that they tend to reflect systematic tendencies of individual's
to misinterpret events in specific ways.

Several attempts have been made during recent years to assess the occurrence of cognitive distortions among depressed or suicidal individuals. The measures developed have been derived from a
range of theoretical models and include the Cognitive Bias Questionnaire (Krantz & Hammen, 1979), the Attitudes Toward Self Scale

(Carver & Ganellen, 1983), the Attributional Style Questionnaire (Seligman, Abramson, Semmel, & von Baeyer, 1979), and the Irrational Beliefs Test (Jones, 1969). Given the central role of distorted or biased cognitive processing in cognitive models of depression, it may be helpful to review briefly research employing these measures at this time.

The Cognitive Bias Questionnaire was developed as a means of assessing depressive thought patterns independently of dysphoric mood (Hammen & Krantz, 1976, 1985). The measure consists of a series of short stories about a person experiencing a potentially depressing event, followed by several multiple-choice questions regarding how the subject would feel if they were the character in the vignette. Responses are scored according to their depressive content and whether or not they reflect cognitive distortion. The validity of this measure was examined by Krantz and Hammen (1979), who studied the responses of one sample of clinically depressed outpatients, one sample of depressed and nondepressed psychiatric inpatients, and four samples of nonclinical control subjects on the scale. Significant correlations were found between the occurrence of depressive distortions and levels of dysphoria for each of the samples. Moreover, depressed individuals demonstrated significantly more cognitive distortion than nondepressed individuals. Depressed and nondepressed students and clinical patients could be distinguished, then, according to the number of depressed and cognitively distorted responses they reported.

These findings were subsequently replicated by Norman, Miller, and Klee (1980), who examined levels of cognitive distortions among depressed and nondepressed psychiatric inpatients. Once again, levels of cognitive distortion correlated significantly with levels of depression. Moreover, they did not differ between patients suffering from primary and secondary depression. As such, cognitive distortions were found to be characteristic of depression in general, and were not specific to particular subtypes or diagnostic categorizations.

Further evidence for the role of cognitive distortions has been provided by Blaney, Behar, and Head (1980), Frost and MacInnis (1983), Carver, Ganellan, and Behar-Mitrani (1985), and Dobson and Shaw (1986). Although Miller and Norman (1986) also found elevated levels of cognitive distortion among depressed inpatients, they found little evidence for the persistence of these distortions following the remission of depressive symptoms and did not find high levels of cognitive distortion to be accompanied by an increased risk of future hospitalizations. Their observations suggested, however, that cognitive distortions may persist within a subgroup of "high distorting" individuals and that these individuals may be at greater risk of relapse. Although research employing the Cognitive Bias Questionnaire, then, has not been fully supportive of the cognitive model of depression (at least in its initial formulation), it has been consistent with the central tenets of the model, and points the way toward important and useful modifications of the theory. Carver and his colleagues have focused their attention on the assessment of distorted beliefs about the self. They developed the Attitudes Toward Self Scale as a means of assessing self-critical beliefs among depressed individuals (Carver & Ganellan, 1983; Carver & Scheier, 1982; Carver, Ganellan, & Behar-Mitrani, 1985). They argued that human behavior reflects a "process of establishing goals or standards of action, followed by attempts to attain the goals or approximate the standards in behavior." From this model, they hypothesized that depression may stem from an individual's tendency to adopt goals or standards that are unreasonably high, or from an increased sensitivity to variations from one's standards. As such, when depressive episodes are initiated by environmental stressors or losses, individuals experience a heightened state of self-awareness. They become increasingly cognizant of their inability to meet their standards of coping, and tend to accept greater responsibility for negative events and outcomes. Their model is quite consistent with Beck's and Ellis's emphasis on cognitive distortions, such as "magnification," among depressed individuals. Depression, according to Carver, is thus characterized by a tendency to overgeneralize from single, discrete failures about the self. Research based on this model has been supportive. It appears that patients' tendencies to generalize from single failures to a "broader sense of personal inadequacy" play an important role in the occurrence of depression.

Similarly, research by Janoff-Bulman (1979) and Peterson, Schwartz, and Seligman (1981) suggest that depressed individuals engage in greater amounts of "characterological self-blame" than nondepressed persons. That is, there is an increased tendency to attribute failures or negative events to deficits in one's character (which cannot be controlled) rather than to one's behavior (which presumably can be controlled). It is this emphasis on the perception of control that distinguishes Janoff-Bulman's approach from other attribution models of depression. Clinically, this may be an important distinction in that suicidal individuals typically manifest high levels of pessimism, and a sense that important outcomes are uncontrollable or unattainable. Further evidence for the role of cognitive distortions in depression has come from studies employing the Irrational Beliefs Test (Jones, 1969), a self-report scale designed to assess the presence of irrational beliefs postulated by Albert Ellis to underlie a range of emotional disorders. Scores on this measure have been found to be highly correlated with levels of dysphoria among students (LaPointe & Crandell, 1980; Nelson, 1977).

Taken together, these studies have convincingly demonstrated an association between cognitive distortions and depression in outpatient and inpatient psychiatric groups, as well as among normal controls. Although questions remain regarding the causative role of depression-specific cognitive distortions in the emergence of depressive disorders and suicide (Coyne & Gotlib, 1983; Hammen & Krantz, 1985) and the persistence of cognitive distortions following the remission of depressive symptoms (Hamilton & Abramson, 1983; Ludgate, Reinecke, & Beck, 1987; Miller & Norman, 1986), these studies provide compelling evidence for a relationship between levels of cognitive distortions and clinical depression, and are consistent with cognitive models of depression.

These findings are supportive of cognitive theory's postulate of a relationship between specific cognitive distortions and levels of depression. There is a need for further improvement in the psychometric and conceptual shortcomings of certain measures (Coyne & Gotlib, 1983; Hammen & Krantz, 1985). Moreover methodological shortcomings in some of the research designed to test cognitive models of depression should be addressed (Abramson, Alloy, & Metalsky, 1988).

Cognitive Processes in Suicide

Although the nature of cognitive distortions among suicidal individuals has received less empirical attention, recent findings suggest that suicidal patients may be distinguished from nonsuicidal controls on a range of cognitive measures. Suicidal individuals have been found, for example, to demonstrate deficits in their ability to generate and evaluate alternative solutions or viewpoints. This "cognitive rigidity" is reflected in their relatively poor performance on measures of social problem solving, such as the Means-Ends Problem Solving Task (Platt, Spivak, & Bloom, 1975; Reinecke, 1987; Schotte & Clum, 1987). Similar findings have been reported for suicidal children (Cohen-Sandler & Berman, 1982).

Schemata

Cognitive distortions are maintained by an individual's basic life schemata and assumptions. Schemata are nonconscious cognitive structures, and are postulated to underlie and maintain an individual's belief system and automatic thoughts. An individual's cognitive structures are postulated to be hierarchically organized, and include a coordinated set of abstract principles about the self, the world, and relationships, specific beliefs and coping mechanisms derived from these assumptions, and a set of cognitive process mechanisms that serve to direct one's attention, and mediate the perception, encoding, and retrieval of specific events. The schemata are very rarely isolated and separate but, like distortions, occur in complex combinations and permutations. An individual's cognitive schemata and assumptions are believed, then, to influence both the "content" of their beliefs and automatic thoughts, and the "process" by which this information is retrieved and used. As such, schemata serve as an organized representation of prior knowledge that guides the perception, memory, and processing of current information (Neisser, 1967). The relationships among the cognitive structures are hypothesized to be relatively stable. The schemata become, in effect, how one defines oneself, both individually and as part of the group. The schemata can be active or dormant, with the more active schemata being the rules that govern day-to-day behavior. The dormant schemata are called into play to control behavior in times of stress. The schemata may be either compelling or noncompelling. The more compelling the schemata, the more likely it is that the individual will respond to the schemata.

One's schemata and assumptions are actively developed, and serve an adaptive function in that they assist individuals to evaluate their circumstances efficiently and guide coping attempts. They are, in short, the unspoken rules and assumptions we live by. As they are assumptions, or "givens," they are not typically open to evaluation. Schemata are theoretically related to the concept of "tacit knowledge" (Franks, 1974; Guidano & Liotti, 1983; Polanyi, 1966, 1969; Turvey, 1974). These schemata and assumptions are typically established early in childhood, and are refined and consolidated by one's experiences throughout life. The specific content of an individual's schema and assumptions typically are not open to disputation. The particular extent of effect that a schemata has on an individual's life depends on several factors: (a) how strongly held the schema is; (b) of how essential individuals see that schema to their safety, well-being, or existence; (c) lack of disputation that individuals engage in when a particular schema is activated; (d) previous learning vis-à-vis the importance and essential nature of a particular schema; and (e) establishment of how early a particular schema was internalized.

As Guidano and Liotti (1983) concisely stated, "self-knowledge is irrefutable." One's schemata are protected from confutation by the activity of cognitive distortions, and by the development of flexible beliefs and assumptions. This notion is similar to Kelly's (1955) construct of a "protective belt," a set of beliefs that serves to protect one's "hardcore" assumptions or personal constructs from disputation. Schemata are in a constant state of change and evolution. From the child's earliest years there is a need to alter old schemata and develop new ones to meet the different and increasingly complex demands of the world. Infants conception of reality is constrained by their limited interaction with their world such that they may initially perceive the world as their crib and the few caretakers that care for and comfort them. As infants develop additional skills of mobility and interaction, they then perceive their world as significantly larger. One way of conceptualizing the change process is to use the Piagetian concept of adaptation with its two interrelated processes, assimilation and accommodation (Rosen, 1985, 1989). Environmental data and experience are only taken in by the individual as the individual can use these data in terms of their own subjective experiences. The self-schema then become self-selective as the individual may ignore environmental stimuli that they were not able to integrate or synthesize. The assimilative and accommodative processes are interactive and stand in opposition, one with the other. There is an active and evolutionary process where all perceptions and cognitive structures are applied to new functions (assimilation) while new cognitive structures are developed to serve old functions in new situations (accommodation). Some individuals may persist in using old structures without fitting them to the new circumstances in which they are involved, but use them in toto without measuring fit or appropriateness. They may further fail to accommodate or build new structures.

The schema of suicidal and depressed individuals frequently center on specific themes of vulnerability to loss or abandonment, and their personal inadequacy or unlovability. Although these schema may be latent much of the time, they can be activated by specific negative life events. Depressogenic schema, then, may be seen as distal causal factors, rendering individuals vulnerable to depression under specific circumstances. Cognitive theories of depression, then, typically take the form of diathesis-stress models of illness. Although depressogenic schema, and their consequent activation of depressive distortions and beliefs, may be seen as sufficient for the emergence of depressive symptomatology, they are not necessary. Cognitive theories typically acknowledge that depression may be precipitated by factors other than the activation of depressive schema.

Empirical research on the nature and development of depressogenic schema is accelerating. The Dysfunctional Attitudes Scale (DAS) was developed by Weissman and Beck (1978) as a measure of depressogenic assumptions. Scores on this measure have been found to be highly correlated with levels of depression among college students (Weissman & Beck, 1978) and psychiatric inpatients (Eaves & Rush, 1984; Hamilton & Abramson, 1983). Unfortunately, however, the measure also has been found to be highly influenced by current mood (Miranda & Persons, 1988; Miranda, Persons, & Byers, 1990), and so appears to contain both state-dependent and trait items. The validity of the DAS as an index of stable depressive schema or beliefs, then, requires further documentation. Recent evidence suggests, nonetheless, that the DAS may serve as a useful predictor of relapse among specific groups of depressed individuals (Ludgate, Reinecke, & Beck, 1987), and that specific subsets of items within the measure may discriminate patients at risk for relapse (Reda, Carpiniello, Secchiardi, & Blanco, 1985).

In a provocative study, Greenberg, Vazquez, and Alloy (1988) observed that depressed and anxious outpatients could be discriminated in terms of their performance on an incidental recall task. Experimentally derived measures, such as this, show promise as measures of underlying schemata.

Further evidence for the role of schemata in depressive disorders comes from the field of social psychology. Investigators examining the attributions made by depressed individuals to specific environmental events suggest that they possess an attributional style that may contribute to ongoing feelings of vulnerability. As noted at the outset, hopelessness and self-reproach are frequently seen as cardinal symptoms of depression. As noted earlier, schemata are believed to be activated by a patient's perception of a personally meaningful deprivation, loss, or disappointment, For example:

A 26-year-old, single woman had become highly depressed and suicidal after her boyfriend of 1 month left her for another woman. Her specific thoughts centered on themes of loss, her personal inadequacy, and the necessity of romantic relationships to her sense of self-worth. As she stated, "I'm a [Ford] Pinto and am defective, so why would a guy want me when he can have a Mercedes?" These beliefs appear to have been long-standing in nature. This women was the youngest of six children, and had been unplanned. Her parents had vowed to have no more children after the fifth one and had told her that she was unwanted as her older brother had been so difficult. She described her father as critical and unsupportive of her mother and the female children. Her cognitive distortions included the "magnification" of personal deficits, such as attractiveness (which was highly valued because of its importance in attracting a man), minimization of personal attributes, and selective inattention of positive experiences.

As with cognitive distortions, the development and activation of schemata need not always be negative. The activation of depressogenic schemata, for example, may serve an adaptive function in that they lead the individual to withdraw from their investment in the source of their loss or disappointment, and to seek the support of others.

As cognitive schemata and assumptions are based on individuals' life experiences and perceptions, they may be highly personal and idiosyncratic. Nonetheless, beliefs and assumptions may be shared by persons with similar experiences, and may be widely accepted by specific social groups.

Assumptions and schemata can, under specific circumstances, serve as the nexus from which cognitive distortions and maladaptive beliefs or automatic thoughts emerge. Although they may be latent much of the time, schemata may be activated by external events that are phenomenologically similar to the experiences that contributed to their establishment. When activated, specific beliefs, distortions, and styles of thinking are seen. An individual's assumptions and beliefs are of various strengths. The degree of belief the individual places in them and the importance of them to their sense of self determines the extent to which they may serve as the source of cognitive distortions and depressive automatic thoughts.

How we respond behaviorally to the activation of specific schemata mediates their effect on our emotions. If one has the belief, for example, that "people should always love me," one might become dependent and helpless, always seeking support and reassurance, and continually vigilant for signs of disinterest or annoyance on the part of others. Alternatively, such an individual might become an outstanding college professor, actor, or politician who constantly seeks approval from others.

The manner in which a person responds to the activation of a schema influences the feedback they will receive from others and from their environment. It is this feedback, and one's selective attention to it, that serves to consolidate the belief system. As such, meaning is not simply attached by individuals to environmental events. It is proactively developed. Individuals do not simply respond to environmental contingencies or events on the basis of beliefs or schemata established earlier in life. Rather, they approach situations and events in a goal-directed manner and actively develop the situation in a manner that is consistent with the belief system.

Schemata may center on a range of issues. They appear to include beliefs about oneself, relationships with others, one's view of the world, and one's future. The schemata of a depressed person, then, might include beliefs that "I am unlovable," "Others are unreliable," and "Life is a struggle." In accord with the cognitive specificity hypothesis, patient's specific clinical presentations are determined by the nature of their schemata and beliefs. Moreover, clinical syndromes may be distinguished in terms of the specific content of the underlying belief system. As we have noted, the beliefs of depressed individuals typically center on themes of personal inadequacy and vulnerability to loss. The schemata of anxious patients, while also including a sense of vulnerability, tend to center on a belief that "the world is dangerous," in conjunction with a belief that it is adaptive to maintain one's vigilance (Beck & Emery, 1985). Borderline disorders, in contrast, may be characterized by the activation of multiple, interacting schemata. These typically include beliefs that "The world is dangerous," "I am inherently flawed and unacceptable," "I am powerless and vulnerable," "I need the support of others," and "Others are malevolent and rejecting" (Freeman & Leaf, 1989; Pretzer, 1983; Reinecke, 1987; Young, 1984). With this in mind, an important component of therapy is the clarification and resolution of dysfunctional schemata. As the schemata and assumptions that underlie an individual's depressive or suicidal. Suicidal thoughts and actions are frequently precipitated by the frustration of an individual's psychological needs (Shneidman, 1985). These may include desires for achievement, affiliation or support, nurturance, autonomy, and the like. Specific needs become salient or important for particular individuals depending on their early experiences and tend to reflect specific schemata.

Cognitive-Developmental Aspects of Schema Formation

The cognitive model postulates that depression may be seen as a manifestation of enduring belief systems, assumptions, and schemata. The relationship between early negative experiences and current symptomatology is not through the invocation of a descriptive personality structure, but is mediated by the activity of specific assumptions and schemata. These beliefs are understandable within each individual's personal meaning system, and although highly personal and idiosyncratic, are available to conscious awareness. With this in mind, we might ask what is the evidence that early experiences contribute to the establishment of maladaptive schemata among depressed and suicidal individuals? Although prospective, longitudinal studies are singularly lacking, there is reasonably consistent retrospective evidence from studies of adults, as well as research with suicidal children and adolescents, that these individuals have been exposed to early events that could contribute to feelings of vulnerability and to a sensitivity to loss. An argument can be made that relatively specific events occur early in the life of individuals that contribute to the establishment and consolidation of depressogenic schemata and assumptions. These persons often are, as a consequence, rendered vulnerable to recurrent episodes of depression and to suicidal thoughts and, possibly, behavior. Later events of a related nature are believed to reactivate latent schemata triggering a range of hopeless feelings and beliefs, as well as cognitive distortions.

The idea that vulnerability to psychopathology may be acquired through early negative experiences is certainly not new to psychological theory. Traditionally, depressed or suicidal individuals are seen as having acquired a constellation of depressogenic traits, habits, or defenses, which together constitute a depressive personality structure. The process or mechanism by which this premorbid personality structure contributes to the emergence of clinical depression and the occurrence of suicidal acts, however, remains poorly articulated. That is, it is not clear how specific events during one's childhood mediate the emergence of depressive episodes or suicidal acts.

It is reasonably well established, for example, that the early social environment of suicidal individuals is frequently quite chaotic, and that they are more likely than nonsuicidal individuals to have experienced the loss of a parent. Among the sources of family disorganization most frequently studied have been parental death, alcoholism, family conflict or hostility, neglect or abuse, and parental divorce or separation. Retrospective studies have been fairly consistent in their finding that suicidal adults can be distinguished from depressed individuals and nonpsychiatric controls on the basis of various forms of early loss (Adam, 1986; Adam, Bouckoms, & Scarr, 1980; Adam, Bouckoms, & Streiner, 1982; Adam, Lohrenz, Harper, &

Streiner, 1982; Bruhn, 1962; Rogers & Wenes, 1979; Bunch, Barraclough, Nelson, & Sainsbury, 1972; Crook & Raskin, 1975; Goldney, 1981).

These findings are consistent with reports regarding the concomitants of suicidal behavior among children (Ackerly, 1967; Cohen-Sandler, Berman, & King, 1982a; Frommer & O'Shea, 1973; Green, 1978; Pfeffer, 1986; Pfeffer & Trad, 1988; Schaefer, 1974). Cohen-Sandler, Berman, and King (1982b), for example, examined 76 children who had been admitted for inpatient psychiatric treatment. They found that, in comparison with depressed and psychiatric control groups, the suicidal children experienced "increasing and significantly greater amounts of stress as they matured, including a number of specific chaotic and disruptive family events which resulted in losses and separations from important people." Moreover, the suicidal children reportedly experienced "significantly greater and increasing amounts of stress as they matured, particularly during the year prior to admission" as well as a "disproportionate number of losses of all kinds." The authors interpretation of these findings is quite consistent with cognitive theory. As they stated, "Suicide attempts of children in this study . . . represent active coping efforts to counteract the sense of helplessness they felt in being unable to effect changes in the stressful, chaotic conditions of their families. Suicide (represents) . . . a last ditch strategy for the young child to alter an intolerable situation, to appeal for help, or, especially, to gain love and attention by arousing parental concern." Moreover, these findings highlight the importance of examining both early loss experiences and ongoing stresses in understanding suicidality. As they cogently stated, "Taking a longitudinal perspective . . . which permits analysis of recurring patterns rather than simply the presence or absence of experiences, illuminates the processes of ongoing and increasing stress and repeated losses, which may be used to identify children at high risk for suicide." We concur and would suggest that such considerations are equally important in understanding suicidality among adults.

Similar findings have been reported in studies of depressed and suicidal adolescents (Barter, Swaback, & Todd, 1968; Berman & Jobes, 1991; Friedman, Corn, Hurt, Fibel, Schulick, & Swirsky, 1984; Garfinkel, Froese, & Hood, 1982; Haider, 1968; Hawton, Osborn, O'Grady, & Cole, 1982; Hendin, 1991; Spirito, Brown, Overholser, & Fritz, 1989). A breakdown of the family structure, as reflected in a parental death or absence, alcoholism or drug abuse; parental illness; and family violence have all been associated with an increased risk of suicide among teenagers. It is worth noting, however, that no well-

controlled studies have been completed of the family dynamics of suicidal children or adolescents.

Parker and Hadzi-Pavlovic (1984) reached similar conclusions after examining 79 women whose mothers had died during their childhood. They found that although there was an increased incidence of
depression among these women, this relationship was mediated by a
"lack of caring" by their fathers and step-mothers after their mother's
deaths. Taken together, these studies suggest that the exposure to
early loss and the subsequent decrease in support (or other associated factors) are associated with an increased risk of later depression
and suicide. As noted, however, the specific mechanism by which
these experiences contribute to later depression and suicide are not
fully understood.

As Pfeffer and her colleagues have obsrved (Pfeffer, 1981a, 1981b,
1985; Frances & Pfeffer, 1987; Pfeffer, Adams, Weiner, & Rosenberg, 1988)
observed, findings such as these also have practical implications in that
they highlight the importance of maintaining the stability of the patient's
family, as well as the value of encouraging the family's active involvement
in the treatment process. Although she was discussing the treatment of
suicidal children and adolescents, we have no reason to suspect that her
suggestions are not applicable in assisting suicidal adults.

Given these observations, the question becomes one of identifying the specific means by which these early experiences contribute to
an increased risk of later suicide. Is there a simple, linear relationship
between the early loss of a parent and an increased risk of later depression or suicide? Probably not. Research suggests that early object loss is
often followed by important, deleterious changes in the child's social
environment. Suicidal ideations, attempts, and completions are multi-
ply determined, and it is reasonable to suspect that a range of factors
mediate the relationship between early object loss and later risk of suicide. In his classic text *Maternal Deprivation Reassessed*, Rutter (1981) observed that the availability of parental support, the developmental level
of the child, and the long-term effects of the parental loss on the stability of the family also influence the emotional development of the child.
There is, in sum, no consensus as to whether the age at which losses
occur, or the nature of the loss, have any specific relationship to the
later development of depressive disorders or suicidality. Moreover, it is
not clear how early losses interact with other developmental experiences or events in placing children at risk.

Although the loss of a parent due to death, separation, or divorce is a traumatic event in the child's life, there are other circumstances and events that may also contribute to feelings of vulnerabil-

ity or a sensitivity to loss in the individual. A cognitive therapy model, with its emphasis on the development of depressogenic belief systems and the acquisition of adaptive coping skills during childhood, suggests that the absence of a supportive adult who is able to provide children with a sense of security and control over their environment, and who can model flexible problem solving under difficult circumstances, may engender feelings of helplessness in children. The evidence reviewed demonstrating a relationship between the early loss of a parent, a chaotic family environment, and later depression is quite consistent with this perspective. It is the lack of continuity in parental care, the decrease in emotional support, and the modeling of ineffective coping strategies that consolidate the children's developing sense that they are incapable of responding effectively to losses or separations.

Attempts have been made during recent years to cast Beck's cognitive theory of depression into developmental terms. Guidano (1987) views the development of depressogenic schemata as stemming from dysfunctional patterns of attachment. As he states, "The central feature of the developmental pathway of depressive-prone individuals is the ongoing elaboration of a sense of loss that parallels the abnormal course of their attachment relationships with their parents."

This perspective is congruent with Adam's (1986) suggestion that suicidal behavior "can more usefully be conceptualized as attachment behavior, with its function not primarily a retreat from the world and its disappointments, but a desperate attempt to maintain relatedness to a vital attachment figure in the face of a threatening situation" (p. 72). It is well established that early losses experienced by infants, as well as difficulties in their relationships with their primary caregivers, can have important effects on their emotional and social behavior during their childhood. Moreover, as Adam (1986) has observed, there are important morphological and functional similarities between the protest and despair behaviors of infants who have been separated from their parents, and the behaviors of depressed or suicidal individuals that serve to elicit the support and reassurance of others. It is tempting, then, to look to attachment theory as we search for the developmental origins of schema and assumptions that render individuals vulnerable to depression and suicide.

Infant attachment is an appealing model for the development of schemata in that it places the emergence of depression and suicide behavior within a normative developmental context. There are, however, important methodological and theoretical difficulties in this endeavor that should not be overlooked. It has not yet been demonstrated, for example, that pathological patterns of social behavior in adult life are functionally related to earlier deficits in the mother–infant attachment relationship, much less that these patterns of attachment are functionally related to the emergence of suicidal behavior. Although Bowlby (1980) suggested that pathological patterns of social behavior in later life (including chronic desires for love and support, emotional detachment, and compulsive self-reliance) are related to disturbed forms of attachment during infancy, this has not been empirically established. There is no longitudinal research, to our knowledge, bearing on the attitudes, beliefs, expectations, and social or emotional development of adults who had manifested "difficult" or "anxious" attachment patterns during their infancy. Moreover, Bowlby's conceptualization of the attachment relationship as a "working model" of a specific relationship with a primary caregiver differs somewhat from current cognitive conceptualizations of the self-schema as an internal structure of tacit beliefs.

Nonetheless, we do believe that attachment theory can serve as a useful metaphor for understanding the consolidation of depressogenic schemata and the development of the "constricted" cognitive focus that characterizes the suicidal individual (Shneidman, 1985). An insecure early attachment may be accompanied by a tacit belief or perception that others are unreliable. This belief, in turn, hinders the development of an ability to form trusting, stable relationships. Subsequent experiences of loss, rejection, or neglect serve as corroborating evidence in the consolidation of the depressive belief system. Individuals, as a consequence, come to view themselves as helpless in facing a chaotic or unsupportive environment. Their self-esteem declines, and feelings of despair or hopelessness emerge. Individuals are thus rendered vulnerable to loss and increasingly sensitive to threats of abandonment or rejection. As Adam (1986) stated, "Whatever other meanings suicidal behavior may have, it serves effectively in signaling distress to others . . . admonishing them for neglect, punishing them for rejection, and coercing them to reestablish a needed bond" (p. 72).

We speculate, then, that difficulties in establishing a secure attachment lead to the development of specific schemata or expectations about relationships that may render patients vulnerable to suicidal ideations later in life. The early loss of a caregiver need not, in itself, place an individual at risk for later depression or suicide. Rather, it is the accumulating experiences of rejection, conflict, and unreliable support that so often follow the loss that consolidate the nascent maladaptive beliefs. It is these tacit beliefs that may render the patient vulnerable to suicidal ideations later in life. These schema and assumptions center on beliefs that it is necessary to have the support of others, and that in order to maintain this support it is necessary to maintain high standards for personal performance. This possibility is supported by a recent study in which it was observed that high expectations for oneself, or perfectionistic beliefs, and a sensitivity to rejection or criticism by others accounted for more than 75% of the variance in predicting the intensity of inpatients' suicidal ideations (Ranieri, Steer, Lawrence, Rissmiller, Piper, & Beck, 1987).

Summary

Cognitive therapy is a short-term, active, directive, collaborative, psychoeducational, and dynamic model of psychotherapy developed for the treatment of depression and is ideally suited for the treatment of the hopelessness and suicidality often related to depression. Understanding the problems of the suicidal individual in terms of the cognitive triad of the negative view of the self, the world, and the future helps to organize the treatment and lend structure to therapy. Working with the patient's cognitive distortions helps to direct the therapist to the dynamic schematic issues that may be fueling the suicidal thinking.

A diverse set of therapeutic techniques has been derived from this theory, and has proved useful in providing suicidal patients with a sense of hope and a means of developing alternative solutions for their difficulties. Within the model the patient and therapist work together to examine cognitive, affective, environmental, and interpersonal factors that contribute to the suicidal crisis, and to resolve underlying issues and beliefs that place the individual at risk for future suicidality.

3

Assessment of Depression and Suicidality

Whenever Richard Cory went down town,
We people on the pavement looked at him;
He was a gentleman from sole to crown,
Clean favored, and imperially slim.

And he was always quietly arrayed,
And he was always human when he talked;
But still he fluttered pulses when he said, "Good morning,"
And he glittered when he walked.

And he was rich—yes, richer than a king—
And admirably schooled in every grace;
In fine, we thought that he was everything
To make us wish that we were in his place.

So on we worked, and waited for the light,
And went without the meat, and cursed the bread;
And Richard Cory, one calm summer night,
Went home and put a bullet through his head.

—Edward Arlington Robinson, *Richard Cory*

To the casual observer, Richard Cory seemed to be an icon of excellence. One to whom all would aspire to emulate. A thorough assessment of the thoughts and emotions that Richard Cory experienced might have identified the suicidal elements. The principle objectives of the assessment of depressed or suicidal patients are, first, to evaluate the degree of current risk and, second, to develop a conceptualization of the individual's difficulties, which will guide the development of a treatment plan. Assessment, then, is a critical issue in patient treatment, regardless of the diagnosis. This assessment of both the presence of a depressive disorder, and feelings of dysphoria, should be completed regardless of the patient's diagnosis or presenting concerns. A complete clinical assessment of suicidal ideation is essential. This assessment must be part of both the initial evaluation and of the ongoing evaluation of the patient in treatment. The therapist must take any indications of suicide seriously and evaluate them with care. The clinician must be sensitive to subtle distinctions in meaning, or subtle meanings of certain behaviors. The statement, "I would like to die" may mean for one patient that life has no meaning and that, at times, he or she wishes to die during sleep. This is very different from the patient who finds his or her life situation untenable and say, "I would like to die. How can I do something about it?" Even the most sensitive clinician cannot safely assume that he or she fully understands the meaning of suicidal ideation without directly asking the patient about the ideas and discussing the thoughts.

The same care must be expressed for the subtle behaviors that may reflect suicidal ideation or intent. The patient who has updated his or her will, taken care of legal odds and ends, or given away possessions may well be sending a message. It should not require the patient writing a note, making funeral arrangements, and always wearing clean underwear to alert the therapist to the need to discuss the patient's behaviors and intentions in great detail.

The assessment and understanding of the patient's view of the available options are critical. The patient who sees few or no options is a far more serious risk than the patient who maintains that options exist although they are limited or undesirable. In making a clinical assessment of suicidality, the therapist must be aware of his or her own cognitions so that information is not lost or never sought in an attempt to provide a modicum of comfort for the therapist. The therapist who is discomforted by the idea of discussing suicide may be actively colluding with the patient's suicidal behavior.

The objectives of this chapter are to review the current literature on several cognitive therapy assessment instruments that may be used in assessing the severity of patients' depression, hopelessness, and suicidal risk and lethality. We conclude with a discussion of issues to be considered in conducting clinical interviews of suicidal individuals. The patients or specific patient types discussed cover the clinical gamut—including inpatients and outpatients, minimally hopeless or hopeless patients, and severely suicidal patients. The principles and issues remain the same; that is, a complete and accurate diagnosis, an evaluation of patient risk factors, an assessment of patients' strengths and an examination of deterrents to completion of the suicidal act.

Assessment of Depression and Suicidal Risk

Depression and suicidal risk may be assessed in four ways: Through patient self-report, the report of significant others, clinician interviews or ratings, and through objective test data. Given the limitations of each approach—in terms of reliability, validity, and clinical utility—a multimodal assessment typically will provide a clearer view of the patient's concerns and allow for a more accurate assessment of suicidal risk.

Self-Report

Patients' self-reports may differ in several significant ways. Some patients will report severe depression and never allude to concomitant hopelessness. Other patients may report their feelings of depression with commonly used synonyms for dysphoric affect, such as "blue," "down," "blah," or "off." Obviously, these terms must be carefully defined and delineated, because these patients may never directly address the issue of hopelessness. A third group of patients reports depression and actively denies any thoughts of suicide. A fourth patient group will readily identify or acknowledge the hopeless and suicidal thoughts with or without depressive affect. A final group of patients seeks help because of the active and upsetting stream of suicidal thinking. With any and all of these patients, their statements must be quickly moved from the vague, general descriptors to more highly specific statements and thoughts. These can be operationalized so that the therapist can fully empathize with the patients' difficulties. Often, patients may expect the therapist to know what they (the patients) mean by the naming of a particular symptom or syndrome. One patient, for example, described the following symptoms: "I just feel bad . . . everything feels awful. I might as well be gone than have to live like this. The last time I was depressed, I told myself that if I ever got depressed again I'd just disappear rather than go through it again."

In addition to asking patients to describe their concerns, it is useful to ask them to complete one or more self-report scales of depressive, hopeless, or suicidal symptoms. Such measures may tap symptoms they may have overlooked, and provide the therapist with a means of quantifying the severity of patients' dysphoria, hopelessness, or suicidal intent or ideation.

Several self-report rating scales have been developed during recent years and have been widely used in the assessment of depression. Of these, the Beck Depression Inventory (BDI) is the most widely used and researched. As Steer, Beck, and Garrison (1986) have noted, the BDI has become "a touchstone against which to compare assessments derived from other measures." The BDI is a 21-item self-report measure developed from clinical observations of the attitudes, feelings, and symptoms experienced by clinically depressed patients (Beck, Ward, Mendelson, Mock, & Erbaugh, 1961). The items were selected to assess the severity of depression and were not derived from a specific theory of depression. Items on the BDI are rated from 0 to 3 by patients in terms of severity. The symptoms and feelings assessed include: (a) mood; (b) somatic symptoms, such as loss of libido, sleep difficulties, and decreased appetite; (c) depressive thought, including feelings of pessimism, guilt, or self-reproach; and (d) suicidal ideations. Factor analyses of the BDI have been conducted by several groups (Beck & Lester, 1973; Foelker, Shewchuk, & Niedoreche, 1987; Louks, Hayne, & Smith, 1989; Wechowitz, Muir & Cropley, 1967).

Large-scale studies of the BDI with normal populations yield a skewed distribution, with a mean score in the range of 4 to 6. With this in mind, scores from 0 to 9 may be viewed as normal. Mild levels of depression are associated with scores of 10 to 20, with 11 to 15 suggesting dysphoria, and 15 or above associated with more serious depressive states. Scores of 20 to 30, then, may be seen as reflecting moderate levels of depression, and scores above 30 reflect severe depression. Studies that have selected outpatients on the basis of meeting Feighner, Research Diagnostic Criteria [RDC], or DSM III criteria for major depression typically report mean BDI scores of approximately 30 (Beck, Hollon, Young, Bedrosian, & Budenz, 1985; Bumberry, Oliver, & McClure, 1978; Murphy, Simons, Wetzel, & Lustman, 1984; Oliver & Simmons, 1984).

Although it was initially developed as a screen for depression among psychiatric patients, application of the BDI has been expanded to a range of normal, medical, and psychiatric populations (Steer, Beck, & Garrison, 1986). The psychometric properties of the BDI, as well as its clinical usage and limitations have been reviewed by Beck and Beamesderfer (1974), Mayer (1977), Kendall, Hollon,

Beck, Hammen, and Ingram (1987), and Beck, Steer, and Garbin (1988).

The BDI can be used both as a quantitative and qualitative instrument. We can assess the level of depression on a session-by-session basis, and can assess levels of depression in the morning and the evening as a means of measuring diurnal variation in mood. The BDI may also be used qualitatively to assess the components of a patient's depression. By doing an item analysis of the scale, the therapist can quickly identify the areas of foci of the depression. Two clients with BDI scores of 33 may be very different in terms of the profile of their scores. For example, client A may endorse items 1 to 11 at the highest level, yielding a score of 33. Client B, however, endorses items 11 to 21 at the highest level, also yielding a score of 33. Although the level of depression is equivalent, the content of their concerns is very different. Clinically, it is often found that items 3, 5, 6, 7, and 8 cluster together, suggesting a self-critical stance. Similarly, items 4, 12, 15, 17, and 21 often co-occur, indicating that the patient's primary concerns may center on a loss of energy, decreased motivation, and feelings of anhedonia. When the BDI score, therapist's clinical assessment, and client report are at variance, the therapist must clarify the discrepancy. It is often quite useful to ask patients whether the BDI score accurately reflects their mood, as well as reasons for changes in item scores from session to session.

The patient presenting with a BDI score of 10 to 14, who reports a chronic, low level of dysphoria, can be particularly difficult to work with. This type of client often is characterized as "anhedonic" or "dysthymic," and reports feeling a chronic, "blah" feeling about life. Although they often are actively working, involved with families or relationships, have friends they see on a regular basis and are successful in limited ways, they appear to experience a Taedium Vitae. Life is for them an underwhelming experience. A dinner at the finest restaurant in town is described as "all right." Their sex life is "fair." They describe a Pavoratti concert as "tuneful." They might avoid a walk along the beach at sunset or sunrise "because of all the sand." Clinically, these individuals present with a low activity level in session and a low motivation to complete homework assignments in conjunction with a normal speech level. They generally see life as an intrusion on their existence. Although they are dysphoric and dissatisfied with their predicament, their level of distress is not sufficient to motivate them to change. Such difficulties may be a manifestation of a depressive disorder, or may stem from a specific loss or frustration. With careful questioning, however, it is often possible to identify specific cognitions and behaviors that exacerbate their depression, and the specific schema that maintain it. As Stengel (1964) succinctly stated, "Man does not weary of life without reason."

In addition to assessing patients' levels of depression, it is valuable to evaluate their feelings of pessimism or hopelessness. An assessment of pessimism can be quite useful clinically in that it is strongly associated with suicidal risk (Beck, Brown, & Steer, 1989); Beck, Kovacs, & Weissman, 1975a; Kovacs, Beck, & Weissman, 1975; Lester & Beck, 1975a; Kovacs, Beck, and Weissman, 1976; Nekanda-Trepka, Bishop, & Blackburn, 1983). The Hopelessness Scale (HS) was developed by Beck, Weissman, Lester, and Trexler (1975) to meet this need. It is a 20-item scale, with items scored either true or false by the patient. Items were selected from a test of attitudes about the future (Heimberg, 1961), and from a pool of pessimistic statements made by psychiatric patients. Nine of the items are keyed false, and 11 are keyed true. The total hopelessness score, then, is simply the sum of the endorsed items. The psychometric properties of the HS are presented in the original Beck et al. (1975) article. The mean hopelessness score of an unselected sample of 2,300 outpatients seen at the Center for Cognitive Therapy was 9.5, with a standard deviation of 5.0. Clinically, then, scores of 0 to 3 on this measure are associated with minimal levels of hopelessness. Scores of 4 to 8 reflect low levels of hopelessness, and scores between 9 and 14 are associated with moderate feelings of hopelessness. Scores of 15 or above are considered clinically severe.

Evidence for the predictive validity of the HS has been provided by Beck, Steer, Kovacs, and Garrison (1985). They conducted a longitudinal study of 207 patients hospitalized because of suicidal ideations (though not for suicide attempts). During the 5 to 10 years following their hospitalization, 14 of these individuals committed suicide. A comparison of these individuals with patients who did not subsequently attempt suicide revealed important differences. The mean HS score among psychiatric inpatients who subsequently committed suicide was 13.27 ($SD = 4.43$), whereas the mean HS score of inpatients who reported experiencing suicidal ideations but did not subsequently commit suicide was 8.94 ($SD = 6.05$). Of data collected during their hospitalizations, only scores on the HS and the pessimism item of the BDI predicted eventual suicide. A score of 10 or more on the HS correctly identified 91% of eventual suicides. It is worth noting, however, that not all persons experiencing strong feelings of hopelessness manifest suicidal ideations or attempt suicide. Within the Beck et al. (1985) study, for example, the cutoff score of 9 yielded a false-positive rate of 88.4%. That is to say, 76 out of 86 suicide ideators with HS scores of 10 or more were misidentified. Increased levels of hopelessness among the general population and among persons suffering from physical illnesses have also been reported (Greene, 1981; Green, O'Mahoney, & Rungasamy, 1982). Although the HS is a strong predictor of suicidal risk, false positives remain an important concern given the low base rate of suicidal behavior, even among high-risk groups such as persons hospitalized because of suicidal thoughts. The measure is best employed, then, in conjunction with other measures of depression and suicidal intent. It remains, nonetheless, a powerful clinical tool. As scores on the HS rise above 9 to 10, so does suicidal potential. A patient reporting suicidal ideations, in conjunction with hopelessness scores above 13 to 14, then, suggests that they are at profound risk, and indicates the importance of immediate evaluation or intervention.

The validity of the HS has been questioned by several authors. Linehan and Nielsen (1981), for example, argue that the measure is not an adequate index of an individual's feelings of pessimism, as the scale is highly correlated with measures of social desirability. Specifically, they reported a negative correlation between scores on the HS and responses on the Edwards Social Desirability Scale. These issues have been further examined by Holden and Mendonca (1984); Holden, Mendonca, and Serin (1989); Mendonca, Holden, Mazmanian, and Dolan (1983); Holden, Mendonca, and Mazmanian (1985), Linehan and Nielsen (1983); Nevid (1983); and Strosahl, Linehan, and Chiles (1984). The principal concern voiced by these individuals is that the HS may yield too many false negatives, as it can be socially desirable to present oneself in a positive light.

Ellis (1985), however, administered the HS, the BDI, and the Marlowe-Crowne Social Desirability Scale (MCSDS) (Crown & Marlowe, 1960) to a sample of 60 psychiatric patients (including 20 who had attempted suicide, 20 suicide ideators, and 20 who were nonsuicidal). Correlations found among the measures led Ellis to conclude that controlling for social desirability "did not affect this correlation substantially, nor did the use of MCSDS scores in a discriminant analysis improve the accuracy of classification into severely suicidal and nonsuicidal groups." Similarly, Petrie and Chamberlain (1983), in a study of 54 patients who had attempted suicide, found that hopelessness was a strong predictor of suicidal behavior and cognitions. Social desirability, in contrast, was not found to mediate the relationship observed between pessimism and suicidality.

Although concerns regarding the impact of patient's response style on the HS are legitimate, high correlations between the HS and measures of social desirability have not been consistently found. Moreover, these relationships may reflect psychometric inadequacies of the social desirability scales or the specific populations sampled. Negative correlations between measures of hopelessness and social desirability are not unexpected within a cognitive framework. Depressed persons would be predicted to present themselves in a negative fashion, given their negative perceptions of themselves, their world, and their future. The finding of negative correlations between these measures by some authors then, may not reflect statistical artifact, or difficulties with the assessment of hopelessness. Rather, it may be a legitimate clinical phenomena, in that depressed or suicidal persons systematically view themselves in a negative manner and present this to others. The situation is reminiscent of the anecdote about the archaeologist who relied on statistical analysis, but did not participate in excavations or reflect on their findings. As his colleague noted, "the only artifacts he found were in his statistics."

The utility of the HS in the assessment of suicidality, then, still obtains. The scale has been found in numerous studies to be a stronger predictor of suicidal ideations and suicidal behavior than severity of depression. Kovacs, Beck, and Weissman (1975), for example, found the level of hopelessness to be a better predictor of suicidal ideations among hospitalized suicide attempters than was the level of depression. When depressed persons are unable to see alternative solutions to serious problems and feel that the current predicament requires an immediate solution, they come to view suicide as a viable way out.

Hopelessness, then, may be seen from a cognitive perspective as a central characteristic of depression, and the link between depression and suicide. Further, the sense of hopelessness that accompanies other psychiatric disorders predispose patients to suicidal ideations and place them at greater risk of suicidal behavior. Beck, Kovacs, and Weissman (1975), for example, reported that hopelessness accounted for 76% of the association between depression and suicidal intent among 384 hospitalized suicide attempters. Similarly, Minkoff, Bergman, Beck, and Beck (1973) reported that intensity of suicidal intent was more highly correlated with hopelessness than with level of depression. When patients who had been hospitalized for depression or suicidal ideations, rather than for suicide attempts, were examined, it was again found that hopelessness, rather than level of depression, predicted suicidal intent (Bedrosian & Beck, 1979; Wetzel, Margulies, Davis, & Karam, 1980). Similar findings have been reported in studies by Bagley and Ramsay (1985); Dyer and Kreitman (1984); Wetzel (1976); Nathan and Rousch (1984); Nekanda-Trepka, Bishop, and Blackburn (1983); Wang et al. (1985); and Whitters, Cadoret, and Widmer (1985).

The Scale of Suicidal Ideation (SSI; Beck, Kovacs, & Weissman, 1979) is available in a multiple-choice self-report format. The content and goals of the measure are discussed later on in this chapter.

Interview of Family and Significant Others

A second source of data is the report of significant others, including the patient's family. This might include historical data relative to the chronicity of the suicidal thinking or behavior, longevity of the problem, family history of depression and suicide, perception of client coping skills previously used to deal with the depression, and the like. These are all important data for the therapist to have. The patient may not be the best reporter of life history at the time of the evaluation. The information gained from significant others, then, is particularly useful in assessing both the patient's current symptoms, and their Axis V diagnosis, their highest level of adaptive functioning during the past year. For example:

A 23-year-old man was referred for treatment because of his constant suicidal statements. His "reason" for wanting to kill himself was his "inability to make friends," "always being alone," and general jealousy about the relationships others seem to have. When questioned about his previous friendships, he stated that he "never had any friends," "never had a buddy," and was "always alone." When his mother was interviewed, she stated that until the past year he had several friends with whom he spent time and went places, and seemed to enjoy.

Assuming that the report of his mother is accurate, the issue for the therapist is why the patient has either distorted, lied, or avoided dealing with the fact that he is able to develop friendships. This becomes the grist for the therapeutic mill.

Although not always possible, interviewing of family members can be a valuable component of an evaluation of suicidal risk. Having the family or significant other (S.O.) complete the same self-report forms completed by the patient. By using an "S.O." version of the forms, the clinician can assess the differences between self- and other-report. For example, rewording the instructions on the BDI to read "Fill out this form as you believe your _____ would complete it for the past week." This can also be done with the HS and the SSI.

Suicidal attempts on the part of children and adolescents, almost invariably are associated with serious family difficulties. Similarly, suicidal crises among adults are often precipitated or exacerbated by difficulties with family members or in other important relationships. As noted in chapter 2, relatively early events in an individual's family history may leave them vulnerable to suicidal thoughts and behavior. Later interpersonal or family difficulties may activate these schemata and precipitate a suicidal crisis. Although the role of the family and others in the attempt may not initially be clear, they often become apparent over the course of the clinical interview. As Stengel (1964) observed, "they [family members] often come into the picture as objects of (the patient's) love and hate, during and after the attempt."

In evaluating the family of suicidal individuals, it is important to assess their feelings toward the patient, as well as their thoughts regarding the suicide attempt. These thoughts and feelings may be openly expressed or may be poorly articulated. Frequently, family members feel an increased sense of sympathy or concern for the patient after an attempt. This may be used therapeutically in encouraging them to assist the patient with therapy and in making environmental changes. Alternatively, family members living with a depressed or suicidal individual may themselves become quite distressed. The resulting reductions in their overall levels of functioning, and in their ability to support the patient, can exacerbate the depressive crisis. Numerous researchers have examined the role of close relationships in the course of depression, and the adverse effects of depression on these relationships (Coyne, 1976; Coyne, Kessler, Tal, Turnbull, Wortman, & Greden, 1987). Quite frequently, interactions between depressed persons and their spouses or relatives are conflictual. Recent research by Coyne et al. (1987), for example, found that more than 40% of adults living with a depressed individual became sufficiently distressed themselves to warrant referral for therapeutic treatment. Interviews with family members can provide important information about the patient's social supports, as well as stresses in the home that may be compounding their difficulties.

Not surprisingly, when the interview of family members reveals that they feel a lack of concern, or even disdain, there is an increased risk for the patient. For example, the mother of a 12-year-old girl was interviewed in the intensive care unit of the hospital. Her daughter had taken 200 Tofranil in the school gymnasium and had experienced a cardiac arrest. When notified by a nurse that "it didn't look as if she would make it,"she responded calmly "and we gave her opportunity." When her daughter regained consciousness and requested a drink, her mother admonished the nurses "not to let her keep manipulating you like that."

Risk is increased, as well, by family members' tendency to minimize or deny the seriousness of the patient's suicide attempt. It is not uncommon, for example, to hear family members comment that the patient was "just trying to get our attention." This tendency to minimize the gravity of the situation may indicate serious interpersonal difficulties within the family, or simply attempts to cope with the crisis. Regardless, denial or minimization on the part of significant others represents a potentially serious impediment to therapeutic progress—particularly with children and adolescents.

The family interview may also be valuable in uncovering other risk factors for suicide. These include a history of psychopathology or suicide attempts among family members and a lack of family stability or cohesion. It may be apparent, for example, that family members demonstrate poor empathy, communication difficulties, or problem-solving deficits. As a consequence, they may be unable to provide each other with a sense of support or security. In short, if the patient is returning to an aversive environment, in which the problems and concerns that precipitated the attempt remain, and there are limited supports to assist the individual in managing these problems—the risks remain.

Family members and other individuals who are significant and meaningful to the patient can be important sources of information and feedback within the therapy and may assist the therapist by acting as change agents. Family members may change their behaviors, and by decreasing the maladaptive ways through which they interact with the patient, they may increase the positive interactions. As they support positive change in the patient's behavior, they serve to keep therapeutic change going outside of the therapist's office. Significant others can also assist in reality testing and providing numerous opportunities for the patient to test new behaviors.

Clinical Interview

The third mode of assessment is the clinician's view of the client's general mood and mental status. There are several specific questions to keep in mind during the clinical interview that will help in assessing current risk level, conceptualizing the patient's difficulty, and ultimately in treatment planning.

1. What reasons do patients have for considering suicide, or for having attempted suicide? Was it motivated by a desire to get a sense of relief from their problems or from a wish to manipulate others?

2. Do patients manifest a specific psychiatric disorder?

3. Do patients currently experience significant feelings of depression or hopelessness? Do they feel their current situation is intolerable and requires an immediate solution? Do they present themselves as clinically anxious, agitated, hostile, evasive, or suspicious?

4. What is the degree of their suicidal intent? What exactly did they do? Did they believe it would be successful? Was the attempt carefully planned or relatively impulsive? Was "rescue" anticipated or likely?

5. What situational or personal factors contributed? How longstanding and intractable are the difficulties that precipitated the attempt?

6. What resources or supports are available to patients? This may include family, friends, clergy, coworkers, or professionals. Are there persons they feel they are able to turn to and in whom they can confide?

7. Do they possess adaptive coping capabilities, or, conversely, have they shown maladaptive coping strategies, such as alcohol or substance abuse? How have they been able to cope with serious problems and stressful situations in the past?

8. What is their current attitude about death and suicide? What does it mean to the patient to be dead? To be alive? To have failed in their attempt? Do they plan to try again? what do they think others, such as their family and friends, feel about their plan or attempt?

9. Are there deterrents? It is often useful to simply ask, "Why not kill yourself now? What's holding you back?" It may then be possible to explore possible reasons for living. Do patients anticipate that change in their predicament is possible? Hope for the future, then, would be seen as a strong deterrent. A patient's concern for the effect of their death on their children or family, however, is less viable as a deterrent, as they could come to believe that "they'd be better off without me." Do patients have religious or moral beliefs that deter them from committing suicide? In some situations, it is helpful to discuss their religious beliefs with them, even if they are not currently active in a church or synagogue. Beliefs and values they had been ex-

posed to during their upbringing may be present but not readily acknowledged.

10. Are there unstated beliefs or presumptions maintaining their desire to die? Examples include beliefs that "I deserve to be punished," "All my life I've known I'd never live past 30," and "Life is meaningless."

11. Are they able to generate and evaluate alternative solutions? Are they flexible thinkers, or do they demonstrate a rigid cognitive style? Are they acceptant of alternatives suggested by the clinician, or do they negate these as untenable?

The evaluation of the suicidal patient, then, will include assessments of the presenting problems, the precipitating stresses or events, and the individual's family history. Particular attention may be given to evaluating stresses within the family, and their ability to support the patient at the present time. The clinician cannot presume that they understand what the patient means by "bad," "awful," "depressed for the last time," or "just disappear." It is essential that each of the stated concerns be explored and clarified, with the goal of developing a specific problem list. If the therapist responds by encouraging the patient to present a vague list of complaints, with the objective of allowing catharsis or "ventilation," there can be little specificity to the therapy. We cannot stress too strongly, then, the importance of operationally defining terms with the patient. Although we might encourage patients to "ventilate" during the session, this should be followed by reflection and clarification of their concerns. It is, in short, active listening. Reflection and clarification of their concerns by the therapist enhances patients' sense of being understood and having spoken their mind, thereby facilitating the development of a trusting therapeutic relationship. Moreover, it provides a structure or means of understanding problems or feelings that otherwise may be poorly articulated in the patients' mind and may lead them to feel overwhelmed.

For example, if the client is crying yet reports no dysphoria, the therapist must clarify exactly what the emotional issue is for the particular patient. The general level of activity during the interview as compared with the reported activity level at home, the patient's appearance during the session, voice quality, and content are all included in the therapist's assessment. When the patient's report and the way they present themselves during the interview are at variance, the therapist needs to clarify the processes that put those two sources of information in conflict. For example:

A 30-year-old woman was referred for treatment of severe depression. She stated that she was very depressed and had been depressed for several years. She reported that she was too depressed to do any work, other than for her father in his business. She had completed college after 7 years with a 4.2 grade-point average (on a 4.0 scale) (as her university graded on a +/- system, she was able to earn a 4.2 by receiving A+ grades). She was extremely well dressed, exotically made up, and well spoken. She stated that she was aware that she did not look or sound depressed, but that her BDI score of 48 was an accurate assessment of her level of depression.

This woman's score on the BDI would be far more consistent with severe depression. Her lack of psychomotor retardation, work history, academic achievement, demeanor, dress, and verbal expressiveness, however, were more suggestive of a histrionic style. Her suicidal gestures, then, appeared not to stem from feelings of hopelessness, but from poor impulse control, a need for excitement, and a desire to be noticed.

Another example follows:

A 46-year-old businessman was referred for treatment of anxiety by his family physician. He presented as teary eyed, and manifested generally depressed affect, psychomotor retardation, and malaise. He remarked that he was far more depressed than was obvious. His score on the BDI was 7, indicating a level of depression within the normal range.

As in any clinical interview, attention should be given to the development of a trusting alliance or "therapeutic collaboration." This is particularly important with potentially suicidal individuals, given their sense of hopelessness and the common belief that they "have to go through it alone." With this in mind, a nonjudgmental, supportive stance is recommended. This would involve active listening, as well as an assessment of the specific automatic thoughts that the person presents and their consequent emotions. Attempts should be made to convey to the patient that you accept their concerns and feelings, and do not deny the legitimacy of their suicidal thoughts.

Several structured interviews have been developed and have proved useful in providing reliable diagnoses of affective disorders in adults and children. These include the Schedule for Affective Disorders and Schizophrenia, which was developed by Endicott and Spitzer (1978), and Diagnostic Interview Schedule (Robins, Helzer, Croughan, & Ratcliff, 1981). More recently, Spitzer and Williams (1983) developed the Structured Clinical Interview for DSM III (SCID), and its revised form, the SCID-R, as an efficient and flexible means of making differential diagnoses according to DSM III–R criteria. Unlike other structured diagnostic interviews, the SCID–R was modeled after clinical interviews, and so begins with an overview of the patient's presenting concerns and past episodes of psychopathology. These relatively open-ended questions are followed by a systematic series of questions regarding specific symptoms. In research conducted at the Center for Cognitive Therapy, Riskind, Beck, Berchick, Brown, and Steer (1987) found the SCID to be highly reliable in providing diagnoses of major depression and generalized anxiety disorder. The percent agreement of independent raters for major depression was 82% and 86% for generalized anxiety disorder. Kappa coefficients were .72 and .79, respectively. Structured interviews, then, appear to be a reasonably reliable means of identifying specific problems experienced by patients and have the virtue of encouraging us to assess a broad band of potential concerns rather than to have our attention limited by the patient's presenting problems.

The therapist's subjective impression of the patient can also play an important role in the evaluation. This is based not solely on lore of master therapists' clinical acumen but also on research. Motto, Heilbron, and Juster (1985), for example, employed stepwise regression analyses in developing a clinical scale to estimate suicidal potential among adults who were hospitalized because of depressive or suicidal states (suicide had been attempted, threatened, or planned). Among the 15 variables derived was "interviewer's reaction to the subject." They found that therapist's having experienced a "neutral or negative reaction" to the patient was associated with an increased risk of suicidal attempts during the 2 years following the evaluation. The authors speculate that this may stem from interpersonal difficulties experienced by depressed or suicidal individuals. As they stated, "if our interviewers had a negative subjective reaction to a patient, the chances of that person developing a firm support system after leaving the hospital were not very good."

A clinician's emotional reaction to a patient, as well as the automatic thoughts elicited by the patient's presentation, behavior, and comments are worthy of careful examination. Although they may, to use a more traditional term, reflect a countertransference reaction, in that they are elicited by the activation of the therapist's underlying schema, they may also be a reflection of behaviors and beliefs of the patient. For example, a clinician reported having felt attracted to a 29-year-old women, who had sought treatment because of a series of depressive episodes and suicidal gestures. Although the patient was not overtly seductive, she was neatly dressed and was quite ingratiating toward the clinician. It became apparent over the course of treatment that this was typical of her behavior toward men. She tended to feel overwhelmed by day-to-day responsibilities. Despite having earned a master's degree from a major university, she was highly insecure regarding her competence. She would, then, adopt a dependent and solicitous demeanor, with the goal of gaining support, reassurance, and guidance from men. She reported, for example, that men regularly "come up to me on the street . . . they say I look confused and ask me if I need help."

A physical exam should be included within the evaluation, particularly when there is evidence of alcohol or drug abuse, or a psychotic process. A mental status exam may be useful as well in assessing patient's reality testing, judgment, impulse control, and lability of affect. Although patients may be hesitant to acknowledge auditory hallucinations, these are not uncommon among severely depressed individuals. Empathetic, albeit forthright, questioning may allow persons to discuss the occurrence of ego-dystonic/mood congruent hallucinations. These may take the form of command hallucinations or of critical voices telling them such things as "Live in fear" or "You must die."

Although schizophrenic individuals are at particular risk for suicide (Bleuler, 1978; Tsuang, 1978), the evidence that this increased risk is related to command hallucinations is equivocal. Nathan and Rousch (1984), for example, conducted a retrospective survey of 24 patients who committed suicide. Although 9 of the 24 had received a diagnosis of schizophrenia, the authors reported that they were "unable to find any evidence that any of these people had had an exacerbation of their psychotic state at the time of their death." As a consequence, they concluded that "a more prominent factor is the feelings of hopelessness patients have about their illness."

These conclusions are consistent with recent work by Drake, Gates, Whitaker, and Cotton (1985). They observed that suicide among schizophrenics tends to occur more frequently during periods of depression and hopelessness than during episodes of intense psychosis. These findings are congruent, then, with observations by Shaffer, Perlin, Schmidt, and Stephens (1974), Yarden (1974), and Brier and Astrachan (1984). Research by Roy (1982) revealed that suicidal risk among schizophrenics was associated with a course characterized by recurring exacerbations and remissions. These patients experience functional deterioration, yet retain a nondelusional awareness of the effects of their illness. Their consequent feelings of hopelessness and despair in conjunction with impaired problem-solving place them at greater risk.

Objective Testing

A fourth means of assessing severity of depression and suicidal risk is through objective testing. Reviews of the literature regarding the assessment of suicidal risk suggest, however, that traditional psychological tests, such as the Rorschach, Bender-Gestalt, Rosenzweig Picture-Frustration Test, Minnesota Multiphasic Personality Inventory (MMPI), and Thematic Apperception Test, may be less accurate as predictors of suicidality than are measures specifically designed to assess suicidal ideations (Brown & Sheran, 1982; Farberow, 1981; Hawton, 1987; Neuringer, 1974a, b; Lester, 1970, 1974). Several scales have been developed during the past 25 years that have been designed to predict suicidal risk (Cohen, Motto, & Seiden, 1966; Devries, 1966; Lettieri, 1974; Zung, 1974). The Scale for Suicidal Ideations (SSI) focuses specifically on patient's thoughts regarding suicide, and appears to be a reliable and valid index of suicidal intent. The scale was developed by Beck, Schuyler, and Herman (1974) as a means of quantifying the severity of patients' suicidal thoughts and impulses. It is comprised of 19 items, which are rated by the clinician on a scale of 0 (least severe) to 3 (severest) and is administered in the form of a semistructured interview. The total can range from 0 to 38 and is derived by summing the item ratings. Separate scores are derived for patients' thoughts and feelings on the day of the interview, and for the "worst point of crisis."

Although certain items, such as "I have written a suicide note" were endorsed infrequently by suicidal individuals, they were retained in the scale because of their clinical utility. Although fewer than 20% of suicide completers prepare suicide notes (Shneidman, 1979), the preparation of one may be seen as a pathognomic sign.

In addition to providing a quantitative index of the severity of patients' suicidal thoughts, the SSI may be used in a qualitative manner. We have found it clinically useful to review the items regarding patients' development of a plan, availability of means, preparation for death, and desires to conceal their feelings from others. As Waters, Sendbuehler, Kincel, Boodoosing, and Marchenko (1982) stated in concluding their review of the literature on the prediction of suicide, "the best indicator of suicidal risk, then, remains a statement of suicidal intent by the patient. The seriousness of this intent is generally associated with the degree of deliberate planning and preparation."

The Suicide Intent Scale (SIS; Beck, Schuyler, & Herman, 1974) is highly useful, then, in that it directly assesses this intent. In addition, the SIS provides the clinician with information regarding the nature and strength of available deterrents. The SIS does not, however, include questions regarding patients' knowledge of the lethality of their plan. As such, it is often quite useful to assess their beliefs regarding the lethality of their plan or attempt as part of the clinical interview of the patient. Clinically, we have found that individuals who have planned or made attempts by relatively nonlethal means, but who believed their plan was lethal, may be at greater risk for future attempts.

Psychiatric Disorders and Suicide

Because of the multifaceted nature of suicidal ideation and behavior, suicidal patients cannot be viewed as a homogenous population (Blumenthal & Kupfer, 1986). It can be argued that persons who complete suicide may be distinguished in important ways from unsuccessful attempters and suicide ideators (Beck, Resnick, & Lettieri, 1974). Moreover, although specific psychiatric diagnoses have been associated with increased risk of self-destructive behavior, including major depression (Fawcett, 1985), bipolar disorders (Jamison, 1986), alcohol abuse (Frances, Franklin, & Falvin, 1986), schizophrenia (Drake, Gates, Whitaker, & Cotton, 1985; Johns, Stanley, & Stanley, 1986), and personality disorders (Frances, Fryer, & Clarkin, 1986), limited progress has been made in identifying commonalities among these patient groups. With this in mind, a multiaxial approach to diagnosis is recommended.

In addition to identifying Axis I diagnoses that suicidal individuals manifest, it is useful to clarify characterological contributions to their difficulties. Several reports indicate that a significant proportion of suicide attempters and completers manifest Axis II disorders (Morrison, 1982), and that personality disorders may increase the suicidal risk of patients with Axis I disorders (Crumly, 1979; Friedman, Aronoff, Clarkin, Corn, & Hurt, 1983). Recent work by Francis, Fyer, and Clarkin (1986) suggests that patients manifesting antisocial and borderline traits are at particular risk for suicidal behavior. In a similar manner, strongly dependent individuals may be at increased risk for suicidal behavior during episodes of depression (Birtchnell, 1981; Pallis & Birtchnell, 1977; Paykel & Dienelt, 1971).

Patients suffering from chronic or progressive illnesses have frequently been found to experience strong feelings of dysphoria and hopelessness. Sawyer, Adams, Conway, Reeves, & Kvale (1983), for example, examined a sample of patients with chronic obstructive pulmonary disease, and found that they tended to develop a sense of hopelessness and discouragement as they came to recognize that recovery was not possible. As they accepted the irreversibility of their condition, several became "susceptible to extremes of depression, and developed suicidal ideations." This finding is particularly important in that elderly individuals, who frequently suffer from debilitating chronic illnesses, are at high risk for suicide.

The importance of developing an accurate diagnosis during the initial stages of treatment cannot be overemphasized. Several large-scale studies have examined the relationship of psychiatric disorders to suicide, with the consensus being that more than 90% of persons who successfully attempt suicide manifest a psychiatric disorder (Barraclough, Bunch, Nelson, & Sainsbury, 1974; Beck, Steer, Kovacs, & Garrison, 1985; Hagnell, Lanke, & Rorsman, 1981). In as much as depression, alcoholism, and substance abuse are the major psychiatric diagnoses associated with suicide (Blumenthal, 1984; Evenson, Wood, Nuttall, & Cho, 1982; Vaillant, 1966; Weissman, 1974), the detection and treatment of these disorders may be seen as central to preventing suicide. As we have seen, several studies suggest that cognitive therapy is useful in treating these disorders. Moreover, there appear to be specific cognitions, beliefs, and schemata that are characteristic of individual disorders. As such, the diagnosis may guide initial interventions in cognitive therapy.

We have, for example, found it helpful in some circumstances to acknowledge that "Suicide is an option, things are bad for you, and death is something that can be considered." This is followed by noting that there may be other alternatives available and that suicide may not be a high priority. In addition to enhancing rapport, this approach may reduce manipulative gains patients may seek through suicidal threats. There is little risk in asking about suicidal thoughts or impulses directly. Rather, patients may be reassured by your candor as well as your willingness to address their most serious concerns directly. By stressing the seriousness with which their statements or behavior are taken, the therapist is conveying a genuine concern and desire to help. Guidelines for the assessment of suicidal patients have also been prepared by Jacobs (1982), Frederick (1981), and Hawton and Catalan (1982).

After the objective materials, self-report, family interview, and clinical assessment of the patient have been completed, a cognitive conceptualization or formulation can be made. This would include (a) a description of the person's most salient or significant automatic thoughts, and the specific emotions that stem from them; (b) a description of possible schemata that underlie these beliefs; (c) a description of the specific environmental or social stresses that have precipitated the current crisis; and (d) a listing of the resources and coping capacities that the patient can bring to bear on their current problems. The objectives, then, are to integrate historical and current life situation material to clarify the factors that have combined to place the person at risk. We may then employ this information to devise techniques directed at resolving their current predicament, providing the patient with a sense of mastery and hope, and shifting their beliefs. In the short term, the emphasis is made on developing the patient's belief that "life is worth living," "death is not a reasonable alternative," and "problems are solvable."

Given that a primary goal of the initial evaluation is to keep the patient safe from self-generated physical danger, the question will arise: Is the patient safe to be released, or is hospitalization indicated? This specific decision rests on several factors, many of them dependent on the clinician's judgment:

1. Has the patient been open and honest in discussing their concerns and feelings?
2. Is there an imminent risk of suicidal behavior (e.g., verbal or behavioral indicators of risk)?
3. Is there concurrent, serious psychopathology such as psychosis, mania, or intoxication that would make them unable (as opposed to unwilling) to care for themselves at the present time?
4. Are there unresolved stressors or problems that are of sufficient severity that the person could not tolerate them until a follow-up appointment?

In the event the patient is not hospitalized either because the clinician does not deem inpatient care necessary, the patient refuses hospitalization, or the patient is refused admission, it is recommended that (a) a follow-up appointment be made for the following day, or at least regular phone contacts until the appointment; (b) the patient be provided with emergency phone numbers; (c) the patient agrees to a "no-suicide contract"; and (d) specific arrangements be made for the patient to stay with a friend or family member for support.

Suicide Notes

The suicide note is often the single most important part of the postmortem psychological autopsy of suicide (Schneidman, Farberow, & Litman, 1970). In an interesting study by Tuckman, Kleiner, and Lavell (1959), suicide notes were evaluated in terms of five variables: (a) person to whom the note was addressed (interpersonal elements); (b) reasons for suicide (stated conscious reasons); (c) affect indicated (or implied); (d) content (patient's main concerns); and (e) the overall tenor of the note (instructions, etc.). The major finding of the study was that there was no difference between note writers and nonnote-writing suiciders in respect to age, race, sex, employment, martial status, physical or mental condition, history of mental illness, place of suicide, unusual circumstances preceding the suicide, medical care and supervision, and history of threats of previous attempts. In summary, the writing of a suicide note is a pathognomic marker of serious intent, but the lack of a note cannot be used to indicate a lack of seriousness or intention to suicide (Beck, Morris, & Lester, 1974).

Assessment of Biologic Markers

Given the research on biologic markers of suicidal behavior, the question remains: Are 5-HIAA assays clinically useful in assessing the suicidal potential of individual patients? The answer is "perhaps" for some patients under some circumstances. Åsberg, Nordstrom, and Traskman-Bendz (1986) reported the results of a 1-year follow-up study of 76 patients with low cerebrospinal concentrations of 5-HIAA. These individuals were 10 times as likely to commit suicide during the following year as patients with normal to above-average levels of the metabolite. Twenty-one percent of their low 5-HIAA group committed suicide compared with 2% of the remaining patients. Similar findings have been reported by Roy, Agren, Pickar, Linnoila, Doran, Cutler, and Paul (1988). It is not clear, however, whether these findings are limited to suicide attempters or can be generalized to individuals with suicidal ideations who have no history of prior attempts. Similarly, it is not known whether 5-HIAA assays have predictive utility above and beyond more conventional (and less costly and invasive) measures of impulsivity and aggressiveness. Reviews of this literature have recently been prepared by Roy and Linnoila (1988) and Roy (1992).

The clinical utility of assessing monoamine metabolites is limited at present for several reasons. Tricyclic antidepressants typically interfere with serotonin turnover and reduce CSF concentrations of 5-HIAA. As such, the measurement of cerebrospinal 5-HIAA concentrations requires that the individual be off all neuroleptic and antidepressant medications.

Moreover, concentrations of 5-HIAA can vary with age, sex, height, season, and the time of day the assessment is made, thereby reducing our confidence in the reliability of the observations. The usefulness of these techniques for estimating the suicidal potential of high-risk inpatients is also limited, as such individuals typically receive psychotropic medications as part of their treatment regime.

These findings are, nonetheless, thought-provoking and suggest several directions for future research. Although, for example, several authors have reported that low cerebrospinal 5-HIAA levels persist after the remission of depression (Traskman-Bendz, 1983; Van Praag, 1977), it is not yet known whether variations in 5-HIAA levels that do occur over the course of treatment are associated with changes in suicidal potential, or whether decreased cerebrospinal 5-HIAA concentrations are associated with a poor response to subsequent psychotherapy or pharmacological interventions. Similarly, the incremental validity of assessing cerebrospinal 5-HIAA levels as part of a clinical evaluation has not been documented, nor has its utility in assessing the suicidal potential of high-risk populations (such as the elderly or persons suffering from alcohol or substance abuse). The validity of this measure as an index of suicidal potential among adolescents has received no study whatsoever. As noted, the assessment of cerebrospinal 5-HIAA concentrations requires invasive procedures and is not applicable with patients receiving antidepressant or neuroleptic medications. The validity of less invasive measures of monoamine activity and related neuroendocrine functioning, including peripheral measures of serotonin activity, increased secretion of cortisol, decreased cortisol suppression after administration of dexamethasone, and the fenfluramine prolactin response test, have received little study. It is not known, for example, whether these measures are also associated with increased impulsivity and suicidal potential. Recent work by Coccaro et al. (1989) suggests that prolactin responses to fenfluramine challenge are blunted among depressed patients, as well as aggressive or impulsive individuals. As such, these less invasive measures show promise as research and clinical instruments. The behavioral and psychophysiological concomitants of reduced 5-HIAA concentrations have not been fully explored. Similarly, little attention has been paid to the study of first-degree relatives of suicidal patients or of nonsuicidal individuals who manifest low cerebrospinal 5-HIAA concentrations. Although researchers typically presume that neurochemical metabolites are a substrate of impulsive or aggressive behavior, few individuals have asked the alternative question: What is the effect of psychotherapy or environmental change on neurotransmitter levels? Do, for example, cerebrospinal concentrations of

5-HIAA increase in tandem with behavioral and emotional improvement over the course of psychotherapy?

Summary

A complete clinical assessment of suicidal ideation is essential. This assessment must be part of both the initial evaluation and of the ongoing evaluation of the patient in treatment. The therapist must take any indications of suicide seriously and evaluate them with care. Depression and suicidal risk may be assessed in four ways: through patient self-report, the report of significant others, clinician interviews or ratings, and through objective test data. Given the limitations of each approach—in terms of reliability, validity, and clinical utility—a multimodal assessment typically will provide a clearer view of the patient's concerns and allow for a more accurate assessment of suicidal risk. The assessment, then, is of value beyond the gathering of information and the preparation of a treatment plan.

The importance of developing an accurate diagnosis during the initial stages of treatment cannot be overemphasized. Several large-scale studies have examined the relationship of psychiatric disorders to suicide, with the consensus being that more than 90% of persons who successfully attempt suicide manifest a psychiatric disorder.

There are several biological markers that may, in the future, prove useful in estimating suicidal potential.

The assessment, then, is of value beyond the gathering of information and the preparation of a treatment plan. It can be used, very effectively, to enable patients to come into touch with the fears, anxiety, dread, anger, and despair that threaten to overwhelm them. By putting these emotions and concerns into words, clarifying them, objectifying them, and gaining distance from them, the person is able to gain a sense of control over them. Moreover, sharing these concerns with a supportive clinician enables the person to feel that their problems are understandable, that solutions may be obtainable, and that they are accepted as a person. As such, assessment is the first step of an integrated treatment approach, which is the topic of the following chapters.

4

Cognitive Therapy: From Conceptualization to Intervention

> Cure her of that: Canst thou not minister to a mind diseas'd,
> Pluck from the memory a rooted sorrow;
> Raze out the hidden troubles of the brain;
> And with some sweet oblivious antidote
> Cleanse the stuff'd bosom of that perilous stuff
> Which weighs upon the heart?
>
> —*Wm. Shakespeare, Macbeth,* Act V, Scene 3.

> Experience is the child of thought, and thought is the child of action.
>
> —*Benjamin Disraeli*

Cognitive therapy treatment follows several discrete steps. The first step requires that a thorough assessment, as discussed in chapter 3, be completed. Using the information from the assessment, the therapist begins to develop a conceptualization of the patient's problems. The conceptualization becomes the guide for the therapist in determining direction and targets for therapy. The cognitive therapist develops hypotheses about the reasons for the patient's suicidal or covertly self-destructive behavior, and determines what reinforcers (internal or external) maintain the patient's suicidal thoughts and behaviors. The conceptualization also suggests strategies for intervention, and the most potentially promising interventions to be tried to effect the strategy. For maximum impact and effectiveness, the therapist will need a range of skills and techniques to implement the treatment strategy. The techniques or combinations of techniques are selected to suit the purpose and goals of therapy, the therapist's conceptualization of the problem(s), the needs of the patient at the specific point in therapy, the resources available in the patient's environment, and the therapist's skill and style.

The goal of this chapter is to describe a case conceptualization approach with the conceptualization then leading to a broad range of strategies and techniques that are used in cognitive therapy. There are several steps in establishing a treatment plan for the suicidal patient. The initial step involves the therapist developing a conceptualization of the problem(s). This conceptualization will, of necessity, be based on family and developmental histories, test data, interview material, and reports of previous therapists, or other professionals. This conceptualization must meet several criteria. It must be (a) useful, (b) simple, (c) coherent, (d) explain past behavior, (e) make sense of present behavior, and (f) be useful in predicting future behavior. The conceptualization process begins with the compilation of a problem list. This list can then be prioritized in terms of identifying a sequence of problems to be dealt with in therapy. The reasons for choosing one problem as opposed to another as the primary, secondary, or tertiary focuses of the therapy depends on many factors. A particular problem may be the primary focus of therapy because of its debilitating effect on the individual. In another case, there may be no debilitating problems. The focus may be on the simplest problem, thereby giving the patient practice in problem solving and some measure of success. In a third case, the choice of a primary focus might be on a "keystone" problem; that is, a problem whose solution will cause a ripple effect in solving other problems. Having set out the treatment goals with the patient, the therapist can begin to develop strategies and the interventions that will help effect the strategies.

Although the available techniques are broadly categorized in this chapter as cognitive (focused primarily on modifying thoughts, images, and beliefs) and in chapter 5 as behavioral (focused primarily on modifying overt behavior), they are not mutually exclusive. A "behavioral" technique such as assertiveness training has many cognitive aspects. Assertiveness training techniques can be used to accomplish cognitive changes such as adjustment in expectancies regarding the consequences of assertion as well as changes in interpersonal behavior.

The decision of whether to use cognitive or behavioral techniques can be heuristically determined using the following model (see Figure 4.1). In any therapy, the mix of cognitive or behavioral techniques is arranged in an inverse order. The greater the patient's pathology (or, conversely, the lower the patient's ability), the more likely the therapist will need to use behavioral interventions.[1] The

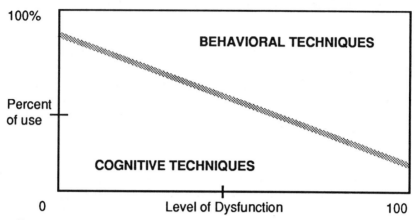

Figure 4.1   Level of Dysfunction and the use of Cognitive or Behavioral Interventions.

less impaired, the more readily cognitive techniques can be used. The therapist can estimate, based on clinical interview, the degree of impairment. By drawing a vertical line at that point, the therapist can ascertain the approximate ratio of cognitive to behavioral techniques.

Development of Treatment Conceptualization

The treatment conceptualization may be thought of as a "picture" of the patient's problems. The greater the congruence of that picture to the patient's internal cognitive or affective state, the greater the therapist's understanding of the patient's internal realities. If the problems are well conceptualized, the patient becomes more understandable and predictable in thought and action. By developing hypotheses about the patient's operant schema based on the patient's verbalizations, behavior, or family information, the therapist can, by direct questioning work toward validating, modifying, or rejecting the original hypotheses. The following examples serve to illustrate hypothesis formulation:

A 44-year-old married man comes for his initial therapy appointment accompanied by his mother after having ingested about 100 aspirin. She refuses to remain in the waiting room and demands to sit in on the session; he quietly agrees.

Given the available data, several hypotheses immediately come to mind. The therapist can begin, quite quickly, to gather the data necessary to confirm or refute any or all of the initial hypothetical alternatives. The hypotheses might include (but are not limited to) the following:

> He is dependent (he brought his mother and easily acceded to her demand).
>
> He is having marital difficulties (his wife did not accompany him).
>
> He is feeling helpless or weak (he brought someone with him).
>
> Mother is overbearing (she may have accompanied him against his will; she demands to be in the session).
>
> Mother is very concerned (she has accompanied him and demands to be in the session).
>
> Wife is unavailable or unconcerned (she is absent).

In the next example, the same hypothesis testing strategy is used:

A 13-year-old girl has made two suicide attempts by taking a sampling of several different pills found in her mother's medicine cabinet, and then quickly telling her mother what she had done. In each instance, the pill-taking followed a problem in peer relationships.

The hypotheses might include the following:

> She is histrionic.
>
> She has poor impulse control.
>
> She has poor problem-solving skills.
>
> She wanted attention.

In both of these cases, the initial hypotheses are available for modification as the therapist collects additional data. The hypotheses also serve to direct the therapist toward the patient's dysfunctional thoughts, assumptions, and schemata.

The working hypotheses can be shared with patients as questions. Rather than interpreting patients' thoughts or actions based on rigid theoretical formulations of suicidal behavior (e.g., suicidal behavior always represents retroflected anger, a cry for help, and the like), the evaluation of the alternatives *must* be based on the data from the patients and their perceptions and beliefs. The statement of the hypotheses as interpretations runs the risk of having the therapist "mind reading" patients' thoughts and intentions. The questioning format allows the patient to maintain integrity and allows the therapist to gather the most accurate data.

Assessment and Testing of Dysfunctional Thinking

The therapist must question what reinforces and maintains dysfunctional thinking and behavior. The major factor would appear to be the self-consonance of the belief system. If a particular belief is only partially believed by individuals it is much easier for them to give it up, because they are giving up a small piece of a belief system as opposed to asking them to challenge what they see and regard as "self." More chronic patients, including those with chronic "neurotic" behaviors and character disorders, who seek treatment often see their symptoms as "me." They will readily verbalize, "This is who we are, and this is the way we have always been." By asking them to challenge or directly dispute their dysfunctional beliefs we are then asking them to challenge their very being directly. When the challenge to self is perceived, individuals usually respond with anxiety. They are then placed in a conflict situation as to whether they would prefer to maintain their particular dysfunctional symptoms or to experience anxiety. As they see themselves defined by the problem, they hesitate to give up the problem because it would leave them nothing but an empty shell. We can see that any challenge to the self needs to be the result of a careful, guided discovery based on collaboration, as opposed to a direct, confrontational, and disputational stance. One of the primary techniques in cognitive therapy involves teaching the patient to identify specific automatic thoughts that occur in problem situations, to recognize the effects these thoughts have on his or her emotions and behavior, and to respond effectively to those thoughts that prove problematic.

Negative, self-deprecating thoughts, for example, become a habitual part of the depressed patient's life. They assail the patient with speed, frequency, and fury. They are often unrelenting, and often enter the patient's awareness without the patient being aware of their presence, or the relationship of the thoughts to his or her ongoing distress. For example, a colleague reported the following interaction:

"During the first session, I had asked a patient how often he thought that he had negative thoughts. His response was that he had them at times but only infrequently. Given his BDI score of 38, I suspected that he would have many, many more. He estimated no more than two to three a day. As a homework assignment I asked him to record as many of his thoughts as possible. I estimated that he probably had several negative thoughts a day, and that by the end of the week he would probably have 50 thoughts recorded. He quickly responded, 'I'll never be able to do it.' 'It would be too hard for me.' 'I'll just fail.' My response was to indicate that he already had 3 and only needed 47 more." The patient's limited awareness of his constant stream of negative thoughts is obvious when he expected to have two to three per day but produced three in a few seconds.

By using self-monitoring techniques patients can learn to recognize dysfunctional thinking as a preliminary step to learning ways to develop control over the negative and self-destructive thoughts. The automatic thoughts become the signposts or directional signals that point to the schemata. The initial introduction to the process of collecting automatic thoughts is done in the session. The therapist can start, even in the first session, to identify with and for patients the content of their negative thinking. The therapist can start by simply drawing a line down the center of the page, and can then teach the most simple "double-column" technique by looking at situations and resulting reactions.

After helping the patient to recognize the specific thoughts that are part of the ongoing stream of consciousness, the therapist then helps the patient to learn how to record the thoughts effectively and to respond to them adaptively. An excellent format for recording automatic thoughts and adaptive responding is the Dysfunctional Thought Record (DTR). It provides a simple and efficient format for the patient to use in recording his or her thoughts and reactions in problem situations, and can then be used as homework and then reviewed within the therapy session (see Figure 4.2).

Educating the patient to use the DTR effectively and efficiently is very important. The goal in using the DTR is not simply to learn to fill out a form, but rather to begin to use a new format for thinking and viewing the world. The thought record offers the structure for examining thoughts and is useful for work both within the session and as homework. Explaining the use of the record, demonstrating how it can be used, and ascertaining that the patient fully understands the use and rationale for the record is part of the therapeutic groundwork.

As therapist and patient explore the patient's reactions in a specific situation, the therapist enters the patient's reports of thoughts and feelings in the appropriate columns. Once the situation has been reviewed and the value of monitoring thoughts and feelings is clear

DAILY RECORD OF DYSFUNCTIONAL THOUGHTS

DATE	SITUATION	EMOTION(S)	AUTOMATIC THOUGHT(S)	RATIONAL RESPONSE	OUTCOME
	Describe: 1. Actual event leading to unpleasant emotion, or recollection, leading to unpleasant emotion.	1. Specify sad/anxious/angry, etc. 2. Rate degree of emtion, 1-100.	1. Write automatic thought(s) that preceded emotions(s). 2. Rate belief in automatic thought(s), 0-100%.	1. Write rational response to automatic thought(s). 2. Rate belief in rational response, 0-100%.	1. Re-rate belief in automatic thought(s), 0-100%. 2. Specify and rate subsequent emotions, 0-100.

EXPLANATION: When you experience an unpleasant emotion, note the situation that seemed to stimulate the emotion. (If the emotion occurred while you were thinking, daydreaming, etc., please note this.) Then note the automatic thought associated with the emotion. Record the degree to which you believe this thought: 0%=not at all; 100%=completely. In rating degree of emotion: 1=a trace; 100=the most intense possible.

Figure 4.2 Daily record of dysfunctional thoughts.

	Situation	Emotional Responses	Thoughts
Client A	I just lost my job		
Client B	My wife left me		
Client C		I'm Depressed	
Client D		I feel very nervous	
Client E			I'm a loser
Client F			My life is over

Figure 4.3   Situations, Emotional Responses, and Thoughts.

to the patient, the therapist can point out the value in recording the thoughts and feelings at the time that they occur rather than relying on memory.

The therapist must demonstrate the use of the DTR format by demonstrating the first three columns. There is no requirement that the DTR be filled out in a left to right linear fashion. If, for example, the patient starts with a feeling, "I'm really depressed," we can start with the emotion column and work both left to the situation and right to the thoughts. If the patient starts with a thought such as, "Boy, did I ever mess that up," the therapist can enter the thought and move to the left by questioning how the patient felt when he or she had that thought, determining what the situation was in which the thought occurred, and then working to the right to respond adaptively.

In Figure 4.3 we can see that patients A and B identify situations that have led to their suicidality. In these cases, the therapist can question the feelings that arise and the thoughts attendant to the feelings. With patients C and D, the presenting issues are feelings. As before, the therapist may question either the thoughts or the situations, in any order. Finally, with patients E and F, the initial presentation is of a thought, followed by a question about the feelings and the situations.

The patient needs to record the situation briefly and objectively.

Judgments, editorial comments, or conclusions need to be limited. Although this is a fairly straightforward procedure, patients often need coaching and practice before they can identify their automatic thoughts accurately and can use the DTR well on their own. The patient may also need help in identifying the attendant emotions and learning to quantify them. Patients are often confused by statements such as "I feel stupid," "I feel like a fool," "I don't feel as though I'll succeed," or "I feel as if nothing will ever go right for me," and some discussion may be needed to help the patient learn that these reflect thoughts rather than emotions despite the presence of the word "feel." Patients with extreme difficulty labeling emotions may need to be provided with a list of possible emotions (e.g., depressed, sad, nervous, lonely, angry, hopeless, happy, excited, etc.) so that they can start with a "multiple-choice" approach. If, of course, the patient insists on listing a thought as a feeling, it can be listed in both columns.

Once the patient can record emotions, he or she can learn to rate the intensity of each emotion. For example, the patient who feels sad can be asked to think of the saddest he or she has ever felt and assign that experience a rating of 100. When rating the intensity of sadness on another occasion, the patient would simply compare the intensity of his or her sadness on the two occasions. Thus ratings of 20 or 30 would reflect mild sadness, whereas ratings of 80 or 90 would reflect intense sadness. Although these ratings are obviously not precise, they are subjectively accurate enough to prove useful.

In completing the "automatic thought" column on the DTR, the patient is taught to quote the thoughts as accurately as possible rather than paraphrasing them. Automatic thoughts typically take the form of a series of grammatically simple statements or questions. As they typically occur in sequence, however, patients may report the stream of thoughts as a single compound thought such as, "What's the use of going on? I'm a loser without any possibilities for the future and someone who nobody would ever want to be with, marry, or even date briefly."

A series of thoughts such as this would be difficult to respond to because of its complexity. It really involves the following five thoughts:

1. "I'm a loser."
2. "I have no possibilities for the future."
3. "Nobody would ever want to be with me."

4. "Nobody would ever want to marry me."
5. "I'm better off dead."

By helping the patient to learn to break the complex thoughts into workable parts, the therapist can help the patient to respond more effectively.

Some patients do not readily recall their internal dialogues that precede their shifts of emotion. They may remark that, "It's just the way I feel. . . . There wasn't anything that came before it." For patients that do not report preceding cognitions, the therapist does not have to pursue doggedly a course of insisting that there *must* be an antecedent thought, thereby coming into conflict with the patient. Nor does the therapist have to invent a construct similar to the unconscious to explain the presence of thoughts unbeknownst to the patient. A more parsimonious approach would be to examine patients' attributions as to their emotions (e.g., "I feel sad because of my being a bad person") and then examine their attributions in the column for dysfunctional thoughts. The patient's degree of belief in the thought (or attribution) can be rated as baseline data against which to measure change of thinking.

After the therapist and patient have jointly agreed on treatment goals and the therapist has developed both a working conceptualization and an overall treatment strategy, the therapist will need a range of skills and techniques to implement the treatment strategy. Cognitive therapy is not the mechanical application of a standard set of techniques. Rather, interventions are selected to suit the goals of therapy and can be flexibly adapted as the conceptualization develops.

Adaptive Responding

A major goal in monitoring automatic thoughts is to lay a foundation for helping patients to respond effectively to them. Suicidal patients may not, initially, think of themselves as worthy of any defense, or assistance in overcoming their difficulties. As such, the therapist must work to point out that anyone deserves a defense, assistance need not be earned, and that their hopeless view is a product of their depression. This can be accomplished by setting up a behavioral experiment to examine what would happen if individuals were to offer a self-defense or accept assistance. It is helpful to keep in mind that patients must often be taught cognitive strategies and interventions through direct didactic work and modeling, and that constant monitoring and feedback of the developing skills are essential.

Some patients protest any attempt to respond adaptively inasmuch as they believe the negative thoughts to be true, and any attempt to refute, question, dispute, or challenge the negative thinking as unreal, contrived, or simply intellectualization or rationalization. These individuals see their ideas as irrefutable, permanent, and unyielding. The therapist might use the following example to help patients understand the need and importance of adaptive responding:

> Suppose that I have been jailed for allegedly committing a crime. I am brought to trial and the District Attorney presents 95 witnesses in 9 days of testimony attesting to my guilt and complicity. At the conclusion of the prosecution's arguments, my attorney for the defense rises and says, "Your honor, ladies and gentlemen of the jury. My client is a nice person, and is more than likely innocent. Thank you. The defense rests."

The therapist then inquires of the patient what they would judge to be the chances of an acquittal. The patient response is usually that the chances of an acquittal are poor to none. The reason for the therapist being found guilty on all charges did not come from the charges but rather from the lack of a defense. The therapist then offers the following scenario:

> I have been charged with a crime and the District Attorney produces 95 witnesses in 9 days of testimony attesting to my guilt. My defense attorney then produces a single witness for the defense, Mother Theresa. She testifies that on the day in question, I was having dinner with her and the Pope. What are the chances for an acquittal?

At this point the patient usually agrees that there is a far better chance for an acquittal based on having such a powerful and credible witness. A third scenario is then offered:

> Suppose the same situation exists, and the defense attorney cannot get Mother Theresa. The attorney does, however, product 92 witnesses in 10 days of testimony attesting to the therapist's innocence. What are the chances of an acquittal now?

The patient can be helped to see that the innocence or guilt is not based solely on the charges leveled against one, but depends, in large part, on the defense one offers.

The cognitive techniques are used to develop adaptive responses to the dysfunctional thinking. The format for intervention is a Socratic questioning method. It seems far more congruent with a collaborative model to question rather than to interpret. When a therapist offers an interpretation it may be perceived by patients as anti-collaborative in that it tells patients that the therapist knows what is going on in patients' minds, and may be viewed as an intrusion rather than a guiding and uncovering. By careful questioning, the therapist offers to patients an idea, hypothesis, or prompt that leads them to reconsider the validity or value of their automatic thoughts.

There are a range of cognitive techniques that are useful in accomplishing this objective. We have included a list of the following techniques at the end of this chapter for easy reference.

1. *Understanding of idiosyncratic meaning*—As we have seen, it is not safe for the therapist to assume that he or she completely understands the terms used by the patient without asking for clarification. If a group of 100 professionals were asked to indicate what they considered the prime descriptor of depression, we would not get unanimity of response. Out of 100 responses, descriptors might include sad, hopeless, sleep difficulties, psychomotor retardation, apathy, and eating problems. Given the varying meanings that words have, one cannot be sure of what the patient means or experiences when they use words such as "depressed," "suicidal," "anxious," or "upset." Therefore it is essential to question the patient directly on the meanings of their verbalizations. While such directed questions may appear to be intrusive, it can be structured in such a way as to make sure that the therapist is not merely in the right ballpark in understanding but is right on target. This might be called the "Columbo approach" to psychotherapy. The television character played by Peter Falk solves crimes not be interpreting and telling people what he thought they had done, but rather by assuming that he did not know and by being willing to ask what appeared to be obvious or even "dumb" questions. For example:

Patient: I'm a loser!
Therapist: You call yourself a loser. Just what is a loser? What does being a loser mean to you?
Patient: You know a *loser*. You know what a loser is, don't you? I'm a *loser*, a *loser*.
Therapist: I'm not sure. . . . I know what I mean when I use the term

loser, but it's important to know what *you* mean when you use the term "loser."

2. *Questioning of evidence*—One effective way to challenge a dysfunctional thought is to examine the extent to which the thought is supported by the available evidence and whether other interpretations would better fit the evidence. People selectively attend to evidence that maintains their ideas and beliefs. It is essential to teach the patient to question the evidence that they are using to maintain and strengthen an idea or belief. Questioning the evidence also requires examining the source of the data. The patient who is depressed often gives equal weight to all sources. A stranger in the street who appears to frown when the patient passes may be used as evidence for the need to kill oneself. The patient who uses selective abstraction has the ability to ignore major pieces of data and focus on the few pieces of data that support their depressive and suicidogenic views. By having the patient question the evidence, a fuller accounting can be had. For example:

Patient: There is no way in the world that he would be interested in me. If he's not, there's not use going on.
Therapist: You raise two issues—one that he's not interested in you, and second that if he's not there's no use continuing. Before you consider killing yourself, how do you know that he's not interested? What evidence do you have that he has no interest?
Patient: Come on. If he were interested in me he would have asked me out . . . and he hasn't.
Therapist: That's true—he hasn't asked you out yet. Has he done anything else to let you know that he's interested? Does he spend time talking to you? How about the small gifts he has brought for you?
Patient: That's all true, but the real test is whether or not he asks me out and then goes out with me.
Therapist: So the evidence at this point is, at least, mixed?
Patient: Well . . . yeah, I guess.

3. *Reattribution*—A common statement made by patients is, "It's all my fault." This is commonly heard in situations of relationship difficulty, separation, or divorce. Although one cannot dismiss this out of hand, it is unlikely that a single person is totally responsible for everything going wrong. Some patients take responsibility for

events and situations that are only minimally attributable to them, whereas others tend to blame someone else and take no responsibility. The therapist can help the patient distribute responsibility among all relevant parties. If the therapist takes a position of total support (e.g., "It wasn't your fault," "She isn't worth it," "You're better off without her," or "There are other fish in the ocean"), the therapist ends by sounding like friends and family that the patient has already dismissed as being a cheering squad and not understanding his or her position. The therapist can, by taking a middle ground, help the patient to reattribute responsibility and not take all of the blame, nor unrealistically shift all blame to the partner. For example:

Patient: It's all my fault. I really screwed things up this time. If I could only have handled things differently the relationship could have worked. If only I hadn't been so demanding. It could have been good. I blew it. What's left?

Therapist: You had mentioned that much that you did in the relationship was good . . . so it sounds as if you did both good and bad in the relationship. Is it *all* your fault that things didn't work out?

Patient: Yeah. Who else?

Therapist: What part did Alice play in the breakup? Did she do anything to contribute to the difficulty? I know that you feel that it was all your fault. I think it might be helpful to examine just what you contributed and what Alice contributed to the end of this relationship.

Patient: No, it's all my fault.

Therapist: Did Alice do anything at all to contribute to the problem?

Patient: You mean besides being a lying, cheating, bastard?

Therapist: Let's start with that. . . .

4. *Examination of options and alternatives*—Suicidal patients are prime examples of individuals who see themselves as having lost all options. Alternatively, they see their options and alternatives as so limited that among their few choices, death might be the easiest or simplest choice. This cognitive strategy involves working with patients to generate additional options. If the therapist takes the position that suicide is unacceptable, wrong, bad, or not a viable option, the therapist runs the risk of being in direct opposition to patients. This potentially conflictual position may force patients into a harder stance vis-à-vis suicide. Moreover, it may distance patients from the therapist and contribute to a loss of credibility for the therapist. Suicide *is* an option. We cannot deny that

position no matter how loudly or long we protest. As such, the therapist's objective is to generate other options. Even one more option increases the suicidal patients options by 100%. For example:

Patient: What else is left for me? My life is as good as over! The only
               thing left for me to do is to die. I'll probably mess that up
               too.
Therapist: Dying is one option. Are there any others?
Patient: No. None that I can think of or want to try.
Therapist: Let's look at that. On one hand you say there are no op-
               tions. On the other hand you suggest there are options that
               you have in mind but don't want to try or that you dismiss.
               I'd like to help you to look at the options, as limited as you
               see them to be.
Patient: It's not just the way I see them, that's the way it is.
Therapist: Alright. . . . It looks bleak right now. Dying seems to be the
               best choice. Let's see if you and I can generate another
               possibility.
Patient: I don't care . . . about anything.
Therapist: You don't care about anything? Nothing at all in the entire
               world?
Patient: That's not true, I do care.
Therapist: Then what can you do? In addition, of course, to killing
               yourself?

5. *Decatastrophizing*—If the patient sees an experience as potentially catastrophic, the therapist can work to help the patient evaluate
whether he or she is overestimating the catastrophic nature of the situation. Questions that might be asked of the patient include, "What
is the worst thing that can happen?"; or "If it does happen, how will
you life be different 3 months from now?" This technique has the
therapist working against the "Chicken Little" style of thinking. Ellis
(1963) calls this technique the "elegant solution" in that he views the
catastrophic thinking as a core issue in many of the cognitive distortions. The patient can be helped to see the consequence of his or her
life actions as not all or nothing, and thereby less catastrophic. It is
important that this technique be used with great gentleness so that
the patient does not feel ridiculed by the therapist. For example:

Patient: She'll think I'm an idiot. A moron. A loser.
Therapist: And what if she does? What would be so horrible if she, or

anyone for that matter, thinks you're an idiot? Does that make you one? What would be so horrible?

Patient: It WOULD be awful.

Therapist: Let's go over that again. What if she does think something about you? First, how do you know what she's thinking, and, second, is what she thinks true?

Patient: (smiling): I can't easily answer either of those questions. Either way, the world will continue in orbit, so it's not that terrible, but it still seems personally horrible.

Therapist: You're right, the world will stay in orbit. Now what?

6. *Fantasized consequences*—In this technique patients are asked to fantasize a situation and to describe their images and attendant concerns. Often, as patients describe their concerns, they can see the irrationality of their ideas. If the fantasized consequences are reasonable and likely, the therapist can work with the patient to assess realistically the danger and develop coping strategies. This technique works by encouraging patients to bring into the consulting room imagined events, situations, or interactions that have happened in the past or that they see as happening in the future. By having patients move the fantasy to the "reality" of being spoken, the images become amenable to adaptation. Patients' fantasies and images are typically being colored by the same dysfunctional attitudes and beliefs that alter their perceptions, and may be overly negative. The explication and investigation of the style, format, and content of the fantasy can yield very good material for therapy work. For example:

Therapist: I'd like you to close your eyes and picture what you think will happen when you get your exam scores back.

Patient: I can picture walking into the kitchen at home. My parents are both there, and my father asks me about the exam.

Therapist: What will he say or do?

Patient: He'll get furious when I tell him that I've failed. He'll yell at me and tell me for the millionth time about my wasting his hard-earned money. He'll tell me that I might as well drop out of school. . . . No, he won't do what I was thinking.

Therapist: What was that?

Patient: My thought was that he would throw me out of the house and make me drop out of school. He probably would tell me that I had been doing a lousy job and then carry on for days about my work.

Therapist: What would he do then?

Patient: He'd be angry for a while, a long while, maybe days, but eventually he'd calm down.
Therapist: "Let's stay with the image. In your image he would throw you out of the house, and have you drop out of school."
Patient: "Nah! He worries if I come home late, he's not going to throw me out. And school - he would pass out if I really dropped out.

7. *Advantages and disadvantages*—Having the patient list the advantages and disadvantages of maintaining a particular belief or behavior as well as the advantages and disadvantages of changing the belief or behavior can help them gain a more balanced view or perspective. This is related to other scaling techniques, and serves to assist the patient to move away from an all-or-nothing position to one that explores the possibility of an experience, feeling, or behavior having both negative and positive possibilities. By focusing on the advantages and disadvantages of a particular behavior or way of thinking, a more reasonable and adaptive perspective can be achieved. The depressed patient who has dichotomized life events sees only one side. By asking him or her to examine both the advantages *and* the disadvantages of both sides of an issue, a broader perspective is achieved. Although there will, undoubtably, be some overlap between the advantages and disadvantages listed, the differences will be important. This technique can be used to examine the adaptiveness of acting, thinking, and feeling in certain ways. Although the patient will often claim that he or she cannot control his or her feelings, actions, or thoughts, it is precisely the development of control that is the strength of cognitive therapy. For example:

Patient: I can't stay in this marriage. If I stay, I'll die.
Therapist: There are many parts to the relationship from what you've described in the past, both good and bad. Leaving had lots of consequences.
Patient: I don't care anymore.
Therapist: Let's explore the possibilities. We can work at making two lists, the first can be the advantages and the disadvantages of staying with Steve. The second can look at the advantages and disadvantages of leaving.
Patient: Aren't they the same?
Therapist: Not really. There will be some overlap, but the lists will, I think, show some very different ideas.

8. *Process of turning adversity to advantage*—As if often the case, for each thing that is lost, something important is gained. There are times that a seeming disaster can be used to advantage. Losing one's job can be a disaster but may, in some cases, be the entry point to a new job or even a new career. Having a deadline imposed may be seen as oppressive and unfair, but may be used as a motivator. This technique asks the patient to look for potential positive outcomes. Given the depressed patient's negative outlook, they typically find the darkened lining to every silver cloud. As such, looking for the positives of a difficult situation can be very difficult. They may simply not see the positive. Patients will sometimes respond to the therapist pointing out positive aspects with greater negativity. They may accuse the therapist of being an unrealistic Pollyanna or Mary Poppins. The therapist can point out that the view that he or she offers is no less real than the patient's unrealistically negative view. For example:

Patient: Now I'm without a job, now what do I do?
Therapist: With the job gone, what keeps you in food service? You've thought of other jobs; in fact we've spoken of some new career directions. What about those?
Patient: That's true, I don't have to sweat quitting. There's no job to quit. It is freeing. I hated that job. But I don't know whether I'm ready to do something new at this point.
Therapist: Let's explore that idea. . . .

9. *Labeling of distortions*—One of the first steps toward self-knowledge is an identification of one's errors of thinking. Many patients may find it useful to label the particular cognitive distortions that they notice among their automatic thoughts. The list of distortions offered earlier in this book can be learned by the patient. Once learned, the patient can see the "personalizing" or "mind reading" that they are doing. Although not essential for improvement, labeling is often helpful for patients in that it assists them to begin to speak the therapist's language, to "see" things from a cognitive therapy perspective, and to learn the style and format of their distortions. *Feeling Good* (Burns, 1980) is an excellent self-help book for educating patients about cognitive distortions. For example:

Patient: This always happens to me. whenever I'm in a hurry, there's always a traffic jam.
Therapist: What are you doing?

Patient: Yeah, I'm personalizing.

Therapist: Do you really believe that the traffic jam had to do with you?

Patient: (laughing): Hey, I'm depressed, not crazy!

   10. *Guided association discovery*—Through simple questions such as, "Then what?"; "What would that mean?"; and "What would happen then?" the therapist can help the patient explore the significance they see in events. This collaborative, therapist-guided technique stands in contrast to the technique of free association, which is basic to the psychoanalytic process. The idea behind free association is that the "free" wandering mind will eventually meander to the hot areas of conflict and concern. The use of what we call the chained or guided association technique involves the therapist working with the patient to connect ideas, thoughts, and images. The therapist provides the conjunctions to the patient's verbalizations. The use of statements like; "And then what?"; "What evidence do we have that that is true?"; and the like allow the therapist to guide the patient along various therapeutic paths, depending on the conceptualization and therapeutic goals. The guided association can be employed in helping patients to identify underlying assumptions or schemata. For example, a 39-year-old, single mother reported feeling depressed and suicidal after her boyfriend, an alcoholic, left her to date other women.

Patient: I kept demanding that we should have a relationship. . . . I kept telling myself that I should like him and that we should have a relationship. So why did he leave me for her? (Pause.) She's better than I am.

Therapist: You think she's better than you?

Patient: Yeah, she can do what I can't. Why can't I (cries)?

Therapist: That seems very upsetting to think that she can do what you can't. What does that mean? Why is it so upsetting?

Patient: That I'm inadequate (continues crying).

Therapist: What about being inadequate? That seems so really awful. It seems so terrible because it means what?

Patient: That I can't ever have a relationship. That I'm not able to grow or change.

Therapist: And not growing or changing. That's bad because of what? What does that mean.

Patient: That I'll be lonely. I won't have a man to share my life with.

Therapist: And that would be terrible because. . .?

Patient: My daughter and I won't have a family. We'll be alone.
Therapist: And being alone. That would be horrible because. . .?"
Patient: It makes me think that she'll be an orphan. There will be nobody there for her, or for me.
Therapist: So, you've mentioned that she's "better than you," you feel that you're "inadequate and aren't growing or changing," that you'll "be lonely," you and your daughter "won't have a family," and that "there won't be anyone there for you or her." Right?
Patient: Yeah . . . that's it.
Therapist: Do you see any connections here? Any common themes among all of these thoughts?
Patient: Well . . . I seem to feel that having a family, a man, is real important. I need the backup, a net under me if I fall. I feel inadequate . . . that I need the relationships to be OK.
Therapist: That's what you need to feel secure? To feel happy?
Patient: That's it.
Therapist: Does that seem typical of you? Like the way that you usually view things?
Patient: It sure does . . . and its been that way for a very long time.

11. Exaggeration or paradox—By taking an idea to its extreme, the therapist can often help to move the patient to a more central position vis-à-vis a particular belief. As with decatastrophizing, care must be taken to not insult, ridicule, or embarrass the patient. This is not a technique that should be lightly or frequently used. Some patients may be hypersensitive to criticism or ridicule and may experience the therapist who uses such strategies as making light of their problems. There seems to be room at the extreme for only one person. The patient may see things in their most extreme form. As a result, when the therapist takes a more extreme stance (i.e., focusing on the absolutes never, always, no one, everyone) the patient will often be forced to move from his or her extreme view to a more moderate position. There is the risk, however, that the patient may take the therapist's statement as reinforcement of his or her position of abject hopelessness. The therapist who chooses to use the paradoxical or exaggeration techniques must have (a) a strong working relationship with the patient, (b) good timing, and (c) the good sense to know when to back away from the technique. For example:

Patient: No one has ever helped me; no one cares.
Therapist: No one? No one in the whole world has ever, in any small way, offered you any help at all?

Patient: Well, maybe my parents did.

Therapist: No teacher, no friend, no coworker has ever in your life ever helped you in any way?

Patient: That's going too far. Of course people have helped me . . . but not when I needed them.

Therapist: Let's look at that. It changes the issue. People have helped, but not when you wanted or needed them to help. Are there ways that you can work to get more help by asking differently? Different people or different ways?

12. *Scaling*—Scaling is particularly useful for the patient who sees things in a dichotomous manner. The technique of scaling or viewing things as existing on a continuum forces the patient to gain distance and perspective. Because suicidal patients are at a point of extreme thoughts and extreme behaviors, any movement toward a midpoint or dimensional focus is helpful. For example:

Therapist: If you put your sadness on a scale of 1 to 100, how sad are you?

Patient: Ninety to 95.

Therapist: That's a lot. Can you think of the saddest you've ever been in your life? When was that?

Patient: That's easy. When my mother died.

Therapist: How sad were you then?

Patient: One hundred!

Therapist: Can you remember a time that you were the happiest you have ever been?

Patient: Not really.

Therapist: No time at all?

Patient: Well if you want me to say something happy. . . .

Therapist: I was wondering if you have *ever* been happy?

Patient: "Yeah. On my 5th birthday. I got a train set.

Therapist: "If that was a happy time, label that 1 . . . or 0 for sadness. Use those two events—your 5th birthday party as 0 sadness and your mom's death as 100 sadness. Compared with those events, how sad you are now?

Patient: Well, compared to that this is a 50, maybe 45.

13. *Replacement imagery*—Not all automatic thoughts are verbal in nature, and therapy loses much if the patient's images and dreams are overlooked as they can be valuable sources of material in the therapy. If the patient has dysfunctional images, we can help him or her

to generate more effective and functional coping images to replace the depressogenic or anxiety-producing ones. Athletes have discovered that the use of coping and successful images can lead to increased performance. This performance might be anything from a higher high-jump to lifting heavier weights. For example:

Therapist: Picture yourself pushing that piece of pie away.
Patient: It's hard. I can't do it.
Therapist: Try. Picture yourself at the table, looking at the pie, and then slowly pushing it away.

Similarly, the content of dreams can be examined from a cognitive perspective.

A 42-year-old, single man had felt depressed about his work and his 80-year-old mother's recurrent illnesses for several years. He had seen several therapists and had received a range of medications, all to no avail. He reported a dream in which he was walking home alone after work and saw a gang shooting across the street. The FBI picked him up, and offered to place him in a witness protection program—providing him with a new identity and $100,000 per year if he would agree to testify.

The outcome of the dream—that he was rescued from his highly aversive predicament by an outside authority—which required no action on his part (other than to tell what he saw), was consistent with his passivity in therapy, and his generally hopeless outlook and lack of a sense of personal efficacy.

Freeman (1981) and Freeman and Boyle (1992) have identified several rules for using dreams in cognitive therapy, and uses the following example of replacement imagery:

A 31-year-old woman reported the following dream: "I was sitting on the couch when out from the opposite wall came this huge snake. It struck at me with incredible speed, not allowing me to move away. It sank its fangs into my arm. All I could do was look at it and comment on the pain and the fact that it was biting me. I woke up feeling anxious and frightened. It was a scary dream."

The basic cognitive elements involved were her helplessness and inability to react, her passiveness in response to being attacked, and her feelings of anxiety when placed in a position that required direct action. These actions paralleled her dysfunctional cognitions in the waking state. She was extremely effective on the job but often felt anxious when called on to be assertive.

The therapist helped her to restructure the experience by asking the patient what she might have done differently in the dream. Her initial response was that she could do very little, that she was at the mercy of her dream content (cognitions). The therapist emphasized that because she was the sole producer, director, stage manager, and casting director (after all, she recruited the snake), she could recast or restructure the scene as she wished.

At first, she restructured the dream tentatively, by visualizing herself trying to hold something over the snake hole in the wall (a "finger-in-the-dike" response). With further encouragement and some modeling on the therapist's part, she restructured the scene so that she immediately severed the snake's head. (When she protested that she did not have a knife, it was pointed out that the knife could come from the same source as the snake—her imagination.) As she restructured the dream scene to one of her taking greater control and asserting herself, there was a rapid affect shift from anxiety to relief.

Another technique has the patient revisualize the dream but for the primary purpose of altering the negative elements. The snake could become a Sesame Street character, or the patient could offer the snake a treat or have a transparent shield. In restructuring the dream or image, a positive outcome can always be effected.

14. *Externalization of voices*—By having the therapist role-play part of the dysfunctional thoughts, the patient can become proficient in adaptive responding. At first, the patient can verbalize his or her dysfunctional thoughts, and the therapist can model adaptive responding. After modeling the functional thought process, the therapist can, in a gradual manner, become an increasingly difficult dysfunctional voice for the patient to respond to. Patients normally "hear" the dysfunctional voices only in their heads. When they externalize the voices, both patient and therapist are in a better position to deal with the voices and messages in a variety of ways. The patient comes to recognize the dysfunctional nature of the thoughts. The therapist can hear the tone, content, and general context of the thoughts and generate strategies for intervention. For example:

Therapist: I'd like to be your negative voice. I'd like you to be a more positive and functional voice.
Patient: I'll try.
Therapist: "Okay. Let's begin. You really don't know what you are talking about!
Patient: That's not true. There are times that I may be over my head, but overall I really do know my stuff.

These techniques may be also used at the termination of therapy to evaluate how effectively the patient has learned to employ the cognitive techniques (Beck, Rush, Shaw, & Emery, 1979). This is achieved by confronting the patient with the automatic thoughts and images that had plagued him or her at the beginning of treatment, exaggerating the beliefs, and then encouraging the patient to respond. The patient gains great confidence in his or her ability to handle future "worst-case scenarios."

15. *Cognitive rehearsal*—By visualizing an event in the mind's eye, the patient can practice particular behaviors using their imagination. Several athletes are using this technique to enhance performance (i.e., lifting more weight, jumping higher jumps, scoring more baskets, or taking a horse over a higher jump). By first generating a reasonable scene and practicing it by using the imagination, the patient can investigate several possibilities. This is akin to having a pilot practice on a simulator to gain skills. For example:

Therapist: I'd like you to close your eyes and picture speaking with your girlfriend. Can you picture that?
Patient: Yeah. I don't like it.
Therapist: What don't you like?
Patient: What I'm seeing.
Therapist: What do you see? Describe it.
Patient: I see her listening to me and then turning away. I start crying and begging her to stay, and then I start feeling embarrassed and want to die.
Therapist: Can you picture not doing the crying and begging?
Patient: Not really.
Therapist: Let's try to construct a picture that you can live with, both literally and figuratively. What would be in a scene that you would like to see happen?

16. *Self-instruction*—We all talk to ourselves. We give ourselves orders, directions, instructions, or information necessary to solve problems. Meichenbaum (1977) has developed an extensive model for understanding self-instruction. According to Meichenbaum's model, which is derived from Vygotsky's theory of cognitive development and socialization, the child proceeds along a sequence from overt verbalization of instructions to subvocalization to nonverbalization. This same process can be developed in the adult. For example, in learning impulse control, the patient can start with direct verbalization by saying self-instructions out loud. With practice, the patient learns to say the instructions without actual verbalizations, and even-

structions come automatically. The patient can be taught to offer direct self-instructions or in some cases counterinstructions. In this technique, the therapist is not introducing anything new to the patient. Rather, the patient is being helped to use and strengthen a technique that we all use at various times. For example:

Patient: What do you expect me to do? I just act this way.
Therapist: How can you deal more effectively with Jon (the son) when he starts to act up?
Patient: I just respond. I need some space. I want to throw him out of the window.
Therapist: What would happen if you could tell yourself the following: I need to just walk away and not respond. I need to walk away and not respond.
Patient: Well, if I listened to myself I would probably be in far better shape.
Therapist: That's interesting! If you could tell yourself, very directly, very forcefully to leave the situation, both you and Jon would do better. Is that so?
Patient: I suppose. But how can I talk rationally to myself when I'm so angry?
Therapist: Let's practice.

17. *Thought stopping*—Dysfunctional thoughts often have a snowball effect for the individual. What may start as a small and insignificant problem can, if left to roll along, gather weight, speed, and momentum. Once on the roll, the thoughts have a force of their own and are very hard to stop. Thought stopping is best used when the thoughts start, not in the middle of the process. The patient can be taught to picture a stop sign, "hear" a bell, picture a wall, or think the word "stop." Any of these can help to stop the progression and growth of the thoughts. A therapist hitting the desk sharply or ringing a small bell can serve to help the patient to stop the thoughts within a session. The memory of that intervention can then be used by the patient to assist his or her thought stopping between sessions. There is both a distractive and aversive quality to the technique. For example:

Patient: I keep thinking about causing a plane to crash. God, I'm sweating just thinking about it. My thoughts can't stop me, I'm really getting upset. . . ."
Therapist: (slapping the desk loudly): *Stop!*

Patient: I . . . I . . . OK."
Therapist: When you start, it's really important to stop before you lose
          control. What just happened? What allowed you to stop?
Patient: The noise, I guess.

   18. *Focusing*—There is a limit to how many things a person can
think about at once. By occupying his or her mind with neutral
thoughts, the patient can block dysfunctional thoughts for a limited period. This might involve counting, focusing on calming and pleasant images, or focusing on external stimuli. Although this technique is short
term in nature, it is very useful in that it allows the patient time to establish some degree of control over his or her thinking. This time can then
be used to introduce other cognitive techniques. For example:

Therapist: I would like to have you subtract the number 17 from 183,
          and then continue to subtract 17s successively."
Patient: That's hard.
Therapist: I know. We want to see if the counting can interfere with
          the rush of suicidal thinking you described.
Patient: Let's see. 183; 166; 159; no, 149; 132; This is silly!
Therapist: Keep going. . . . 132. . . .
Patient: OK. . . . 132; 115; 98; here I go—81; 64; 47. Is that right . . .
          30; 13; that's it.
Therapist: Good. How are you feeling?
Patient: I feel better. The thoughts did seem to go away a little.

   19. *Direct disputation*—Although we do not advocate arguing
with a patient, there are times when direct disputation is necessary.
A major guideline for necessity is the imminence of a suicide attempt. When it seems clear to the clinician that the patient is going to
make an attempt, the therapist must directly and quickly work to
challenge this hopelessness. Although it might appear to be the
treatment technique of choice, the therapist risks becoming em-
broiled in a power struggle or argument with the patient. Disputation coming from outside the patient may, in fact, engender passive
resistance and a passive-aggressive response that might include suicide. As such, disputation, argument, or debate are potentially dangerous tools. They must be used carefully, judiciously, and with skill.
If the therapist becomes one more harping contact, the patient may
turn the therapist off completely. For example:

Therapist: I understand that you are terrified of going crazy, but obvi-
          ously I'm not as concerned as you are. Would you like to
          know why?

Patient: I guess so.

Therapist: The reason that I'm not afraid of your going crazy is that this isn't the way craziness starts. You're very scared, but there are not signs of craziness. Being afraid of craziness is very different from being crazy.

Patient: You mean I'm not crazy?

Therapist: No, you're not crazy!

20. *Development of cognitive dissonance*—When there are conflicts among one's beliefs, or between beliefs and behavior, anxiety results. Although there are several explanations for this cognitive dissonance phenomenon, it is sufficient to recognize that it exists and can be used therapeutically. Patients who are considering suicide often experience conflict regarding their family, or cultural or religious beliefs. Their previous learning tells them that suicide may be seen as bad, wrong, or sinful. As long as there is dissonance, suicide is less likely. When they resolve their dissonance they feel less pressure and can effect a suicide. The goal of using dissonance with suicidal patients is to generate anxiety and then help them to resolve it in a more effective way. Patients may complain that their death will be meaningless or go unnoticed. Having them examine the effect of their death on children or family can be effective as a deterrent. By fueling patients' dissonance and increasing the anxiety level, the therapist can move patients toward resolving the dissonance in more functional ways. For example:

Therapist: What effect will this have on your kids?

Patient: They'll survive!

Therapist: I'm sure that they will survive but with what effect? How will what you do influence how they think, feel, or behave in the future?

Patient: I don't want to think of it.

Therapist: I know, but it is something that's there, that you've got to at least look at.

Patient: Why? Why do I have to look at it? Once I'm gone. . . .

Therapist: Once you're gone the effect will linger.

Summary

The therapist must develop an armamentarium of cognitive techniques and the skill to move quickly between the various techniques.

By using these interventions, the therapist teaches patients the techniques and encourages them to use the techniques on their own. The particular techniques to be used, and the order in which they are used vary from patient to patient and from time to time. The interventions are derived from the therapist's conceptualization of patients' problems, an understanding of patients' thinking and schemata, and the strategy for intervention that the therapist chooses.

Notes

1. This would hold true for working with children. The less cognitive the level of integration, the more likely it is that behavioral techniques would be more effective.

In working with client's with lowered intellectual ability, the behavioral techniques would similarly be the treatment of choice.

2. We prefer the term *adaptive responding* to the more frequently used *rational responding*. Often the thoughts are not irrational, but dysfunctional in a particular time or place. For example, wanting a dish of chocolate ice cream is not irrational. If it necessitates going out to buy it during a blinding snow storm when most every store is closed, however, this response is not adaptive.

3. These can be viewed as a "menu" of interventions. We have found that it is useful to copy this menu in large letters and post it in the therapy office. This allows both therapist and patient to have potential interventions in sight at all times.

APPENDIX 4.1
Cognitive and Behavioral Techniques

Cognitive
1. Understanding of idiosyncratic meaning
2. Questioning of evidence
3. Reattribution
4. Examination of options and alternatives
5. Decatastrophizing
6. **Fantasized consequences**
7. Advantages and disadvantages
8. Process of turning adversity to advantage
9. Labeling of distortions
10. Guided association/discovery
11. Exaggeration or paradox
12. Scaling
13. Replacement imagery
14. Externalization of voices
15. Cognitive rehearsal
16. Self-instruction
17. Thought stopping
18. Focusing
19. Direct disputation
20. Development of cognitive dissonance

Behavioral
1. Activity scheduling
2. Mastery and pleasure ratings
3. Graded task assignments
4. Social skills and assertiveness training
5. Fixed role therapy
6. Bibliography
7. Behavioral rehearsal/role playing
8. Relaxation/meditation
9. In vivo exposure
10. Biofeedback

5

Behavioral Interventions, Treatment Compliance, and Relapse Prevention

Actions speak louder than words.

—Anonymous

There are times when the approach with the suicidal patient will be cognitive-behavioral. That is, the clinical decision will be to intervene with the suicidal thoughts and ideations as the focus of the therapy. At other times, especially with the more depressed and vegetative patient, the therapeutic approach may have to be behavioral-cognitive, with the initial interventions (or indeed the major focus of therapy) being behavioral. The exact point of delineation between cognition and behavior is debatable, and the case can be made that cognitions are simply one type of behavior.

The goals in using behavior techniques are twofold. The first goal is to use direct behavioral strategies and techniques to alter suicidal behavior as quickly as possible. The behavioral interventions can be used to achieve the short-term but rather immediate impact often necessary with suicidal patients. The second goal involves the use of the behavioral techniques as short-term interventions that allow for the collection of data about the suicidality in the service of longer-term cognitive change. In effect, the behavioral work can be the ongoing and longer-term "laboratory" work of therapy.

We discuss several of what we consider the most effective behavioral strategies and techniques for working with the suicidal patient. The use of particular behavioral techniques, alone or in combination with the cognitive techniques, is based on several factors. The clinician's assessment of the patient's needs and ability (either physical or emotional) to comply with the therapeutic regimen, the therapist's skill in using particular strategies or interventions, issues of resistance or noncompliance, and, most important, the treatment conceptualization. Once the therapist has developed the treatment conceptualization, shared necessary parts of it with the patient, and assessed the time and resources available to effect the treatment, certain behavioral techniques can be introduced. This discussion of the behavioral work is in no way meant to be a complete discussion of behavior therapy techniques or approaches.

Working with the suicidal patient can be an uphill struggle against great inertia or an ongoing battle against keen and powerful resistance. The patient may well respond to any interventions with the pessimistic thought, "What's the use? Nothing will change." We address the issue of noncompliance later in this chapter.

The techniques that are discussed include the following:

Activity scheduling

Mastery and pleasure ratings

Graded task assignments

Behavioral rehearsal

Social skills and assertiveness training

Bibliotherapy

In vivo exposure

Relaxation, meditation, and breathing exercises

Activity Scheduling—Common self-statements for many patients include, "I'm overwhelmed"; "There aren't enough hours in the day to do all that I need to do"; "Given my inability to do what needs to be done, I might as well die"; and "I just sit around all day doing nothing. What's the use of going on? I'm just a waste." The same individuals who are feeling overloaded and unable to cope with what they view as be insurmountable demands rarely consider attempting to cope with their perceived load by scheduling time to do what needs to be done. It might only require planning an hour, a day, or a week or two weeks in advance. Given that suicidal patients are feeling hopeless, the notion of a future orientation, even for an hour, may seem out of line with their present thinking. The goal of activity scheduling is not simply to maximize patients' potential for productivity but to make use of the available time. For depressed patients generally, and for suicidal patients who see themselves as "doing nothing," the activity schedule can become evidence that can be used to show what patients are, or are not, doing. Three uses of the schedule are assessment, planning, and mastery/pleasure ratings.

By using the activity schedule early in therapy, the therapist can (a) assess patients' present use of time, (b) help to plan better and more productive use of time to attack the hopelessness, (c) begin to socialize patients to the idea of doing homework, and (d) work with patients to test the idea that they are doing nothing. If the activity schedule is completed during the session, the therapist can either coach the patient on the best use of the schedule, or fill the schedule out based on patients' data. Care must be taken to avoid accepting patients' hopelessness and labeling large blocks of time as "sitting," "in bed," "watching television," or "doing nothing." Even when watching television, other behaviors, no matter how minimal, are probably being manifested. We should note that the cognitive and the behavioral are not mutually exclusive. The very work of completing an activity schedule frequently elicits negative cognitions, which in turn need to be addressed rather quickly. If the task seems to be overwhelming to the patient, the therapist can work on a day at a time, starting with the day of the session.

The following activity schedule was completed by a 60-year-old physician recently diagnosed as having metastasized bone cancer. He had been successfully treated for the medical problem and presently had residual pain from the treatments (see Figure 5.1).

As can be seen, he was doing very little. He was feeling useless, seeing no chance for doing more, and therefore concluded that he might as well succumb to the cancer and die. Any attempt to schedule activity on the part of his wife and son had been met with, "What's the use, there is nothing I can do." The goal of activity scheduling was to start with very simple and nonstressful activities. If activities could be developed that were even slightly engaging, the data could be used to help refute his idea that he could do nothing. In his mind, nothing could be done to him or for him; therefore, death was his only alternative. Figure 5.2 illustrates an increased activity level.

Using the activity schedule prospectively would involve the therapist and patient working collaboratively to begin to schedule activities for the rest of that day and the following day. Follow-up to the activity schedule can be done by telephone so that there can be rein-

WEEKLY ACTIVITY SCHEDULE

NOTE: Grade activities M for Mastery and P for Pleasure 0-10

	M	T	W	TH	F	S	S
MORNING 6-7							
7-8							
8-9							
9-10							
10-11							
11-12	Get up						
12-1	Eat						
1-2	Watch T.V. →						
AFTERNOON 2-3							
3-4							
4-5							
5-6						Visit by son →	
6-7	Eat						
NOON 7-8	T.V. →					T.V.	
8-9							
9-10							
10-11							
11-12							
12-6							

Remarks:

Figure 5.1 Weekly activity schedule.

WEEKLY ACTIVITY SCHEDULE

NOTE: Grade activities M for Mastery and P for Pleasure 0-10

	M	T	W	TH	F	S	S
MORNING							
6-7							
7-8							
8-9							
9-10		Wake up		Wake up		Wake up	
10-11	Wake up	Eat		Shower	Wake up	Go for	Wake up
11-12	Eat	Play cards	Wake up	Lunch	T.V.	ride	Rest
12-1	T.V.	with my wife	Lunch	T.V.	Lunch		Lunch
AFTERNOON							
1-2		Lunch	T.V.		Walk	Lunch out	Lunch
2-3	Go for a walk	Walk	T.V.		with wife	Ride home	Football
3-4					Shopping		
4-5	Dinner	Dinner		Dinner			
5-6	Nap	T.V.		T.V.		Dinner	Dinner
6-7	T.V.	T.V.	Son	Friends	Eat out	T.V.	T.V.
EVENING							
7-8			visits	come over			
8-9					T.V.		
9-10				T.V.	T.V.		
10-11				T.V.			
11-12				T.V.			
12-6							

Remarks:

Figure 5.2 Weekly activity schedule.

forcement of activity done, decatastrophizing of the noncompliance, emphasis on the therapeutic relationship, and strengthening of the therapeutic alliance. Activity scheduling, once initiated, needs to be checked at each session so that the patient does not get the message that the scheduling work is not important. For suicidal patients, having a goal, meaning, and focus to their lives may serve to lessen their suicidality temporarily. Their ongoing activity scheduling can then be used to help structure their lives and to serve as evidence of their ability to do more than they may have seen themselves as capable of doing. A common patient belief that interferes with compliance is the notion that activities *shouldn't* have to be scheduled, and that activities *should* happen naturally and spontaneously. As with other "should" statements, these cognitions can be dealt with immediately and directly.

A third use of the activity schedule is to have the patient rate not simply activities, but specifically the mastery and pleasure derived from the activities. Inasmuch as suicidal patients rarely experience either mastery or pleasure, it becomes a therapeutic focus to assess and develop mastery and pleasure activities as techniques for lessening the suicidality.

Mastery and Pleasure Ratings—Given the negative view of the world, the self, and especially the future, it is no surprise that depressed patients engage in fewer enjoyable activities, and derive less satisfaction from the activities they do pursue, then do nondepressed patients. Because of their lack of activity and involvement with family, peers, friends, and colleagues, they receive lower rates of reinforcement than do their nondepressed (and active) peers. Clinically, this is reflected in their engaging in relatively few behaviors or activities that provide them with a sense of mastery (M) or pleasure (P). Generally speaking, mastery refers simply to the sense of accomplishment, meaning, or value an individual places on a given activity. Pleasure (P) refers to how much they enjoyed the activity—how much fun it was. An objective in employing mastery and pleasure ratings with depressed and suicidal patients, then, is to encourage them to pursue a wider range of pleasant and stimulating activities. This, in turn, serves to alleviate dysphoria, and instill an increased sense of competence and worth. As might be anticipated, this is often difficult for highly depressed patients given their pessimistic thoughts and low sense of personal efficacy. This can be overcome by structuring the task, and formally assisting patients to list, evaluate, and test their mastery and pleasure. The activity schedule can be used not only for assessing the present levels of mastery and pleasure, but also to generate and plan more and greater mastery and pleasure experiences. Patients' significant others can be used, in many cases, to help patients to be more active. By having patients examine what they might ideally like to do, we can begin to assess the reality and likelihood of their doing what they desire.

For example, a 52-year-old woman was depressed and hopeless about ever working as a creative artist again. She had worked in a variety of media and was especially interested in sculpting. She could not, she claimed, find the time to do her artwork, given the incessant demands of others on her time and energy. She rated sculpting as having a 9–10 rating on a 10-point scale. Mastery was equally high (8–9). The therapeutic goal was to attempt to plan an hour per day that she could set aside to do her artwork; however, she refused, saying that it would take her that much time to get ready to work. Taking more time would result in her taking time away from other activities that she was loath to do. By working toward an effective time schedule, time was set aside to allow her some artwork rather than none, thereby allowing her both mastery and pleasure in her life with a concomitant lessening of her hopelessness and suicidal ideation.

A second example is of a 32-year-old woman who indicated that her pleasure rating for the hours of 7–10 p.m. on a Friday evening were 7, the highest they had been in weeks. She had gone to the theater, something she did 3 times a year. When she was asked whether she could schedule more theatergoing as part of her pleasure activities, she responded that it had never occurred to her to go more often. (We should note that in Philadelphia, or any other large city, one could probably go to the theater daily if one counts professional, semiprofessional, dinner, neighborhood, university, and traveling theater. In smaller cities, one might be able to go only weekly, or even monthly. This was still greater than her present frequency.)

Graded Task Assignments—Patients who are feeling hopeless often see themselves as unable to change what they are doing. They see themselves as incapable of altering the manner in which they react and respond to people and situations, and powerless to change the situations in which they often find themselves. Graded task assignments are derived from behavioral "shaping" strategies. Each small, sequential step approximates the eventual goal and helps patients to begin to expand their activities in a gradual manner. It is important to avoid taking too large an initial step, for patients may experience failure as they weren't observant enough to know to "watch the first step." For suicidal patients any step may appear too large. Several smaller steps are far more effective than fewer large steps.

Ideally, the small steps can be reinforcing as the patient starts to do more. However, for some patients, especially those who are demanding and perfectionistic, their response to small sequential steps is often "so what," "big deal," or "it's not enough." The therapist must also be aware that a shaping strategy may not always have the desired result. A colleague reported the following interaction:

A suicidal patient was severely depressed bed bound, hopeless, and unwilling to become active. The therapist initiated a sequence of behaviors starting with having the patient place his foot out from under the covers, touch the floor, followed by a series of steps eventuating in having the patient leave the bed, walk across the room, and touch the opposite wall. When the patient finally left the bed and touched the wall, the patient turned to the therapist and said, "big deal" and went back to bed. While the shaping was appropriate to move the patient from inaction to action, the hopelessness was not addressed. Clearly, the initial behavior in the sequence must be well within what the patient can easily do, and the action must have meaning for the patient and be part of an integrated treatment focus.

Behavioral Rehearsal—The session can be used to practice potential behaviors or interactions, for example, dealing directly with a significant other, a boss, or a friend. The therapist can give feedback on the patient's performance, and coach the patient on more effective specific responses and response styles. With some patients the therapist may need to demonstrate or to model different behaviors. This strategy may be used for skill building or practice of existing skills. For example:

Bob felt himself unable to discuss his fears with his wife. His concern was that he would sound too angry and aggressive. By role playing the interaction in various possibilities, the patient was able to leave the session feeling greater confidence in his ability to address several issues with his wife.

Social Skills and Assertiveness Training—When a patient describes having social difficulty or the therapist assumes that the patient has social difficulties based on the therapeutic interaction, we cannot assume that the problem exists because the patient does not want to behave differently. There may be a skills deficit and not just a motivational deficit. Part of the work of therapy may involve helping the patient gain the social skills that they have missed as part of their normal development and that are now part of the hopelessness. Although there are groups or classes easily available for learning assertiveness skills, there are few classes or groups for learning social skills. There are groups for schizophrenic or retarded patients; however, there are few groups or resources available for social skills training for the "normal neurotic" patient. This will often place the requirement of social skills training on the individual therapist. For example:

Norman entered therapy and rather quickly began to talk about his chronic loneliness. He thought that no woman would ever want to be with him, and that it was of little use to continue to try to go to bars, clubs, or parties. Norman's social skills were poor, and his assessment that his skills were poor was quite accurate. One goal of therapy was to work at building social skills.

Bibliotherapy—For the patient for whom it is appropriate, reading, in addition to the therapy, can be very helpful as homework. The reading materials can range from spiritual readings such as *The Road Less Traveled* (Peck) to readings from the Bible to fairy tales Self-help books such as *Feeling Good* (Burns, 1980), *A New Guide to Rational Living* (Ellis & Harper, 1975), *Cognitive Therapy and the Emotional Disorders* (Beck, 1976), *Getting Undepressed* (Emery, 1988), *Talk Sense to Yourself* (McMullin & Casey, 1975) *Woulda/Coulda/Shoulda* (Freeman & DeWolf, 1989), *Coping With Depression* (Beck & Greenberg, 1978) or *The Ten Dumbest Mistakes That Smart People Make and How to Avoid Them* (Freeman & DeWolf, 1992) can help patients do some of the therapy work on their own, with, of course, the therapist's guidance. It should be stressed that the bibliotherapy is part of the overall psychotherapy and not used instead of the therapy work.

In Vivo Exposure—For many problems, the most effective manner of intervention may be direct modeling in an in vivo setting. Agoraphobia, social phobia, or social anxiety difficulties respond well to the therapist working with the patient in the very situations that generate the "heat" or hopelessness. This technique is useful not so much in helping the patient to become less hopeless, but in assessing and building skills that may be contributing to the feelings of sadness and perceptions of hopelessness. This is far more effective than getting patient reports of the problems several days later.

Relaxation, Meditation, and Breathing Exercises—A frequent concomitant of suicidal ideation and depression is anxiety. For these patients the use of progressive relaxation, focused breathing, and meditation can be helpful to distract themselves from the suicidal thoughts and contribute to their gaining a sense of control over their lives. Having patients breathe according to a pattern (e.g., a square or rectangle) (see Figure 5.1) can be helpful. Patients are asked to imagine the figure, and breathe in through their nose to a count of two or three (whichever is more comfortable). They then hold their breath for a similar count. This is followed by exhalation through the mouth in a two/three count, followed by holding the breath for a count of two or three. This pattern is repeated many times. The pattern serves to stop hyperventilation, and the image of the figure serves as a distractor.

Homework

Part of the socialization process to the cognitive model includes an explanation of the importance of homework, the purpose of the homework, and the potential benefits of the homework. The homework can begin in the first session by having the patient produce something relatively simple and straightforward for discussion at the second session. A good homework assignment for this first therapy session can be the activity schedule, as discussed earlier.

Basic to the practice of cognitive therapy (and essential in working with the suicidal patient) is the recognition that therapy is not totally accomplished in the hour or two per week that the patient is in the therapist's office. The cognitive therapy patient is not being "worked on" so much as collaborating with the therapist. A major part of the patient's contribution to the collaboration is doing self-help work at home. Clinical experience has indicated that the patients who do more self-help work make progress more quickly in therapy. Self-help work includes any and all of the cognitive and behavioral techniques indicated previously. The particular homework, nature and number of interventions, and amount of work all need to be appropriate to the problem, within the skills of the patient, and collaboratively developed. We must note that homework for the suicidal patient must be developed with a graded task focus. Setting homework beyond the present energy level or attentional level of the patient may, in point of fact, add to the patient's hopelessness. Conversely, accomplishing even simple tasks outside of the session can add to the patient's hopefulness. The homework review needs to be noted during the agenda-setting phase of the session and then included and discussed as part of the session material.

Patients who are relatively more autonomous may be more likely to do homework than dependent patients. Autonomous patients often want to leave therapy as quickly as possible. If they believe that doing homework will expedite the course of their therapy, they will be more than happy to do it. Conversely, the more dependent patients will be reluctant to do homework as they believe that doing homework will shorten their stay in therapy and thereby cause the loss of their therapist.

Overcoming Treatment Obstacles

Noncompliance, or "resistance," often carries the implication that the patient does not want to change or "get well" for either conscious or unconscious reasons. If the patient "makes progress" (thereby becoming less suicidal), we consider that the result of good therapy. If, however, the patient resists our therapeutic work and remains suicidal we often consider it a result of the patient's intransigence or resistance. There are, however, many reasons for the patient's resistance or noncompliance other than the patient not wanting to change or their lack of compliance indicating a pitched battle between intrapsychic structures. The "battle" between therapist and the suicidal patient is more problematic than with other patients because of the consequences of the suicide. Clinically, we can identify several reasons for noncompliance that appear in any combination or permutation, and the relative strength of any noncompliant action may change with the patient's life circumstance, progress in therapy, relationship with the therapist, or vulnerability status.

Lack of patient skill to comply
Lack of therapeutic skill to develop compliance
Environmental stressors precluding compliance
Patient cognitions regarding possible failure
Patient cognitions regarding consequences to others
Congruence of patient and therapist distortions
Poor socialization to the model
Secondary gain
Lack of collaboration or a working alliance
Poor timing of interventions
Fear of changing
Lack of patient motivation
Patient rigidity foils compliance

Lack of patient skill to comply—Therapists cannot make the assumption that every patient has developed the skills to act in particular ways, or to perform a particular set of behaviors effectively. For many patients their difficulty in life may parallel their inability to comply with therapeutic regimen, both based on inadequately developed skills. Although their skills may be adequate for "getting by" in some areas, their skills are not adequate for more difficult or involved tasks. It may be the lack of skills to do more than "get by" in life that fuels the hopelessness and acts as a goad to their suicidal thoughts. Given that the patient may never have developed skills, or not developed them to the level necessary for adequate functioning, the therapist may need to teach particular skills to help the patient move along in therapy and thereby in life. For example:

Fred was a 39-year-old lawyer, diagnosed as having an avoidant personality disorder, who had recently been divorced. The divorce was the outgrowth of his ex-wife having had an affair and borne her lover's child. The wife's behavior was seen in the divorce proceedings to be part of her extended pattern of marital problems. She has been married 4 times previous to her present marriage, had actively pursued and wanted to marry her lover, making him her sixth husband. What Fred found so wonderful about his ex-wife was that she pursued him during their brief dating experience and that he became sexually involved with her within the first week of their meeting. This was an extremely unusual experience for him in that he had not dated throughout college or law school. He had a few blind dates set up by younger associates in his firm, but was quite lonely and inexperienced at dating. He entered therapy during the divorce because of his thinking that he could never find another woman, he would always be hurt, always be alone, and therefore life was not worth living. Having samples the joys of marriage, he did not want ever to have to live alone again.

   He saw the goals of developing a social life as unrealistic for him. "It's not me—what's the use?" he would repeat over and over. A homework assignment during the eighth session involved his calling a woman whose number was given to him by a colleague. The therapist asked Fred to role-play the telephone call to the woman. Given his limited experience, Fred had no idea of what to say in such a call. After practicing several different approaches in the session, Fred attempted the call. His limited experience, combined with his characterological avoidance, would have made it difficult or even unlikely that he would have complied with the homework. He could possibly use that failure as further evidence for his hopelessness about ever having a mate again and one more reason that pointed to suicide as the best alternative.

   Lack of therapeutic skill to develop compliance—Just as patients come into therapy with a particular set of skills, so do therapists. Because of limited experience with a particular patient problem or population, or the unavailability of consultative services, the therapist may not be fully skilled to work with a particular patient group or type. The therapist working within the context of an agency or hospital setting may be able to call in colleagues for consultation or to seek supervision on the particular case/problem. If the therapist's skills are poorly developed to cope with a problem effectively, transfer to another therapist is the ethical requirement. If, however, another therapist is not available, it would be incumbent on therapists to develop, enhance, and upgrade their skills constantly through additional training. Postgraduate courses, continuing education programs, seminars, workshops, or institutes would be part of the professional growth of the therapist, no matter what their training.

Dr. B. was a postdoctoral psychology fellow. She was referred a case of an 18-year-old female student, identified as having an obsessive-compulsive personality disorder, with a presenting problem of psychogenic urinary retention. This situation was not only unhealthy and painful, but socially problematic because the student lived in a university dormitory that required that she share toilet facilities. Comments such as, "I can't go on this way" prompted the resident adviser in the dormitory to refer her for therapy.

Given the therapist's lack of experience with this problem, it was quickly brought to supervision. The supervisor also had limited experience in treating this problem, so that information was sought from the Psychiatry Department, the Student Health Center, and from the Behavioral Medicine Department. None of the local references contacted had experience with female urinary retention difficulty. Calls were made to colleagues around the country to collect as much data as possible on treatment of the disorder. In addition, Dr. B. spent time at the library searching for literature on treatment. Given the unusual nature of the problem, there was the need to develop strategies and interventions so that the therapist and supervisor could effectively work with the patient. The therapist, using her research into female anatomy, exercise, and muscle control found the solution in a women's physical workout book, the Koegel exercises. The patient was taught the exercises in the session and was able to gain greater control over her bladder. The behavioral therapy was done concurrently with the cognitive work of identifying and responding to the dysfunctional thoughts about urinating in a public toilet. This led to the schematic work of modifying the schema related to cleanliness, goodness, and perfectionism.

Environmental stressors precluding compliance—There may be individuals or circumstances in the patient's environment that may either fuel suicidal thinking or preclude changing it. Even when the patient and family have acknowledged changes as important, relatives acting on family schemata may work actively against the patient making changes. Without malice or intent, the significant others may work toward maintaining the patient's dysfunctional thoughts and behaviors. Overtly, patients may be verbally assaulted for going to therapy, assailed for talking of "private family matters with a stranger," or teased or stigmatized for being a "psycho" and needing to get their head "shrunk." Covertly, the message may be sent by the withdrawal of significant others while the patient is in therapy.

Al was a 30-year-old single man. He lived at home with his parents. He was a college graduate presently employed as a customer service representative for a large corporation. In college he made two suicide attempts by swallowing large numbers of aspirin. He was also hospitalized for food poisoning.

Even though he made ample money to support himself, his parents continued to press for his living at home. Their concern was that if he lived on his own, he would not take care of himself, and would begin to eat and gain weight. They were concerned that he would "kill himself with food" and would then go up to his previous high weight of 290 lb. Although he presently weighed 225 lb, was in therapy, and was committed to losing weight, their concern was obvious both overtly and covertly. This frightened him and kept him from living on his own.

Patient cognitions regarding possible failure—Given the hopelessness that is attendant to suicide, the patient has cognitions of failing to be able to make changes successfully in thought or behavior. They think that they will always be the same, never change, never be happier, healthier, richer, or more successful. With this as the *sina qua non* of suicidal thinking, the therapist needs to help the patient to examine their cognitions carefully as described in chapter 4. Examining the cognitions and the underlying schemata, and learning to respond in an adaptive manner to these negative and self-deprecatory thoughts is a major goal of the therapy work.

Mitch was a 29-year-old college junior. His dating experience was very limited. For 2 years he watched other men in his dorm date and then moved into an apartment off campus so that he would not have to see the active social lives of his dorm-mates. He thought, "How can I ask a woman out? There's no way in the world she would go out with me. And if I was able to ask her out, what would happen? She'd go out with me once, and never again. So what would I gain? A single date and then if I like her and ask her out again I'd get turned down. She would tell others what a jerk I am and the entire school would know that I was a loser. I'm better off not opening myself up to failure and ridicule. In fact, I'm better off dead. No one would even miss me."

Patient cognitions regarding consequences to others—Another set of cognitions involves patients having catastrophic ideas about the effect of their attempting to change on others. Patients often catastrophize the results or consequences of their changing. They need not only to decatastrophize the potential but also need to examine whether there are still advantages to changing. Change, if possible, might be seen as a cruel and unwarranted blow to someone in their life. This perception may be a totally negative distortion, possibly fueled by the other person (see section on environmental stressors, which was discussed earlier).

Marta, a 42-year-old women, lived with her mother. She was employed as a secretary working for a state government office. Marta was the youngest of three children. Both of her siblings were married, but Marta had never been married and had always lived with her mother. Her mother, by Marta's description, was hypochondriacal and was constantly going to the doctors at Marta's expense. When Marta refused to pay for the doctor's appointment any longer, her mother launched into a diatribe about what a bad daughter Marta was. Although Marta voiced in therapy her goal of someday being able to move out and live a life of her own, she nevertheless was reluctant to do so, in part because of her thoughts about her mother's health, ability to cope, and imminent death. If she were at home, Marta thought she would extend her mother's life. Her moving would, in effect, kill her mother. If, however, Marta were to die, she would no longer have to be responsible for her mother. Her siblings would have to take over the burden.

Congruence of patient and therapist distortions—This therapist blind spot may be fatal to the patient in that the therapist and patient may share a particular dysfunctional idea, for example, that things are hopeless, that the patient's views are accurate, or that nothing can be changed. This sharing of beliefs, based on congruent underlying schemata, can result in the therapist "buying into" the patient's hopeless ideas and beliefs and being an unwitting supporter of the suicidal thinking.

Dr. M. was working under supervision. Her work was very careful and precise. She was prone to become obsessive when stressed and anxious. Her general belief was that when stressed, extra care, effort, and worry will help to reduce her stress. Her extra caring and work was a major factor in her ability to graduate from a major university with a 4.0 grade-point average. It often took her a much longer time than she would have liked to complete her work as she tended to worry about its completeness and quality. In presenting a patient for the first time in supervision, she described the patient as "perfectionistic, obsessive, and internally demanding," which contributed, in large part, to the patient's suicidal thinking. The patient's internal demandingness also fueled the patients' general hopelessness about being perfect in all that he did. When Dr. M. was questioned by her supervisor as to her goals for this patient, Dr. M. responded, "I would like to help him get rid of all the perfectionism that makes him feel so hopeless." When it was pointed out to her that her own demandingness might help her to "buy into" the patient's problems, that is, ". . . all of the perfectionism," Dr. M. tried to develop a case to support the need for perfectionistic striving always to do one's best.

Poor socialization to the model—Patients who do not understand what is expected of them will have difficulty complying with the therapeutic regimen. It is essential that the therapist assess the level of understanding of the model throughout the therapy with any patient, but it is especially important with suicidal patients given the risk. Often their ability to listen and understand the goals and rationale for the therapy may be impaired by their hopelessness. The therapist cannot assume that the patient, having read any books about cognitive therapy, guarantees adequate socialization to therapy generally, or to cognitive therapy specifically. Further, there may be proactive interference because of previous therapy that was not successful. Patients who have been in therapy previous to their coming into cognitive therapy have, ideally, been socialized to that previous therapy model and will continue to use the same strategies and approaches to therapy and to life in general unless and until they are taught differently.

Ed was a 42-year-old physician referred for cognitive therapy subsequent to his analyst dying. He had been in psychoanalysis for 15 years to deal with his chronic depression and periodic suicidal ideation. He had been seen 3 or 4 times a week for most of that time. After his analyst died he tried to continue his analysis with another analyst for several months, but terminated the analysis by mutual consent and sought cognitive therapy. His presenting problems were hopelessness and a current suicidal ideation.

Ed would come into each session and begin to speak immediately and to free associate. Although the therapist tried to keep the session focused using agenda setting, Ed would wander all over, bringing in dreams, fantasies, and generally discussing everything that came to mind. Although the therapist kept reviewing the need for a focus and structure, Ed kept presenting crises to be dealt with on a frequent basis. It seemed clear that the previous socialization to what therapy is, or is supposed to be, was the major factor in Ed's difficulty in therapy. Constant redirection, and scheduling a 10- to 15-minute period of free association at the beginning of the session helped to keep the rest of the session directed and focused, with rather good therapeutic results. Rather than dealing with the rather vague suicidal issue, the hopelessness was tested against Ed's life experience. In addition to focusing on what he had missed or lacked, he was now able to balance his negatives with positives.

Secondary gain—There may be situations in which the patient may not change because of the gain that accrues from continuing dysfunctional and suicidal thinking and behavior. In the case of suicidal behavior or ideation, this may force family members to treat the patient with "kid gloves," not put any pressure on the patient, avoid confrontation, and generally allow the patient to do whatever he or she wishes rather than chance an increase in the suicidal potential. This gain may be gotten from family, friends, employers, or other individuals with whom the patient has interaction. This type of patient needs to look at the "primary loss" that goes into achieving the secondary gain, that is, what they must surrender in terms of autonomy, achievement, and happiness to garner the so-called gain. The patient needs to be helped to get this gain in other ways.

Al was a 38-year-old unemployed carpenter. He had not worked regularly in 5 years. His time was spent at home, watching television and doing minimal housework. He was listed as disabled and collected a disability payment from the state. His wife worked part-time. He stated that he was unable to work because of severe anxiety. He reported that if he exerted himself in any way, he was concerned about getting a heart attack or stroke. The anxiety was so powerful that he often verbalized his wish to die so as not to have to be so very anxious. Even though he had never had any major illness, his wife was so concerned about his health and the potential for his death that she never asked him to do anything at home. If pressed to find work, Al would consider killing himself rather than expose himself to the excruciating pain of the anxiety.

The net result of Al's threats and behavior was that a community mental health center social worker kept writing letters for him that allowed him to not be pressured into working. His wife worked, took care of the house, his two children, and did all of the chores. Al's day involved getting up at 11 a.m., reading the newspaper until noon, and then watching television. When his children came home from school, he would take a nap and get up in time for dinner. After dinner he would watch television, or listen to records or tapes until bedtime.

Given the enabling stance of both his wife and the social worker, it was very difficult to work with Al. He terminated therapy because of the anxiety that the therapy caused. In his case, it was difficult to help him to see that he was surrendering to the anxiety to limit the anxiety. Thoughts of coping with the anxiety were simply dismissed as "too painful," and Al did not want to experience any pain. Ideally, a family-centered approach that included his wife in the therapy might have been more effective.

Lack of collaboration or a working alliance—Collaboration is an essential ingredient for all psychotherapy. If the patient and therapist do not have a good working alliance it would seem to follow that the patient may be less motivated to work with the therapist, do homework, follow the therapist's direction, or generally work toward making changes. The lack of collaboration, if not based on socialization difficulty or the skill of the therapist, may be due to the patient's cognitions relative to cooperation or collaboration. Certain patients may actively work to thwart the therapist. This type of passive-aggressive behavior may be motivated by any of a variety of patient cognitions (e.g., issues of control, fear, competition or displaced anger may all serve to cause difficulty in the therapy). This patient may be directly challenging or more covertly avoidant as in the classic "yes, but" response.

The suicidal patient may not have the emotional or cognitive ability at this point to collaborate 50-50. The therapist may have to provide 80% or 90% of the effort with the patient providing the balance. By working with the patient using what Burns (1980) calls the "Judo technique," the therapist does not try to meet the patient head to head, no matter how provoked, but rather to back off and not fight with the patient. The patient's forward momentum can then be used in the service of the therapy rather than as fuel for conflict.

Mary was a 31-year-old married woman referred because of severe depression (BDI = 49). Any attempt to establish collaboration was met with, "This won't work, so why bother?" Any homework was not done with the same comment. Any discussion of options or alternative of behavior were met with a smile and a, "Yes, but. . . ." She would often inquire as to whether the therapist thought that she was hard to work with inasmuch as her previous therapists had told her that directly or implied as much before their transferring her to other therapists. Without a working agreement or alliance, the therapy was stymied. Attempts to develop the working alliance were met with, "What's the use?" The therapist tried to break through the hopelessness by interpreting the difficulty in relating to the patient. It appeared to be less an issue of the patient's hopelessness than her inability, fear, or difficulty in agreeing to work with any therapist. The patient finally told the therapist that, "I have no power anywhere in my life. At least here I can assert my power and win."

Poor timing of interventions—Interventions that are untimely can have the effect of the patient not seeing the importance or relevance of the therapeutic work, thereby appearing to be noncompliant. If the therapist, because of his or her anxiety about the suicidal risk tries to push or rush the patient, the result may be the loss of collaboration, the missing of sessions, a misunderstanding of the therapeutic issues, or a premature termination of therapy—a possibly fatal issue with a patient who feels hopeless.

B. R. was a predoctoral psychology intern working at an outpatient center. As a result of her anxiety and internal pressure to succeed, she tended to attempt to interpret schemata without gathering enough data to support her interpretations or interventions. As a result, patients often responded by telling her that she was not understanding them, which further built her anxiety and often caused her to make more grandiose leaps of interpretation and mistiming.

Fear of changing—For some patients, changing means giving up ideas, beliefs, of behaviors that they see as **essential** to their survival. Although this may seem paradoxical in that their thinking makes them suicidal, these patients fear the change as unknown. They often choose the familiarity of their pain to the uncertainty of a new mode of thinking or behaving.

Arlene has been chronically depressed and suicidal for 3 years. She had four hospitalizations for suicidal ideation, though she had never made an attempt. When confronted by her therapist with her style of thinking, she would state, "This is how I am. I've never been different." Although she realized that her suicidal thinking was not only painful to herself and significant others, she had great difficulty changing her perspective because of her maintenance of her position that "This is me." Change for Arlene meant giving up her tiny corner in which she hid from the world, left her feeling that there was no way that she could cope with the world, and made her extremely anxious.

Lack of patient motivation—As part of the clinical picture, the suicidal patient has a lack of motivation for most things including life itself. It is then consistent for the patient to have a lack of motivation for therapy. One of the major parts of the therapy work would have to focus on building motivation for therapy. For some patients the motivation for therapy comes from the insistence of a significant other who is concerned for the life and well-being of the patient. The patient may state explicitly that were it not for the significant other, he or she would not be in therapy.

Sam was a 59-year-old jeweler who had been severely depressed and suicidal for years. His concern was his failing business. He saw no way to regain the lost income, customers, and status that he had once had. He went to work, allowed the store to become piled up with boxes of what he described as "junk," and sought no new business. He approached therapy in the same way. As the therapist helped Sam to begin to organize and structure his life and his work, Sam was able to feel better, less suicidal, and willing to comply with more of the therapeutic regimen.

Patient rigidity foils compliance—With some patients, their personality rigidity foils their ability to comply with therapy actively. Patients who are obsessive-compulsive, paranoid, among other problems have difficulty with compliance. They may question the therapist's motives or goals. They may be unable to break out of the rigid position that they see themselves as having to maintain.

Elena, a 28-year-old nurse, saw the therapy (and the therapist) as extensions of her mother's need to control her. By maintaining her right to kill herself, she saw herself as being able to overcome her mother's power. The therapist had to take great care not to feed the delusion as it might have meant Elena's making an attempt to die.

Relapse Prevention

Based on the medical model, a problem (disease) once treated with the proper medication, procedures, or rest will be "cured." However, even after treatment a patient may not be "cured" so that these thoughts of suicidal thinking recur. The individual may continue to have brief or more frequent thoughts of suicide. These may come at anniversary dates of significant events (i.e., previous suicide attempts, death or birth of relatives, patient's birthday, or beginning of therapy). Greenberg (personal communication) framed it for a patient in the following way: "These thoughts [of suicide] are like a pimple or a rash. They are annoying, uncomfortable and may even cause some limitation of your activities, but they don't have to be life threatening." For the suicidal patient, however, the recurrence of the hopelessness or more direct suicidal thoughts is often perceived as compelling proof of his or her illness.

The termination of formal treatment does not mean the end of therapy for the suicidal patient. Having been socialized to the cognitive therapy model, the patient has learned that cognitive therapy is a coping model as well as a mastery model. Translated for the patient, this means that there may be a recurrence of thoughts of suicide in the future. These opportunities will be used to practice the various cognitive therapy skills that have been acquired in the therapy. The therapy continues as an ongoing process for the patient. When and if necessary, there can be booster sessions scheduled on some regular basis, possibly 2 to 4 times per year. For some patients, the booster sessions may be scheduled on an as-needed basis rather than ending the therapy on some official date. By tapering off sessions the patient will have the opportunity to experience life sans therapy. They will have the chance to try out the coping techniques, experiment with various cognitive and behavioral interventions, and then have the opportunity to discuss the success or difficulties in the upcoming session.

The relapse prevention approach, based on work by Marlatt (Marlatt & George, 1984; Marlatt, Baer, Donovan, & Kivlahan, 1988) provides an especially useful model. Although originally developed for understanding and treating substance abuse, it has great merit for conceptualizing and treating other behavioral problems. It consists of (a) helping the patient to be keenly aware of specific situations that are high risk (e.g., being at a family gathering), (b) being aware of both overt and covert cues that may trigger certain thoughts and actions (e.g., being compared with a sibling or peer), (c) being aware of specific cognitions that may be precursors to suicidal thinking (e.g., "they don't think that I'm as smart as my cousin"), (d) identifying early warning signs of relapse (e.g., staying home from work), (e) developing specific and concrete plans for coping with high-risk situations (e.g. not attending family gatherings or not getting into conversations with certain persons), (f) practicing behaviors and responses that can reduce the negative reaction (e.g., disarming techniques such as saying, "Yes, you are right," or "Would you excuse me for a moment?" and not returning to the conversation), (g) overlearning specific cognitions that can be used to cope with the distortions (e.g., "She has a need to put others down, and don't have to agree"), and (h) having a "safety net" in place to help if all else fails (e.g., write down dysfunctional thoughts and challenge them, call a friend and discuss the experience, or call the therapist). If the patient leaves therapy with the expectation that they will never be depressed again, will never have periods of increased vulnerability, will never experience negative affect, will never be confronted by negative or adversarial individuals, the therapist has not done his or her job.

Termination

Termination begins with the initial therapy sessions and is part of the ongoing therapy process (Beck et al., 1979). The goal of therapy with the suicidal patient is skills acquisition and survival. Given the high-intensity problem that was the reason for therapy, there is most often a strong and immediate bond between patient and therapist. Bringing closure to the therapy relationship is an essential ingredient in termination. The future professional availability of the therapist must be stressed. Invitations for personal friendship, business, love, or sex must be dealt with clearly and definitively. Any ambiguous or unclear messages may not only serve to confuse the patient but put the patient in jeopardy. The therapist must act within the canons of ethical behavior, which dictate that such personal relationships may be of questionable ethical character. The tapering off of sessions will often serve to also help the patient to reassert his or her independence.

The tendency to think in all-or-nothing ways may predispose the patient toward having difficulty distinguishing between a minor lapse and a major relapse (Brownell, Marlatt, Lichtenstein, & Wilson, 1986). A brief flash of hopelessness does not have to mean that an avalanche will follow. The immediate application of the therapy techniques will often quiet the initial rumblings. At the point of termination from therapy, the therapist can help the patient to build a "survival kit" (Krantz, personal communication).

Toward the end of therapy, the therapist can review with the patient specific coping techniques. Using the externalization of voices (Burns, 1980), the therapist can give voice to the negative and dysfunctional thoughts and have the patient quickly and easily respond. At the point where the patient cannot respond, it indicates the need for further exploration and training in coping. When the patient gets stuck and has difficulty in responding, the therapist can switch roles and model a more effective series of responses. By switching roles again, the patient can then practice the adaptive responding. Homework might include practicing certain responses in the following manner. The patient was asked to tape-record dysfunctional thoughts onto a cassette recorder with about a 10-second gap between thoughts. The taped gap was the opportunity for the patient to respond. By practicing again and again, the overlearned dysfunctional responses can be replaced by the newly overlearned functional and adaptive responses. For example:

You're no good

You deserve to die

You'll never be successful

Another part of the survival kit is the use of index cards or Post-its™ to place coping messages in one's environment strategically, (e.g., the shade of an office lamp, the dashboard of the car, the refrigerator, etc.). These might read, "Keep cool," "This too shall pass," "Ignore them" or "I'll feel better soon."

Finally, it is important to develop, with the patients, a list of resources to use if they begin to have difficulty. This should include the telephone numbers of the therapist, friends, a hot line, or a self-help group.

Summary

The behavioral techniques are a powerful part of the therapeutic work. with the vegetative patient they are the first course of intervention. With all patients they are valuable in developing motivation, building skills, enhancing existing skills, offering direct input via role-playing depressogenic and suicidal thinking, and developing direct behavioral changes. They can be used as part of the session work and as part of the homework that is part of the cognitive therapy model.

The therapist must be aware of the myriad reasons for a patient's noncompliance with the therapeutic regimen. These include lack of patient skill, lack of therapist skill, environmental stressors that preclude compliance, patient cognitions regarding failure in therapy, patient cognitions regarding the consequences to others of the patient changing, congruence of patient and therapist distortions, poor socialization to the model, secondary gain, lack of a working alliance, poor timing of interventions, fear of changing, lack of patient motivation, and patient rigidity. It is essential to plan strategies and techniques that effectively deal with the relevant issues, and that move the therapy along within the collaborative relationship between patient and therapist.

Therapy ends with a planned and organized program of termination. This will involve tapering sessions off rather than stopping abruptly. By reviewing the reasons for therapy and the skills acquired, and by continued practice of the skills, the patient can develop relapse prevention skills. This will allow him or her to continue the therapy treatment long after the formal cognitive therapy ends. The therapist can continue to be available as a resource or, if necessary, for booster sessions.

Note

For a full description and discussion of cognitive and behavior therapy techniques cf. Bellack, A. S., and Hersen, M. (1987). *Dictionary of behavior therapy techniques*. New York: Pergamon; and McMullin, R. (1986). *Handbook of Cognitive Therapy Techniques*. New York: Norton.

6

Working with Children, Adolescents, and Significant Others

"Grandmother!" said the child, "oh take me with you! I know you will leave me as soon as the match goes out—you will vanish like the warm stove, like the New Year's feast, and like the beautiful Christmas tree." And she hastily lighted all the remaining matches in the bundle, lest her grandmother should disappear.

But in the cold morning hour, crouching in the corner of the wall, the poor girl was found—her cheeks glowing, her lips smiling—frozen to death on the last night of the Old Year. The New Year's sun shone on the lifeless child; motionless she sat there with the matches in her lap, one bundle of them quite burnt out.

—Hans Christian Andersen, *The Little Match Girl*

The little match girl died trying to maintain her wonderful vision. There was no suicide note, no indication to the world of a plan to commit suicide, and no apparent motive. The observer would guess, as stated by Andersen, "She has been trying to warm herself, poor thing!" Was her death an accident, an incident brought about by her naiveté, or the result of a psychotic delusion? Obviously, the rationale for her actions will never be known. This is often the dilemma confronting the therapist working with youths[1] who have acted in ways that may cause their own death. The deaths of children and adolescents in our society has been termed epidemic. The suicide attempts and completions of suicides involving young people have traumatized localities and become front-page news across the country. With the media coverage by newspapers and television, church, community, and school programs have all been mobilized in an attempt to curb what appears to be this upward trend. When a youth dies because of an illness, automobile mishap, or as a result of war, the loss is difficult. In these situations, the grieving parent may even be given status (e.g., the "Gold Star Mothers" of World War II). When a child or adolescent ends his or her own life by choice, the loss seems, somehow, magnified. They have chosen not to be among us.

Given the immensity of the problem, the multifaceted nature of the issues that lead to youth suicide or the sequelae of the suicide, we cannot cover all of the issues in a single chapter. We have directed our attention to those conceptual, assessment, and treatment issues that are part of the cognitive therapy treatment of suicidal behavior in children and adolescents. Several excellent books focus on the issue of youth depression and suicide (Cf. MacLean, 1990; Diekstra & Hawton, 1987; Berman & Jobes, 1991; Patros & Shamoo, 1989; Hafen & Frandsen, 1986; Husain & Vandiver, 1984; Joan, 1986; Lonetto, 1980; Orbach, 1988; Peck, Farberow, & Litman, 1985; Pfeffer, 1986, 1989; Rutter, Izard, & Read, 1986; Sudak, Ford, & Rushforth, 1984; Trad, 1987; Wells & Stuart, 1981).

The actual increase in youth suicide is almost impossible to pinpoint. The figures offered may be underestimates, or conversely, the apparent increase may be spurious because of previous underreporting. "It is well recognized that deaths from suicide are likely to be underreported to a marked extent, so that official statistics fail to represent the true incidence of suicide" (Hawton, 1986). In terms of attempts, Hawton (1986) states, "Surprisingly, little information is available concerning trends in nonfatal suicidal behavior in the United States" (p. 58). As such, it is possible that younger people are exhibiting a greater risk for suicide. If that trend continues, the youth cohort may be at an even greater risk when they enter the more traditionally high-risk ages. Toolan (1975) suggests that suicides by children and adolescents are underestimated and that as many as 50% of all suicides by children and adolescents have been disguised as accidents.

Lukianowicz (1968) and Hawton (1986) identify several reasons for the current lack of certainty regarding the nature and size of the increase in suicide in the young.

1. Given the relative rarity of child and adolescent suicide, it may not be entertained as a high probability determinant of death.

2. Even rarer is the death by suicide of a small child, so that deaths in this group may be listed as "accidental." Subsequent statistics will thereby be skewed.

3. Because children and adolescents have limited access to lethal weapons or drugs, they may use behaviors that may also be seen as "accidental" (i.e. carbon monoxide, single-vehicle automobile accidents, ingestion of household chemicals).

4. Suicidal threats or gestures from children may not be taken seriously.

5. Assessment of death by suicide may be related to socioeconomic class. The death by overdose of a child or adolescent in a "barrio" may be listed as accidental, whereas the death of a middle-class adolescent may be investigated in terms of possible suicide.

6. Suicide gestures or attempts may not be reported because of the disgrace, negative publicity, or disturbance to the family.

7. Cause of death on death certificate may reflect an attempt on the part of the physician to ease the burden of guilt on the family.

8. As it is uncommon for children to leave suicide notes, it becomes relatively more difficult to document their suicidal intent.

In point of fact, childhood suicide has risen far less sharply than has suicide among adolescents and young adults.

An argument over whether the increase is slight or dramatic is moot. Commonly held clinical mythology suggests that suicidal urges, thoughts, and gestures might be part of the normal developmental process. The adolescent, under the pressures of performance (either self or other imposed), social stressors involved in dating, physical changes, and hormonal shifts might act impulsively. Pfeffer (1984) argues against the hypothesis that "suicidal tendencies of children arise from normal developmental turmoil" (p. 171) and that "there is no empirical evidence to support the possibility that expression of suicidal impulses is a normal developmental process synonymous with episodes of transient developmental turmoil" (p. 172). It would be unfortunate to relegate the suicidal thoughts, wishes, or actions of youth to an ill-defined developmental crisis. By definition, a developmental stage or crisis is endemic to the age, and there is no evidence that all (or even most) youth experience these ideas, thoughts, or wishes. Developmental changes in social, emotional, cognitive, and physical maturity over the course of childhood, influence not only the expression of defensive symptoms, but how these feelings are expressed by the child (Kovacs & Beck, 1977; Kovacs & Paulauskas, 1984).

Child's Concept of Death

When Tom (the cat) chases Jerry (the mouse) off of a table, or Wile E. Coyote runs off of a cliff or explodes while chasing the Roadrunner, the characters always survive. Children's shows constantly place the main character in danger only to see him or her escape once again. For many children death is a vague and foreign state. Pfeffer (1986) states, "Many suicidal children believe that death is a temporary, pleasant state that will relieve all tensions." We often code death so that it is supposed to be less upsetting for a child (e.g., "Grandma went away"; "Your dog has gone to heaven where it's very beautiful"; "Grandpa is sleeping very peacefully"; "Aunt Ella is with Jesus"). Because of these explanations, children may think of death as (a) temporary or transient, (b) beautiful and to be desired, (c) a place of peace, or (d) an opportunity to be closer to God/Jesus/ the Saints, Patriarchs, and Matriarchs.

Nagy (1988) identified several stages in the development of a child's conception of death. In stage 1, children under the age of 5 see death as a temporary state that is reversible. Death may be seen as sleep, a trip, or denied completely. In stage 2, children aged 5 to 9 see death as a specific figure or person (i.e., the grim reaper who comes to collect the dead), or a personage connected with the dead (i.e., a "zombie"-like figure who is associated with death). In the final childhood stage, after age 9, death is seen as an ongoing process that happens to everyone according to established rules. Piaget (1970) described four animistic stages, the first three of which correspond to Nagy's stages. These stages are part of Piaget's overall theory of cognitive development (Flavell, 1963) but are not identical with the Piagetian stages. During the earlier stages, life/consciousness is attributed virtually to any object, whether it lives or moves. Dolls are believed to have thoughts and feelings, blankets can have emotions, and a door can be angry. True understandings of death come when the child can master abstract thinking, during the stage of formal operations, after age 11 or 12. Developmental changes in children's understanding of death have been examined by Brent (1977), Kofkin (1979), Brent (1984), and Schaffer (1974).

We may find the same lack of acceptance of death as a permanent state in adolescents who have, ideally, entered the stage of formal operations and can therefore understand the abstraction and realities of death. McIntire and Angle (1971) found that 17- and 18-year-old suicidal adolescents had fantasies of death being reversible, and that consciousness and awareness would somehow continue after death.

Pfeffer, Conte, Plutchik, and Jerrett (1979) found that the specific factors that significantly correlated with suicidal behavior in children included general depression (including hopelessness, feelings of worthlessness, a strong wish to die, and general dysphoria), depression and suicidal behavior in either or both parents, combined with the ideas that death is temporary and a pleasant state.

Jung saw life as a constant process of death and rebirth. These life-death patterns were archetypes that could be traced cross-culturally (Progoff, 1956). The dual themes of death and resurrection, powerfully represented in Western culture, are also seen in the stories and myths of cultures far preceding our own. Given religious and cultural ideas about reincarnation and returning to heaven or paradise, the stage may be set for children and some adolescents to see death or dying as acceptable. After all, if Wile E. Coyote never really gets damaged or dies, why should they?

Husain and Vandiver (1984) have identified several characteristics of suicidal children. These include constitutional factors such as hypersensitivity (or vulnerability), suggestibility, serious psychological pathology (e.g., schizophrenia, severe neuroses, or hyperactivity and impulsiveness associated with neurological problems, developmental disturbances rooted in youth experiencing stress with fewer perceived resources to cope, lowered school performance, low frustration tolerance, and depression and its concomitants including low self-esteem, hopelessness, loneliness, aggression, and impulsiveness. The vulnerabilities described earlier (chapter 2), apply equally to children. Certain of these factors may be even more powerful in that children have not developmentally achieved certain skills such as problem solving and impulse control. The factors related to adolescent suicide, according to Husain and Vandiver (1984), include all of the preceding, in addition to magical thinking and withdrawal.

Assessment

The assessment of suicidal thinking or behavior in children and adolescents is an essential part of the treatment process and involves the same general goals as in assessing adults. The assessment of suicidal ideation and behavior is made using clinical interviews; personal and family history; the reports of parents, teachers, friends, and siblings; and the information from objective scales (Reinecke, 1992; Lang & Tisher, 1978; Poznaski, Cook & Carroll, 1979; Puig-Antich & Chambers, 1978).

The issues that need to be assessed include the following:

1. Degree of suicidal intent
2. Stressors that might increase the ideation, risk, or likelihood of an attempt
3. Individual's conception of death and dying
4. Familial history of suicide

5. Level of impulsivity, acting-out potential, or impulse control
6. Previous attempts
7. Individual's coping skills, resources, and deterrents
8. Risk of subsequent suicidal actions
9. Attitudes of significant others to suicide, death, and dying
10. Attitudes of significant others to seeking or receiving outside help

One of the major areas of difference between the evaluation in children and adults is the availability of data from school performance, teacher anecdotal records and comments, and the information that may be obtained from religious school. Given that the children are living within a family setting, home behavior is also available for evaluation.

In addition, the post hoc assessment of motivation for having made a suicidal attempt involves the following:

1. Events that preceded the attempt
2. Degree of suicidal intent before, during, and after the attempt
3. The individual's rationale for the act
4. Diagnosed psychiatric disorder(s)

Interview Strategies

Basic courses and books on interviewing and counseling may suggest, advise, or even "prohibit" the use of closed-ended questions in an interview or prohibit the counselor's use of questions entirely. This stems from the view that asking questions is intrusive (i.e., moving the interview in directions the clinician may choose, thereby violating the patient's autonomy). More specifically, closed-ended questions serve to bring an interview to a close rather than opening the interview up to allow further explorations of ideas. In general, many of us have been taught that counseling involves the use of open-ended questions, restatements of patient verbalizations, or reflection of words or feeling tone. In interviewing almost all children and adolescents, we strongly advise the extensive use of closed-ended questions. Open-ended questions can, and do, evoke great anxiety for children and adolescents (and adults). Questions or statements such as "Tell me about why you are here" may be met with silence, a shrug, or a grunt from many youths. Many youths who are referred for crisis intervention, consultation, or therapy because of suicidal ideations or a suicide attempt, they may not come of their own accord, may not trust the therapist, may feel guilty, may wish to keep their thoughts secret, or may not be able to give voice to their thoughts. Open-ended questions may defeat the very goals of the therapeutic exploration. By using closed-ended questions that require minimal response on the part of the young patient (we use this strategy with all anxious patients, to some degree) we can work to lower the anxiety level as the patient feels less threatened and less "on the spot." Several closed-ended questions can then be followed by an open-ended question, which is then followed by closed-ended questions. This allows the child to recover from the open-ended question and not become, or remain anxious.

We find that honesty works best with children. Questions such as "Why are you here?" may be seen as dishonest by the child who knows that the therapist knows why he or she was referred. If, however, the therapist's question is: "Do you know why your mom/dad/parents/teacher/pastor wanted you to come to see me?" the child can be encouraged to share his or her ideas or perceptions about the referral. If the child says, "I don't know," the therapist can share the reason for referral (e.g., "Your mom said that you told her that you took some pills, and she was very concerned about you hurting yourself" or "The doctor who saw you in the emergency department said that you had taken a number of pills"). The goal of the interview is to gather information, establish rapport and communication with the young patient, and begin to intervene in the suicidality. An essential part of therapy with adults is rooted in the idea of confidentiality. The honesty required in working with young patients involves informing them that you will be speaking to their parents, teachers, or siblings, as needed. Further, the therapist is legally and ethically bound to discuss with the appropriate significant others any suicidal actions or serious suicidal ideation on the patient's part. We cannot promise the young patient absolute confidentiality. The issue can be phrased in the following manner, "There are times that you may say things that I may need to talk about with your folks. When you start saying something like that, I'll point it out. You can then decide how we proceed with the idea(s) you're talking about."

Family Factors

The "family connection" between troubled families and suicidal youth has been well established (Bedrosian & Epstein, 1984; Haider, 1968; Orbach, 1988; Pfeffer, 1986, 1989; Pfeffer, Conte, Plutchik, &

Jerrett, 1979; Shafii, Carrigan, Whittinghill, & Derrick, 1985). Issues of separation, divorce, loss through death, physical or emotional abuse, violence and aggression in the home, depressed parents or relatives, suicidal parents or relatives, substance abuse in the home, school failure, and social stress all can play a part in the formation and maintenance of suicidality in the young (Pfeffer, 1986).

Interviewing the family of the suicidal child is often quite difficult. Issues of loss, grief, guilt, and anger come through rather quickly, coupled with fear and concern for the child's safety. Rapport is essential with the parents or guardians, as they will probably be an important part of the therapy process (either positively or negatively). The more exact the specific behavioral descriptions of the child's actions, both before and after an attempt, that the parents can offer, the better chance the therapist will have to understand the child's general behavioral style. Based on these descriptions, hypotheses can be drawn regarding the family's cultural, family, and religious schemata relating to death and dying. Information about the patient's early developmental history and family history are important, and the family members may be the only individuals able to offer this information. For example:

Evan came for therapy at age 23 with the complaint of needing friends. He was severely depressed (BDI = 38) and suicidal. He described his depression as going back "as far back as I can remember." His family history included his father's death when he was 2 years old. He was killed, Evan said, in "the war" (meaning World War II). In reviewing the interview notes afterward, the therapist realized that Evan's father would have been killed in 1948, 3 years after the war ended. Evan was not confronted with this information but was asked to give permission for the therapist to speak with Evan's mother to gather additional data. When Evan's mother was asked about her husband's death, she reported that he died in World War II. When she was asked the year of his death, she became evasive, "sometime near the end of the war." When the therapist pointed out that the year of the death appeared to be 1948, she began crying and told the following story: "I left Evan's father when Evan was two. He drank and talked crazy after he came back from the army. I moved out and went to live with my parents. His father broke into my parent's house, shot me, shot my father who was holding Evan, and then shot himself. Evan fell to the floor. I've never told him about this. He thinks his father died in the army." Similarly, the more exact the information from teachers and siblings, the better.

The therapist needs to assess the family pathology, relative strengths of the family members, and family willingness and commitment to participate in therapy and to be likely allies for the therapist within the broad family constellation. This might include grandparents, aunts and uncles, siblings or even neighbors. The therapist must then decide on the therapeutic configuration that will net the greatest therapeutic gain. Based on the issues listed previously, the therapist may choose to work with the entire family or specific members but only if the family members are willing to come to therapy. Whenever there is a family disorganization brought about by divorce, death, or parental separation, there is a high level of stress engendered. The stressors will be intrapsychic (e.g., related to the idiosyncratic cognitive content the event(s) has for the child), interpsychic (e.g., related to the interaction between parents and children), and external (e.g., related to realities of changes in residence, level of security, financial issues, etc.). It is not the separation itself that will predispose a child to attempt suicide, but the overall pattern of family interaction. There would be a lesser risk of suicidal behavior when loving parents make it clear that the child will not be destroyed in the separation. For example:

Michael, aged 6, was referred because of self-destructive behavior in school. He had been stabbing himself with a pencil until he bled. He was accompanied to the first session by his parents. They were the personification of young urban professionals. They were both well dressed, well educated, and apparently concerned. They sat in the office, holding hands, and inquired as to whether the therapist thought that Michael could be helped. The therapist decided to do a psychodiagnostic evaluation of Michael to (a) gather data and (b) use the testing to develop rapport. The WISC–R and Bender Visual Motor Gestalt were both indicative of superior intelligence and perceptual motor functioning. The Children's Apperception Test (CAT; Bellack & Bellack, 1949) was administered. Michael responded to the first picture with the following story:

(What's happening in this picture?) "This is a family on a picnic. This is the daddy bear. This is the mommy bear, and that is the baby bear with the mommy. They're having a tug of war." (What happened before?) "They were kind of bored, so they decided to have this, you know, a game." (What's going to happen afterward?) "The rope is going to break, and the mommy bear will fall on top of the baby bear and kill him. Then the mommy and daddy bear will go away and forget him." (How will they feel?) "They'll be happy. That's all."

The remainder of the CAT cards expressed similar themes. Michael was then asked to play in the waiting area while the therapist spoke with his parents. When the parents were asked about any marital conflict, the mother warily asked what Michael had told the therapist. It emerged that she had told the child not to discuss, in any way, what goes on in the house. It was, she told the child, "none of the doctor's business." When confronted with assurance that the child did not discuss the marital issues, the dam broke, and the parents both described in great detail their anger and the state of the marital collapse. The ongoing argument was who would get stuck with "him" (the child). Neither parent wanted to be tied down with a child as they contemplated starting their new (single) life.

A commonly held idea is that the suicide of a parent predisposes a child to suicide. The evidence is however, equivocal. Adams, Bouckoms, and Streiner (1980), and Roy (1980) conclude on the basis of their studies that the death of a parent during the childhood years was associated with increases risk for both depression and suicidal behavior in later life. Although there appears to be a significant relationship between depressive disorders in parents and depressive disorder in children (Greenhill, Shopsin, & Temple, 1980), other studies question the relationship between parents who commit suicide and suicidal children. Pfeffer (1986), points out that "studies of suicidal parents and the effects on children have major methodological flaws. Hence, conclusions must be considered tentative" (p. 142). There can be little doubt that children respond powerfully to the loss, death, or suicide of a parent. They may blame themselves for not being a better, more loving, smarter, better behaved child. The suicide becomes especially powerful when the child either witnesses the suicide or is the discoverer of the body.

Although there is no strong empirical evidence to support the idea that school failure or failure in social interactions will cause a child to become suicidal there is evidence that depression will negatively influence school performance. Many depressed children fall behind academically. Their failure may then be seen as such a blow to self-esteem that the child becomes hopeless about ever recovering.

Social and Environmental Factors

In concluding their examination of the relationship of social factors to suicide among children, Husain and Vandiver (1984) remarked:

> "Suicidal behaviors appear more prevalent for children of low socioeconomic backgrounds, especially those in urban areas whose play areas often serve as the method of their suicidal behaviors (e.g., jumping from roofs, jumping from subway platforms and running into traffic on their busy neighborhood streets).
>
> Puerto Rican children who are unaccustomed to life in the urban areas of the United States make more suicide attempts than would be expected from their population. It was noted that blacks also had

higher suicide rates some years ago when they were moving into urban areas in large numbers, but these figures have ceased to rise so dramatically since assimilation and acculturation have taken place." (p. 30)

Methods of Suicide

There is no "favorite" technique for self-destruction (McIntire & Angle, 1981). The choice of a method for suicide will depend, in large part, on age of the individual and the availability of the method. Bergstrand and Otto (1962) summarized the results of their study of 1,727 (351 boys, and 1,376 girls) children and adolescents in Sweden who had attempted suicide and found that girls tended to take drugs, and boys tended to hang themselves (see Table 6.1).

As discussed in chapter 3, suicide notes have traditionally been one of the major ways in which suicide has been diagnosed (Shneidman, 1985). Children and adolescents are, as a group, less likely to leave notes. Several reasons have been advanced for this. First and foremost is the lack of a "written tradition" in children and adolescents. Any parent who has asked a child to leave a note indicating where they were going, or anyone who has expected a teenager to write a telephone message down will vouch for this general lack of committing ideas to paper. In cases in which notes have been left, the two outstanding themes have been love and hopelessness, and fallacies in their cognitive processes are apparent.

Therapeutic Interventions With Children

The particular strategies and interventions used with children will, as discussed earlier, depend on the needs of the patient, the skills of the therapist, and the availability of the significant others. Not only are specific techniques tailored for each patient, but the treatment configuration as well. The choice of a particular treatment configuration needs to be altered as treatment progresses. It should be noted that though the therapist's choice may be starting with one therapeutic configuration, other configurations can, and should, be added as needed and appropriate.

Therapeutic configurations include the following:

Child alone

Child and parent(s), each seen separately

Parent(s) alone

TABLE 6.1
Choices Are Often Age Related

Ages 6–12	Ages 10–14
Jumping from heights	Firearms
Ingesting poison	Explosives
Hanging	Hanging
Stabbing	Drug overdose
Drowning	Poisoning by liquid or solid
Running in traffic	Poisoning by gas
Burning	

From Pfeffer (1986). Reprinted with permission. Pfeffer, B. (1986). *The Suicidal Child*. New York: Guilford Press.

Child and parents alternate between individual, couples, or family therapy

Limited family therapy (selected family members participate)

Extensive family therapy (all family members expected to participate)

Child alone—This is probably the least desirable possibility. The reasons for the therapist seeing the child alone would be situations in which the parents refuse to cooperate with the therapy, the parents are not available (e.g., dead), the parent(s) are far too disturbed (e.g., actively psychotic) to cooperate with the therapy, or the parental conflict would, at this point, serve to exacerbate the child's difficulties.

Eric, age 10, was found walking on train tracks. Eric's father was in prison and his mother was a chronic psychiatric patient who was presently out of the hospital but refusing to take her medication. She actively hallucinated, and was delusional and not available for therapy to assist Eric. The therapist's choice was to work with Eric alone, offer support, and try to work with available social welfare authorities to help arrange a better and more appropriate living situation for Eric with a paternal aunt.

Child and parent(s), each seen separately—In this configuration, the parent(s) are willing to be seen, but there may be compelling reasons to keep the parents and child in separate therapies. These reasons may include the need of the parents to discuss and deal with issues of sex, abuse, or violence directed toward each other and the children. Children may not be able to understand the interactions or the psychological abstractions involved, and would be confused by ongoing involvement in the parent's therapy. The scheduling of sessions might involve each unit seen on a weekly basis, or on alternating weeks.

Joanne, age 16, had taken a number of pills after a particularly vociferous interaction between family members. She was the eldest of six children, having four sisters (ages 13, 10, 6, and 4) and a brother, age 8. Her mother stayed home and cared for the house; her father was an electrical contractor and home builder. There were ongoing family fights about money and care of the home. The father was having an affair with the divorced mother of a friend of Joanne's. Her father would make comments at the dinner table relating to his wife's lack of sexual interest, ability, skill, and knowledge. A typical comment was, "Your mother wouldn't know an orgasm if it bit her on the ass."

The therapy initially involved working with Joanne in individual therapy, concurrently with working with the parents in marital therapy. As some progress could be made with the parents (specifically working with the father on achieving greater impulse control), this was altered later on to include family sessions.

Parent(s) alone—This model used by Freud in his treatment of Little Hans involves the parent(s) needing specific parenting skills or information. Once given the skills and information, the parent and child may be seen for combined therapy.

Alicia, age 8, was referred to the school psychologist by her teacher who described her as "the saddest little girl I've ever seen." The teacher also noted that Alicia made frequent comments about death, dying, and disappearing. The only child of very young parents (mother, age 23; father, age 24). Alicia was conceived when her parents were in high school. They married shortly after they discovered that the mother was pregnant. The parents had no parenting skills, had no family nearby, had few friends, no church or social support group, and no opportunity to learn appropriate parenting skills. In working with the parents over approximately 3 months, they were helped to identify specific areas of concern for Alicia, start behaving differently toward each other and toward Alicia, and enter a parenting group. This was followed by family therapy.

Child and parents alternate between individual, couples, or family therapy—This is a combination of the first three configurations. The exact number of sessions and the frequency with each party is dependent on the needs of the individuals. It may, for example, involve seeing the child on a weekly basis, the parents biweekly, and the family on a monthly basis.

Janice was a 12-year-old junior high school student, referred by her mother after Janice ingested 20 aspirin tablets after becoming angry at her girlfriends. This was

the second time that Janice has ingested large amounts of some medicinal substance. The first time, a year earlier, went unreported. Mrs. H. reported that Mr. H.
thought these behaviors were silly "girl stuff." If they acknowledged the seriousness of these gestures, they would, he said, be "giving in to her." He refused to
come to therapy telling his wife to "send his regrets," but he has to work to earn the
money to pay for the therapy. Mrs. H. was willing to come, as was Janice. They
were seen in combination therapy. Sessions were alternated with Janice seen once
weekly; Mrs. H. was seen weekly for 4 weeks and then every other week. Once a
month Janice was seen with Mrs. H.

Limited family therapy (selected family members participate)—In the
limited family therapy configuration, not all family members may be
included. Certain members may, initially, be excluded. This exclusion
may be based on (a) the child excluded being very young, (b) a significant other unable to cope effectively on an emotional level with the
suicidal behavior, (c) a family member being a covert, though active,
reinforcer who may need to be dealt with separately.

Steven, age 11, had spoken to his friends about wanting to be "more quiet." He
had given away several of his toys to friends. The question of Steven's possible
suicidal wishes was brought to light by the mother of a friend who was made
aware of the toy gifts and contacted a local child protection agency. His parents
had been divorced for 5 years and their separation was, at best, acrimonious. He
lived with his mother and maternal grandmother. Even after being informed of
the agency's concern for Steven's welfare, both the mother's and the grandmother's response was to blame Steven's father. After the professionals' concern regarding the seriousness of the problem was made clear to both the mother and
the father, both agreed reluctantly to meet separately with a therapist. The
mother then called and informed the therapist that they (the parents) had agreed
to meet together. When the mother and father were seen together, the grandmother was in the waiting area and verbally attacked the father. She had to be
restrained from attacking him physically. Clearly, it would be impossible for the
parents and the grandmother to meet together. The initial configuration was the
mother and grandmother weekly, the child weekly, and the father biweekly.
Later on, Steven and his mother were seen weekly, with the father and Steven
seen biweekly. The grandmother was seen individually in an attempt to have her
temper her remarks and actions.

Extensive family therapy (all family members expected to participate)—In
this model the entire family would be included in the therapy. The goals
would be the identification of the family schema, challenging the maladaptive assumptions that may be part of the dysfunctional family system,
and alleviating stress upon the parents and siblings of the suicidal child
(Pfeffer, Adams, Weiner, & Rosenberg, 1988).

Inpatient Versus Outpatient Treatment

A suicidal child can be well cared for in both inpatient and outpatient treatment. The main reasons for hospital or residential placement include the following:

1. *Gathering of data*—There may be a need to gather data regarding the child's physical, emotional, behavioral, and cognitive condition. The data will be part of the assessment of the child's needs so that appropriate referral can be made subsequent to hospitalization.

2. *Need for a secure environment*—The child may need to be taken out of an abusive or dangerous setting.

3. *Need for eliminating the potential for self-harm*—For the child who has attempted suicide or has threatened suicide, a setting where there is observation and supervision would be necessary.

4. *Need for medication*—In situations in which medication is required, titration to therapeutic levels is more easily followed on an inpatient basis.

5. *No support system*—If there is no home or other support system that can be called on to help the suicidal youngster, a residential placement can be used to protect the child from others or himself or herself at the same time offering a supportive and therapeutic environment.

6. *Assessment and evaluation*—It is important to assess and evaluate academic, social, and physical skills in vivo.

7. *Medical treatment*—Subsequent to a suicide attempt, medical treatment may be necessary for the medical sequelae.

The goals of outpatient and inpatient treatment with children have been summarized by Pfeffer (1986) (See Tables 6.2 and 6.3).

The negative aspects of inpatient treatment include the separation from family, school, and friends; the stigma of hospitalization; the child's sense of a loss of control; and any negative aspects to the setting itself (i.e., staffing shortages, overcrowding, etc.).

Major cognitive strategies used with children would include cognitive restructuring, decatastrophizing, and rational/adaptive responding. An excellent technique that is most effective with children was developed by Gardner (1972). Called the mutual story telling technique (MST), it allows the therapist to restructure the child's distorted thinking actively and directly.

The MST is described by Gardner in the following way:

> I introduce the child to the game by first pointing to a stack of tapes, each of which has a child's name clearly written on the end of the box.

TABLE 6.2
**Goals and Interventions During Outpatient Psychotherapy of
Suicidal Children**

Beginning phase of treatment
Goal 1: Develop therapeutic alliance
  Interventions
    State that therapy can help.
    State that the therapist and the child will work together to solve the problems.
    If appropriate, state that others (parents, teachers) will also help.
Goal 2: Protect the child from harm
  Interventions
    Emphasize the dangerousness of the suicidal behavior
    Urge and encourage the child to inform the therapist of the child's suicidal ideas and urges
    Emphasize that suicidal or other self destructive behavior is a poor alternative in dealing with problems.
    If necessary, work with youth agencies to find alternative living arrangements.
Middle phase of treatment
Goal 3: Decrease suicidal tendencies
  Interventions
    Develop and discuss alternative solutions to problems.
    Discuss the child's unfulfilled wishes, and develop and outline acceptable compromise gratifications.
    Possibly act as advocate for the child.
Goal 4: Decrease depression
  Interventions
    Suggest ways to structure the day so that there are appropriate eating and sleeping times.
    Discuss how the child can form new supportive relationships to replace lost or problematic ones.
    Discuss how their thinking affects how they feel.
    Talk with the child about positive aspects of the situation.
    Start to develop adaptive self-talk techniques.
Goal 5: Enhance self-esteem
  Interventions
    Compliment and reinforce the child's appropriate and independent behavior.
    Develop ways for the child to act independently and successfully.
    Support the child's ideas about developing friends and support individuals.

Continued

TABLE 6.2
Continued

Help the child to accept perceived shortcomings and difficulties.

Identify the thoughts and ideas that contribute to lowered self-esteem and challenge them.

Goal 6: Modify self- and other-aggressive responses

Interventions

Develop and outline alternative ways, other than suicide, of responding to frustrations.

Help the child to accept disappointment by outlining other ways of obtaining satisfaction.

Remind the child that it is unacceptable in life for anyone to be injured by the child's anger and actions.

End phase of treatment

Goal 7: Cope with feelings involving separation and loss

Interventions

Discuss thoughts and feelings (e.g., loss, sadness, anger, joy about ending treatment.

Discuss ways to develop and maintain new relationships.

Review, practice, and rehearse problem-solving strategies.

Goal 8: Relapse prevention

Interventions

Discuss specific warning signs of suicidal tendencies.

Make agreement that the child will reenter therapy if ideas or clues of suicidal tendencies emerge.

Review the therapeutic tools (i.e., how thoughts affect feelings).

Develop a list of alternative behaviors (written, if possible).

Give the child a list of telephone numbers of support people with the therapist's number at the top of the list.

Taper sessions off (biweekly, monthly).

Follow up.

I tell the patient that each child who comes to my office has his or her own tape for a tape recording game which we play. I ask the child if he or she would like to have a tape of their own. The child generally wants to follow the general practice, and having his or her own tape enhances his or her feeling of belonging. If the child assents, I take out a new cassette and let the child write his or her name on the box.

I then ask the child if he or she would like to be a guest of honor on a make-believe television program on which stories are told. If the child agrees—and few decline the honor—the recorder is turned on and I begin:

"Good morning, boys and girls, I'd like to welcome you to

TABLE 6.3
Goals and Interventions During Inpatient Psychiatric Treatment of Suicidal Children

Beginning phase of treatment

Goal 1: Adjust to hospital routine

Interventions

Discuss child's and parents' responses.

Explain hospital program to child and parents.

Introduce child to peers and staff.

Goal 2: Develop therapeutic alliance

Interventions

Explain the helping role of the hospital.

State that the therapist, child, parents, and staff will work together to solve problems.

Integrate child into unit program.

State that therapy can help.

Goal 3: Protect the child from harm

Interventions

Emphasize the dangerousness of the suicidal behavior.

Establish an agreement with the child to inform the staff of the child's suicidal, or assaultive ideas or urges.

Emphasize that suicidal or other self-destructive behavior is a poor alternative in dealing with problems.

Observe the child's behavior at all times.

Middle phase of treatment

Goal 4: Decrease suicidal tendencies

Interventions

Develop and discuss alternative solutions to problems.

Discuss the child's unfulfilled wishes, and develop and outline acceptable compromise gratifications.

Goal 5: Decrease depression

Interventions

Help and encourage the child to participate in the unit program as one of the ways to structure the day.

Discuss how the child can form new supportive relationships to replace lost or problematic ones.

Discuss how their thinking affects how they feel.

Talk with the child about positive aspects of the situation.

Start to develop adaptive self-talk techniques.

Goal 6: Enhance self-esteem

Interventions

Compliment and reinforce the child's appropriate and independent behavior.

Continued

TABLE 6.3

Continued

Develop ways for the child to act independently and successfully within the unit program.

Support the child's ideas about developing friends from among peers on the unit.

Help the child to accept perceived shortcomings and difficulties.

Identify the thoughts and ideas that contribute to lowered self-esteem and challenge them.

Goal 7: Modify self- and other-aggressive responses

Interventions

Develop and outline alternative ways, other than suicide, of responding to frustrations.

Help the child to accept disappointment by outlining other ways of obtaining satisfaction.

Remind the child that it is unacceptable in life for anyone to be injured by the child's anger and actions, or vice versa.

Isolate the child during episodes of uncontrollable anger, and allow a quiet time for the child to calm himself or herself.

Reinforce impulse-control behaviors.

Discipline child for uncontrollable aggressive actions toward self, staff, or peers.

Goal 8: Enhance peer relationships

Interventions

Support and reinforce the child's participation in therapeutic activities.

Support and reinforce the child's participation in free-time activities.

Offer social skills training as necessary.

Reinforce prosocial behavior with peers, staff, and family.

Goal 9: Enhance school achievement

Interventions

Reinforce appropriate classroom participation and success.

Reinforce the child's attempts to remediate any learning problems.

Provide meaningful academic experiences.

Provide tutoring or other help, as necessary.

Goal 10: Diagnose and treat neurophysiological disorders

Interventions

Examine child, observe behavior, evaluate nursing observations, and electroencephalograms if needed.

Use appropriate medication, as needed.

Goal 11: Evaluate need for and monitor medication

Interventions

Make sure the child takes medication as indicated and prescribed.

Observe the child for signs of medication-induced decreases in symptoms.

Continued

TABLE 6.3
Continued

Observe the child for adverse medication side effects.

Titrate medication to optimal levels.

End phase of treatment

Goal 12: Cope with feelings involving separation and loss

Interventions

Discuss thoughts and feelings (e.g., loss, sadness, anger, joy) about ending treatment.

Talk to the child about the loss of hospital friends.

Talk to the child bout going to a new living arrangement, whether he or she is to return home or to another living setting.

Discuss ways to develop and maintain new relationships.

Review, practice, and rehearse problem-solving strategies.

Goal 13: Relapse prevention

Interventions

Discuss specific warning signs of suicidal tendencies.

Make arrangements so that the child will continue therapy after discharge.

Make an agreement that the child will contact and discuss with the therapist if any ideas or clues of suicidal tendencies emerge.

Review the therapeutic tools (i.e. how thoughts affect feelings).

Develop a list of alternative behaviors (written, if possible).

Give the child a list of telephone numbers of support people.

Follow-up to make sure that the child is in an appropriate treatment and living arrangement.

Dr. Gardner's "Make-Up-a-Story Television Program." As you all know, we invite children to our program to see how good they are at making up stories. Naturally, the more adventure or excitement a story has, the more interesting it is to the people who are watching at their television sets. Now it's against the rules to tell stories about things you've read or have seen in the movies or on television, or about things that really happened to you or anyone you know.

Like all stories, your story should have a beginning, a middle and an end. After you've made up a story, you'll tell us the moral of the story. We all know that every good story has a moral.

Then after you've told your story, Dr. Gardner will make up a story too. He'll try to tell one that's interesting and unusual, and then he'll tell the moral of his story.

And now, without further delay, let me introduce to you a boy who is with us today for the first time. "Can you tell us your name?" (The recorder is then started.)

I then ask the child a series of brief questions that can be answered by single words or brief phrases such as his/her age, address, school grade, and teacher. These simple questions diminish the child's anxiety and tend to make him/her less tense about the more unstructured themes involved in making up a story." Further diminution of anxiety is accomplished by letting the child hear his/her own voice at this point by playback, something which most children enjoy.

At this point, the child is encouraged to tell a story, after which the therapist retells the story with a more adaptive moral, lesson or rule. (Gardner, 1971, p. 28)

As Gardner points out in discussing one of his cases, "Of course, feelings of inadequacy involve more than mere cognitive distortions, but the patient's awareness of the inaccuracies of his thinking is a necessary step in the alleviation of this symptom. The confrontation in my story helped Joey (the patient) reach this first step" (p. 287).

Working With Adolescents

Working with adolescents presents certain problems not always part of the therapy of children. First and foremost is that they are bigger. An old joke asks, "where would a 300-lb gorilla sit in a restaurant?" The answer is, "Anywhere he wants." Given that they are older and can, if they choose, leave home, we must take into consideration the autonomy needs of this group. Another factor involves the level of cognitive development. Ideally, they are operating at a level of abstract and conceptual reasoning not available in younger children. This allows using their reasoning ability as a tool in the therapy.

Given that an important issue for adolescents is the search for identity (Erikson, 1954), the therapist must be willing and able to deal with the sometimes stormy and erratic behavior that is part of the adolescent search. Issues of rapport and understanding are of great importance, along with flexibility to alter the therapy as needed.

DiGiuseppe (1989) sees a contributing difficulty being that adolescents of today may have less coping skills than adolescents in the past. He sees this stemming from the lack of expectations placed on adolescents of today in terms of part-time work, school performance, or responsibility at home. The concept of doing chores at home, working for pocket money by having a paper route, babysitting, and lawn mowing seem to have changed.

The adolescent can be assessed with the tools discussed in chapter 3 and the more traditional cognitive therapy approaches discussed in chapters 4 and 5 can be used.

Bedrosian and Epstein (1984) describe the cognitive therapy approach with adolescents and point out that the directness of the model, the structure of the model (ideal for adolescents who are asking, "Who am I?"), and the collaborative nature of the model all "can help the depressed adolescent develop problem-solving skills, as well as enhance self-esteem and (develop) a realistic optimism" (p. 364).

The adolescent, often exhibiting the histrionic style described earlier, will need help in finding more reasonable outlets for the high level of arousal that they experience. This may include activity in sports or other less hazardous activities. Drugs, life-threatening activities (e.g., playing "chicken" on a highway) can be dealt with by examination of the thoughts, finding alternative ways of thinking and behaving, and by the use of active coping self-statements. In many cases, the adolescent will be limited by age, mobility, or legal constraint from leaving difficult or problematic settings at school or at home. A focus of the treatment may be to help the adolescent exist in a less than optimal school or household setting.

The predisposing factors that have been related to adolescent suicide attempts include the following:

1. Constitutional factors, that is, heightened suggestibility (vulnerability), hypersensitivity, and gross psychopathology
2. Low stress or frustration tolerance
3. Poor anger or impulse control
4. Depression
5. Low self-esteem
6. Loneliness
7. Magical thinking
8. Accident proneness
9. General behavior disorders
10. School failure

Although many nonsuicidal adolescents may suffer from one or more of these problems, they must be seen as sensitizing factors, if not direct causative factors. The therapist working with adolescents must be prepared to do a great amount of direct behavioral work including assertiveness training, social skills training, anger-control training, and relaxation training. By increasing and enhancing skills, the overwhelming hopelessness experienced by the adolescent can often be lessened.

An issue of great importance with adolescents is the phenomenon of the so-called cluster suicide. Cluster suicides are found throughout history. Coleman (1987) describes cluster suicides among the Greeks, Romans, Vikings, Hebrews, early Christians, New World slaves, Russians, Japanese, Vietnamese, and Pacific Islanders. More contemporary clusters occurred in France, England and Wales, and Czechoslovakia.

It might be argued that the apparent increase of teen suicides during recent years is a manifestation of social pressures on them. Teenagers are exposed to a range of stressors and tensions coming from competition in school; conflict at home; developmental changes in body size, contour, and appearance; availability of drugs; and conflicts about dating and sex (Gone & Herb, 1974). Nonetheless, many of the stresses experienced by adolescents are the same today as they have been in previous ages. The perceived pressure of the times is relative to the ability of the adolescent to cope. For example, to the children brought up on the 1950s, air raid drills, in preparation for the inevitable nuclear attack by the Russians, were a way of life and a constant stressor. Air raid shelters, with "safe" and protected food, were supposed to be part of the basement of every home to allow family survival after the blast. Disease, war, changing moral codes, and the stressors of school and work have been with adolescents throughout history.

The pattern starts when an adolescent commits suicide. This is often followed by other adolescents lionizing or beatifying their dead peer. The dead adolescent may be known to the other adolescents or reported in the media. This may, in fact, "inadvertently tip the balance for another troubled adolescent" (Davidson, 1989). Although recent research indicates that direct acquaintance with a peer who has committed suicide, or indirect exposure through television or other media, is not highly associated with teenage cluster suicide (Davidson, Rosenberg, Mercy, Franklin, & Simmons, 1989), suicidal teens often have a history of self-destructive behavior, and are sensitive to the death of a peer. Flowers may be brought to the grave, pictures are distributed and set up on home "altars," along with flowers and candles. There is a sense of anguish among the youth at the loss of one of their own. This is coupled with an almost magical and wondrous image of the dead. The adolescents who are most prone to make the copycat attempt are vulnerable for all the reasons discussed earlier. Issues of personal or family history, personal or family pathology, general level of personal hopelessness, and a limited personal deterrence combine to place an adolescent at risk. These factors are then exacerbated by the histrionic style of many adolescents. Impulse difficulty, tendency to catastrophize and magnify problems, a propensity to minimize support networks or personal skill, a selective abstraction of information, and a personalization of events outside of them all combine to increase the risk of the adolescent.

Adolescent treatment programs involving large-scale education, media campaigns, required counseling, suicide "rap"groups, church involvement, or legislative involvement may have no effect, or may even cause greater difficulty. As Coleman (1987) points out, "Avoid holding large school assemblies and public address announcements about the latest suicide. There is evidence to the effect that these actions tend to memorialize and romanticize the suicides, thus extending the problem." Further, "The reports of the suicides should not be sensationalized. Media blitzes about the suicides may backfire." They should, instead, be downplayed in the local press and in the community more generally.

Important interventions with adolescents would include the establishment of a crisis intervention system including a multidisciplinary team of psychiatrists, psychologists, educators, counselors and police; a crisis hot line (see chapter 5); individual therapy for adolescents and their families, and ongoing education and information for the community.

Significant Others (SOs) and Survivors

As we have previously noted, the potential impact on SOs makes it important, useful, and often essential to involve the SOs in the therapy. In addition, the therapist must be prepared to be available to the survivors of a suicide. Obviously, family involvement in the therapy involve issues of balancing confidentiality with the need to inform, individual needs with group expectations, and proximal and distal goals of the therapy. As described in this chapter, the family involvement is essential when working with children and adolescents. The family involvement is equally as important when working with suicidal adults, and might involve doing conjoint, family, or a broader "systems" therapy.

Early contact with SOs is important (Beck et al., 1979; Bedrosian, 1981). Beck and colleagues believe that, in the absence of any obvious contraindications (e.g., the SOs are physically unavailable, the SOs reject involvement or are too disturbed to be of help, or the patient refuses to meet with the SOs) the significant others should be interviewed immediately after the initial interview with the suicidal patient. Such an interview with the SOs would yield data regarding the patient's symptoms and level of functioning, the reactions of those close to the patient, and the nature of the interactions of the SOs with the patient. This information may help identify sources of distress and alert the therapist, family, and patient to the types of experiences or situations that might trigger suicidal ideation or behavior (Perlmutter & Jones, 1985a,b).

Meeting with SOs early in therapy identifies the therapist to the family and allows him or her to explain the treatment goals and rationale, treatment plan, including the role of homework, and the nature of the cognitive therapy approach. Early education about the nature of therapy and, indeed, the nature of the patient's illness helps dispel misinformation, erroneous beliefs, and distortions possibly held by SOs.

Family and friends may be useful in assisting the patient in carrying out behavioral assignments. They may be aware of community resources the patient needs or might benefit from, and may accompany the patient to these resources and provide encouragement and feedback. They may practice new skills with the patient such as conversational skills (e.g., giving and receiving criticism, issuing invitations) or skills in daily living (e.g., filling out applications, taking a new bus route). Providing feedback that is specific, realistic, and timely can be extremely helpful. If a depressed patient tends to minimize success or discount progress, the "second opinion" of an observant friend or family member may help the patient to reach a more realistic evaluation of his efforts. It is important that SOs provide accurate feedback. In an effort to be encouraging, friends and family may be oversolicitous, and their comments appear patronizing or insincere.

Identifying the problem as the family's or the couple's rather than just the patient's is often appropriate, whether at the outset of therapy or later as the goals of therapy change. Cognitive therapy can be applied to couples and families as described in the work of Abrahms (1983), Baucom and Epstein, (1990, 1991); Bedrosian (1981, 1986, 1991), Epstein (1982, 1986); and Teichman (1984; 1986).

People may have cognitive distortions about relationships as well as about themselves and the world. These distortions may very well lead to the conclusion that life is a hopeless morass that cannot be negotiated, or the distortion that relationships and support that one thought available was not there or easily obtainable. Bedrosian (1983) identified three types of cognitions about relationships: (a) inferences about the internal states of others (e.g., "they don't care about me"), (b) expectations of the other (e.g., "they should do more to make me feel better"), and (c) rules about relationships (e.g.,

"When you're married, you should unconditionally care and accept whatever your partner says or does"). To this we can add (d) the patient's expectations and demands of oneself within the context of relationships (e.g., "I should be more available and accepting. If I'm not, I don't deserve to live"). Inferences about another's thoughts and emotions go beyond mind reading to include inferences about motivations and attributions of behavior (Epstein & Schlesinger, 1993). Often, the inferential process becomes quite complex, with partners and family members substituting their own fantasies for actual fact finding. Similarly, SOs hold explicit assumptions about how relationships should go. They behave in accordance with these expectations and take for granted that those close to them share the same expectations. Very often this is not the case and conflict occurs when the behavior of others differs from one's expectations. The suicidal individual, already feeling vulnerable, tends to overreact to the expectations of self and others. If partners make their expectations clear with one another they can be responded to in a realistic way. The goal of therapy is to make these rules explicit and challenge their validity as well as the advantages and disadvantages of maintaining them.

Having cognitive distortions seems to be a fact of human life, for no one is privy to all information and perfect understanding at any given time. The therapist working with couples or families has many distortions to deal with—those within each individual as well as distortions in communication between them. The threat of suicide is likely to shake the fundamental assumptions that families and friends have bout the patient, themselves, and life itself. At such times, underlying assumptions are accessible and, therefore, workable.

If available and appropriate, an individual's friends and other members of his or her extended social network can be invaluable assets to the therapy and offer unique assistance not only during a suicidal crisis, but also in preventing one and in the recovery after one. Sometimes a patient will feel closer to, understood by, and trusting of those outside his or her immediate family. Roommates, teachers, physicians, clergy, and fellow members of a support group may be the first to see the warning signs of suicide or be the first to hear the patient express suicidal wishes.

In one case, a family physician called the therapist to tell her that their mutual patient handed him all her medication for her upset stomach. The medication was not lethal, but the patient did not know that. The physician had known the patient since childhood, was well aware of her family's problems, and detected that she did not feel safe having medication at her disposal.

In another case, a therapist received a distressed call from a Vietnam veteran who had barricaded himself in his house and had been ready to kill himself if the Viet Cong attacked. He had been waiting all night. The first person he called was someone from his Vet Center support group. This friend helped to avert suicide because of his credibility based on shared experience, his empathy with the patient, and his ability to help the patient test reality.

In these examples, it is clear that non-family individuals play key roles in both assessments and interventions. They, like families and spouses, provide information to expand the therapist's data base and may participate in therapy in various ways, from providing feedback and reinforcement for change, to assisting the patient in challenging maladaptive assumptions actively.

Being involved in a social network can be therapeutic in itself. Increasing the general level of activity, particularly activity with others, can improve one's mood, decrease loneliness, and encourage reality testing. Moreover, some self-help and support groups probably reduce suicide risk. For example, Alcoholics Anonymous not only reinforces abstinence (thereby reducing vulnerability to suicide risk), but provides substitute behaviors (attending meetings), an available contact person (sponsor), a full-time crisis hot line, and basic commonsense ideas about dealing with or avoiding crisis. Similarly, support groups on college campuses for medical students, community groups for gays and lesbians, and church groups can all serve to reduce stress, isolation, and hopelessness.

An often neglected group of potential therapy assistants are the clergy. As trusted members of the community and authorities on religious teachings, clergy are often consulted by patients, families, and therapists. Patients incorporate religious beliefs along with other assumptions about themselves, the world, and the future as part of the basic schema. Freeman (1987) points to the importance of the therapist understanding the patient's religious schema as central to understanding the substrate that generates the hopeless and self-destructive automatic thoughts. Some religions prohibit suicide and view it as a sin. Others take a less explicit stand and have no sanctions against it. Clergy have information that is useful to therapists, such as the Church's sanctions against suicide (e.g., suicides cannot be buried in sanctified ground) or deterrents to suicide (e.g., It is up to God to decide when your life is over), or the belief that destruction of the self is a violation of the commandment about killing. Consulting a clergy member can help the therapist identify solutions to the patient's hopelessness and generate more deterrents to suicide.

It is extremely helpful for a therapist to develop several clergy consultants. These would be clergy who represent the major religious groups in the patient population. (Those therapists working in hospital settings usually have a Pastoral Care department. Therapists in proximity to a university can call the faculty advisers to various religious groups.) When patients of a particular religion present themselves for treatment, the therapist can gain important insight into the schema about self-destruction by understanding their religious beliefs. Because most of us are not sure about the "rules" of our own religion vis-à-vis suicide, much less the rules of other religions, it is essential to consult an expert from that group.

Survivors of Suicide

What is the result of a completed suicide? The problems that may have driven the person to suicide may still remain for the survivors to cope with, along with the pain of the loss. Often the pain, confusion, and anguish experienced by those who have lost someone to suicide go untreated. Frequently, families of suicide victims withdraw from others, and those around them similarly keep their distance, neither offering nor suggesting help. Susan White-Bowden, whose first husband and son both committed suicide, states, "Even if you don't think it's necessary, counseling is essential after a suicide because you are dealing with guilt. My children needed counseling immediately, but no one suggested it" (Brozan, 1986, p. 85). Another survivor of suicide found neighbors pulling away, not speaking of her mother's death. Counseling in her rural area was unavailable, and it was not until a year later that she entered therapy while in college. She felt tremendous isolation from those outside her family and an exaggerated sense of duty and responsibility to family members. It is not unusual that families bond together against the outside world at this time of crisis. Isolation or the denial of how shattering the suicide is can be detrimental, however.

The reactions of survivors to the suicide of a friend or loved one vary and can include distortions of reality, tortured object relations, guilt, disturbed self-concept, rage, identification with the suicide, depression and self-destructiveness, search for meaning, and incomplete mourning. We shall elaborate on these reactions.

The reality of the suicidal act and its context may be distorted by survivors as a result of their denial and repression of painful facts. SOs may have contradictory beliefs about the suicide, and each may assign a different meaning to the act. Misconceptions and distortions of the truth can be perpetuated until a myth exists. For example, a family may label a suicide as an accident and promote this belief until others, lacking information, believe it. SOs may also blame each other for the suicide. For example, a father told his daughter that the fact her mother died wearing a sweater she'd given her was significant.

Survivors of suicide often distrust human relationships, fearing that something will happen to other loved ones. A newly married woman, for example, experienced difficulty having close, intimate feelings for her husband following her mother's suicide. Concurrently, she worried greatly if she did not know his whereabouts. Survivors also report being afraid of being overprotective or even invasive of others. O'Donnell Timchuyla, whose teenage brother shot himself, worries about her own children's adolescence, stating, "I wonder if my experience with [my brother] will shade everything" (Brozan, 1986, p. 85).

Guilt is a dominant emotion among survivors of suicide (Grollman, 1971). They may believe they could have or should have prevented the suicide. They may also think the suicidal person was punishing or blaming them by dying. In addition, survivors may feel guilty about any transgressions they ever did to the dead person, exaggerating its importance and attributing blame to themselves. In a search for meaning, individuals may over generalize from individual events, personalize responsibility, and draw conclusions without evidence. Finally, survivors may feel guilty about their response or reaction to the suicide. One adolescent found his father dying from a gunshot wound and screamed, "You bastard! How could you do this?" He felt tremendous guilt, believing this was the last thing his father heard. A mother whose 35-year-old son committed suicide felt guilty in that it was her strong belief that, "As a mother, I should have known he was so unhappy. I should have been with him, not let him do it." When the therapist asked how she could have been with him every moment of the day, she responded that, "she just would." It was pointed out to her that she has to sleep, would have to go to the bathroom, and could not spend every moment of her life with her son because he would not have allowed it.

Intense feelings of shame, stigma, and helplessness can disturb a survivor's self-concept. Survivors may have had beliefs and attitudes about who commit suicide, stereotypes about the kind of families they come from, and confidence that the deceased gave no warning signs. They may be mind reading and prejudging the reactions of their friends, neighbors, and community. They may be surprised by the intensity of their own feelings. All these factors affect how a survivor views himself or herself.

The rage and anger felt by survivors does not have much of a socially acceptable outlet. The self-destructiveness that accompanies depression may stem from this impotent rage. Drug and alcohol abuse as well as reckless behavior (e.g., getting into fights) are not uncommon. Accompanying the anger or underlying it are feelings of rejection, desertion, or abandonment. One young woman, for example, found herself angry that her mother was not around to care for her while she was ill. Her mother had been dead for 3 years.

Identification with the suicide has received increased attention because of recent work on suicides in families. Pamela Cantor, president of the American Association of Suicidology, is quoted as saying, "Children whose parents have committed suicide are at particular risk for several reasons. They have seen suicide as a way of coping and model after them. And there is some evidence of a genetic predisposition in certain specific and limited cases [i.e., decreased levels of serotonin and bipolar affective disorder]. It's like being the child of an alcoholic. You either copy it or you avoid it like the plague" (*New York Times*, 1986, B5). Susan White-Bowden believes her son modeled his father's suicidal behavior because "I never said to them, 'What he did was wrong and it was bad'" (Brozan, 1986, p. 5). Conversely, some children of suicidal parents fear that they themselves may become suicidal.

Searching for and assigning meaning to a threatening event, including suicide, is a way to assume control over it. Understanding it reduces feelings of helplessness. In the face of personally threatening events, individuals readjust themselves around a number of themes. These include a search for meaning in the experience, an attempt to regain mastery over the event in particular and over one's life in general, and an effort to enhance one's self-esteem, to feel good about oneself despite the setback. Some illusions or adaptive defenses—looking at things in a positive light in the absence of fact—yield adaptive functioning. Meaning is derived by finding a causal explanation, mastery is achieved by believing one has some control over threat-related events; and self-enhancement occurs by comparing oneself to those less fortunate or by construing some personal benefit from this experience.

Incomplete mourning is the consequence of some of the factors mentioned previously—evasion or denial of fact and the mutual withdrawal, if any, and friends, neighbors, and relatives. Social isolation prevents reality testing and perpetuates the cognitive distortions accompanying guilt, rage, and depression. To break through the isolation of survivors of suicide, support groups have been founded. All survivors cannot be approached in the same way. Not everyone wishes to explore and share their grief fully. For some a measure of denial is important, whereas others wish to find out everything about the events and problems precipitating the suicide. Participants in this program report the major concern of survivors as being unable to meet the needs of those around them, for each was adjusting at his or her own pace. The differing needs of bereaved survivors suggests that the idiographic approach of cognitive therapy may be especially helpful.

Therapist as Survivor

Bongar (1991) states that "A psychologist involved in direct patient care has better than a 1 in 5 chance of losing a patient to suicide during his or her professional career—for the average psychiatrist the odds are better than 50-50" (pg. 4). The suicide of a patient can be an incredibly crushing experience for a therapist. The experience can be especially difficult because the therapist has often expended an amount of caring, personal effort, time, energy, and emotion on helping the patient and so may view the suicide as a personal failure. We are all subject to the cognitive distortions that have likely fueled the suicide. The therapist, above all others, is the acknowledged expert who is expected (by self and others) to prevent suicide. The typical therapist, whether a psychologist, psychiatrist, social worker, counselor, or nurse, is not often in a life or death position. With few exceptions, most therapists are not accustomed nor trained to cope with the death of a patient. The rarity of the experience and the lack of sophistication in dealing with it makes a therapist even more vulnerable to significant cognitive distortions and extreme reactions in response to a patient's suicide (Binder, 1978; Brown, 1987; Goldstein & Buongiorno, 1984; Henn, 1978).

From the therapist's side, therapy represents a total focus on the patient. The therapist's attention is focused on helping the patient develop strategies for coping with interpersonal and intrapersonal problems of life, making a therapist appear to be a very altruistic and unselfish character. The therapist's personal investment in caring is a commodity that cannot be bought and must be available on the part of the therapist to be shared with his or her patients. The following quote is from a psychiatrist in response to the experience of having a patient commit suicide (Freeman & White, 1989).

> I had only seen him three times and there were some real questions I had about whether there were significant organic factors with this guy, but I never did get a chance to check him out because he killed himself right after our third session. I couldn't help but feel that there was something I could have done or should have done but didn't do. Maybe I should have been more attentive to what he said. I am sure he must have given me clues as to how suicidal he was. I experienced the same stages as anyone who is faced with death. At first there was disbelief and non-acceptance, followed by resignation, and finally an acceptance of his death. I am still uncomfortable with it, but the thing that helped most was that offer to talk about it. Some people seemed embarrassed and put off and were very ill-at-ease in discussing it. That situation upset me a whole lot. Those people who offered themselves to talk with me about the experience were the most helpful. Even though I didn't take people up on it, I knew that I had a support system were I to need it. I know it helps to know a resource exists whether I use it or not. I really had a need to talk.

An essential beginning for the therapist in dealing with the suicide of a patient is to talk with a colleague, a supervisor, or peer and to make explicit the concerns, thoughts, and emotions that the therapist is having at that time. The therapist working with suicidal patients needs an opportunity to talk with peers to air specific cognitive distortions and to speak with supervisors about the particular treatment so that an assessment can be made as to whether or not the most appropriate and efficacious interventions are being tried. If, however, after our best efforts the patient does attempt suicide, it is incumbent on the colleagues and coworkers to help the therapist by not treating him or her like a leper, but by offering as much support and caring as if the therapist had lost a loved relative. The loss of a relative is often easier to adjust to in that it is a personal loss, whereas the lost patient is not only a personal loss, but also a blow to one's professionalism, therapeutic competence, and ability to help.

Summary

For many reasons, our children are special, not just personally but to society. The loss of the next generation, perhaps a country's greatest resource, cannot be tolerated easily. Whether we see children as the carriers of our genes, the active agents who allow us to live vicariously, the pathway for us to earn status, or simply and naturally the objects of our love and altruistic caring, the loss of a child is devastating. The questions that follow from a youth suicide revolve around the issue of what we have, individually and as a society, done wrong to eventuate in (or cause) the death of a child.

Any increase in youth suicide is of concern. And regardless of whether current increases are statistical or not, a reasonable goal would be to reduce the suicide rate among youth. If there were a downsurge of youth suicide, the therapeutic goal would be to understand the causes for the downsurge and attempt to accelerate it. The therapeutic goal is to decrease the suicidal potential for any youth.

The assessment of suicidal thinking or behavior in children and adolescents is an essential part of the treatment process, and involves the same general goals as in assessing adults. The issues that need to be assessed include degree of suicidal intent; stressors that might increase the ideation, risk, or likelihood of an attempt; individual's conception of death and dying; familial history of suicide; level of impulsivity; acting-out potential or impulse-control problems; previous attempts; the individual's coping skills; resources and deterrents; risk of subsequent suicidal actions; and attitudes of significant others to suicide, death, and dying; and attitudes of significant others to seeking and receiving outside help. Pfeffer and her associates have developed a number of approaches that are very useful in identifying and treating suicidal potential in children between the ages of 6 and 12 (Pfeffer, 1981a, 1982, 1985; Pfeffer & Trad, 1988).

The conceptualization and the succeeding treatment interventions need to be applied within the context of a good working relationship.

In interviewing almost all children and adolescents, we strongly advise the extensive use of closed-ended questions. Open-ended questions can, and do, evoke great anxiety for children and adolescents.

The therapist needs to assess the family pathology, relative strengths of the family members, and family willingness and commitment to participate in therapy and to be likely allies for the therapist within the broad family constellation. This might include grandparents, aunts and uncles, siblings, or even neighbors. The therapist must then decide on the therapeutic configuration that will probably net the greatest therapeutic gain. Therapeutic configurations include child alone; child and parent(s) each seen separately; parents alone;

child and parent alternate between individual, couples, or family therapy; limited family therapy (selected family members participate); and extensive family therapy (all family members expected to participate).

The potential impact on SOs makes it important, useful, and often essential to involve the SOs in the therapy. In addition, the therapist must be prepared to be available to the survivors of a suicide. As described in this chapter, family involvement is essential when working with children and adolescents. Involvement of the patient's family is equally as important when working with suicidal adults, and might involve doing conjoint, family, or a broader "systems" therapy. Family involvement in the therapy involves issues of balancing confidentiality with the need to inform, individual needs with group expectations, and proximal and distal goals of the therapy.

Meeting with SOs early in therapy identifies the therapist to the family, and allow him or her to explain the treatment goals and rationale, treatment plan including the role of homework, and the nature of the cognitive therapy approach. In fact, family and friends may be useful in assisting the patient in carrying out behavioral assignments, offering unique assistance not only during a suicidal crisis, preventing a crisis, and expediting recovery from a crisis.

Being involved in a social network can be therapeutic in itself. Increasing the general level of activity, particularly activity with others, can improve one's mood, decrease loneliness, and encourage reality testing. Moreover, some self-help and support groups probably reduce suicide risk. For example, Alcoholics Anonymous not only reinforces abstinence (thereby reducing vulnerability to suicide risk), but provides substitute behaviors (attending meetings), an available contact person (sponsor), a full-time crisis hot line, and basic common sense ideas about dealing with or avoiding crisis. An often neglected group of potential therapy adjuncts is the clergy. They can offer support, information for therapist and patient, and guidance as to the early religious schema that might be operative for an individual.

The reactions to suicide by survivors include reality distortion, tortured object relations, guilt, disturbed self-concept, impotent rage, identification with the suicide, depression and self-destructiveness, search for meaning, and incomplete mourning. Guilt is a dominant emotion among survivors of suicide. They may believe they could have or should have prevented the suicide. They may also think the suicidal person was punishing or blaming them by dying. In addition, survivors may feel guilty about any transgressions they ever did to the dead person, exaggerating their importance and attributing blame to themselves. In a search for meaning, individuals may over-generalize from individual events, personalize responsibility, and draw conclusions without evidence. Finally, survivors may feel guilty about their response or reaction to the suicide.

The final issue addressed was the suicide of a patient. This can be a crushing experience for a therapist. The experience can be especially difficult because the therapist has often expended an amount of caring, personal effort, time, energy, and emotion on helping the patient and may view the suicide as a personal failure. The therapy that we recommend for the patient is also the treatment of choice for the therapist—cognitive therapy.

Notes

1. To facilitate the discussion, we have chosen the general term *youth suicide* to refer to issues involving both children and adolescents. When a more specific reference is made to one or the other group, we have used the terms *child* or *adolescent*.

2. The authors are grateful to Dr. Gardner and to Jason Aronson Publishers for permission to reproduce this material.

7

Cognitive Therapy with High-Risk Populations

> Which is the side that I must go withal? I am with both: each army hath a hand; And in their range, I have hold of both, They whirl asunder and dismember me,
>
> —*William Shakespeare*, King John *(Act III, Scene 1)*

Although epidemiological studies indicate that the incidence of suicide remains low in the general population, there are several groups who demonstrate substantially higher rates of self-destructive behavior. These groups include the elderly (Barraclough, 1971; Haas & Hendin, 1983; Lyons, 1984), chronically ill individuals (Louhivuori & Hakama, 1979; Maris, 1981), and Native Americans (McIntosh & Santos, 1981). In this chapter, we review factors that contribute to the increased incidence of suicide among these groups, and the manner in which cognitive therapy techniques can be adapted to meet their specific needs.

Suicide Among the Elderly

There are several reasons why the phenomenon of depression and suicide among the elderly are worthy of special consideration. Although there is little evidence of increased rates of major depressive disorders among the elderly (Weissman & Meyers, 1979), recent studies suggest that suicide rates increase with age. Although recent concern has been given to the increasing incidence of suicide among adolescents, the tragic fact remains that the rate of suicide among elderly persons is 2 to 3 times as great. Whereas only 13% of the population is 65 years of age or older, they account for 25% of suicides (Sartorius, 1974; Sendbuehler & Goldstein, 1977). Figures published by the Centers for Disease Control indicate that suicide rates for Americans older than 65 years of age increased by 21% between 1980 and 1986 (Meehan, Saltzman, & Sattin, 1991). The authors reported that nearly 37,000 elderly Americans killed themselves during this period, yielding a suicide rate of 21.5 suicides per 100,000 population in 1986. The increase in suicide rates is most significant among black men, who demonstrated a 42% increase in suicide during this period. More recent figures for 1990 show a rate of 18.1 per 100,000 for persons between 65 and 74 years of age, rising to 26.1 suicides per 100,000 for persons between 75 and 84 years of age. As a group, elderly persons tend to employ more lethal means in attempting suicide than younger persons. Suicide among the elderly appears, then, to be a clinically important but largely overlooked phenomena. It reflects, at the least, unnoticed levels of hopelessness and despair among a large segment of our population. As Salzman (1982) succinctly stated, "depression among the elderly is a lethal disease" (pg. 27). Given current trends, we anticipate that the scope of these problems will increase as the postwar baby boom generation ages. Second, although the occurrence of depression and suicide among elderly persons is mediated by the manner in which they perceive themselves, their world, and their futures, our understanding of these phenomena must be cast in developmental terms. That is, elderly persons' vulnerability to depression may be seen as a function of their success in meeting the developmental tasks of aging, and of their ability to develop new means of coping with a range of financial, social, and personal stresses that accompany the aging process.

The value of adopting a developmental perspective is not only of theoretical interest. Rather, it has practical implications. For example, the diagnosis and treatment of depression and suicide are somewhat different among the elderly than for other age groups. Cognitive therapy must be adapted, then, given the developmental aspects of the aging process. Several vegetative signs of depressive disorders are relatively common among nondepressed elderly persons. These symptoms include insomnia, early morning awakening, and decreased appetite. These vegetative signs, then, may be unreliable indicators of depression for these patients. Moreover, depressive symptoms can accompany a range of illnesses and medical disorders commonly experienced by elderly persons. Such illnesses include endocrinological disorders, such as hypothyroidism and hyperthyroidism. Although the former often is accompanied by symptoms of clinical depression, the latter can present as an apathetic thyrotoxicosis—including symptoms such as psychomotor retardation, hypersomnia, and depressed affect. Symptoms of mood disorders also accompany hyperadrenal states (Cushing's syndrome), which may be characterized either by euphoria or depression. Ettigi and Brown (1978) reported that approximately 10% of patients with this disorder commit suicide. Hypoadrenalism (Addison's disease) is also accompanied by symptoms suggestive of clinical depression. Symptoms of adrenocortical deficiency include apathy, fatigue, irritability, social withdrawal, "lack of initiative," and dysphoria. Depressive symptoms also may accompany hypoglycemia (islet cell adenoma), hypoparathyroidism and hyperparathyroidism. With these concerns in mind, evaluations of depression among the elderly, particularly where vegetative signs are apparent, should be augmented by a more comprehensive medical evaluation.

Other illnesses and disorders that produce depressive symptoms include systemic lupus erythematosus, pancreatic carcinoma, and pernicious anemia. The latter disorder can stem from poor nutrition or decreased protein intake, and may be of particular concern among poor individuals. Depression may accompany a range of neurological disorders including Parkinson's disease, phakomatoses, arteriosclerotic brain disease, localized cerebral lesions, closed head injury, and epilepsy. In these cases, the patient's depression may be directly related to the disorder's effects on brain function and metabolism. It may not simply be that such patients are aware of the disorder and of the likelihood that their condition may deteriorate.

Depression among the elderly may also be iatrogenic, in that a range of medications taken for other illnesses can produce similar symptoms. Depressive symptoms can be produced, for example, by propranolol, methyldopa, levodopa, vinblastine sulfate, ethionamide, and rauwolfia preparations. This possibility of iatrogenic effects is heightened among patients who are receiving medications for several illnesses. The interactions among medications can produce a range of depressive features. These issues have been reviewed by Glassman and Salzman (1987).

The elderly also differ from younger patients in that they seldom seek psychiatric or psychological treatment of their own accord. Although they may feel quite depressed, and may experience suicidal ideations, it is relatively uncommon for them to seek professional help spontaneously for these difficulties. When they do speak with their physician, counselor, or home care workers, they may wish to discuss other concerns or physical disorders. This tendency not to seek psychological help appears to stem from several factors including stigma attached to seeking psychiatric assistance and a range of beliefs commonly held by older persons. Elderly persons may, for example, have developed beliefs that they "should be able to handle these problems on their own," that seeking professional assistance will "prove I'm crazy" or "mean I'll be institutionalized," or that "I shouldn't be a burden to others by bringing these problems up." It may be necessary, then, to ask elderly patients and their family members specific questions regarding the presence of depressive symptoms or thoughts, and to clarify and resolve beliefs that reduce their motivation to participate in treatment. This is particularly important given the observations that most elderly patients in whom depression was eventually diagnosed visited their physician regularly during the previous year, and that better than 80% of elderly persons who committed suicide saw a physician within 1 month of their death. Moreover, better than half of these patients died of an overdose of medication prescribed by their physician (Murphy, 1979). Among the high-risk factors for suicide among the elderly include being a man living alone, having few active supports, recent loss of a spouse or significant other, high levels of hopelessness, and, of course, depression.

The developmental aspects of the aging process have also influenced the way in which we conceptualize depression and suicidality among older persons. Recurrent themes in the literature center on how elderly persons handle loss, cope with the social aspects of aging, and maintain self-esteem in the face of retirement and other role changes. Loss has been explicitly described as an important factor in the ontogeny of depression within the cognitive and psychodynamic literatures, and has been implied within behavioral approaches. The elderly are, in fact, faced with multiple losses as they grow older. The family and friends that were available to them earlier in life may themselves be ill and unavailable, or may have passed away. The activities that provided them with a sense of enjoyment may no longer be available, and they may have few opportunities to participate in endeavors that give them a sense of accomplishment or competence. With this in mind, Zetel (1965) has suggested that the developmental task of aging is the acceptance of these losses, as well as the acceptance of goals that remained unmet in life. Successful adaptation, from this perspective, involves developing the ability to adjust to losses and the adoption of a more "passive" attitude toward life. Depression among the elderly also may be viewed from within the context of learned helplessness theory (Abramson, Metalsky, & Alloy, 1989; Alloy, Abramson, Metalsky, & Hartlage, 1988). Older persons may find themselves in an increasing range of situations in which they are relatively helpless. They may, for example, find themselves out of control concerning a physical illness or their financial situation because of a fixed income, or they may feel "left alone" by the death of a spouse or friend. Unable to control these situations, they may lose sight of their ability to influence events in their life and may withdraw in apathetic depression. Suicide, then, becomes seen as a legitimate alternative in light of unresolvable and demoralizing problems facing them. These suggestions are supported by Vezina and Bourque (1984), who conducted a study of depressive thoughts, attitudes, assumptions, and coping strategies in a sample of 50 elderly persons. Their results revealed that depressed elderly persons experienced significantly more depressive attitudes and negative cognitions than did elderly persons who were not depressed. Although the types of strategies that the depressed and nondepressed groups employed in coping with their depression did not differ, significant differences between the groups were found in their use of these strategies. Depressed persons reported using appropriate coping techniques less frequently, and less effectively, than their nondepressed peers. Our understanding of the role that other cognitive variables, such as attributional style, locus of control, selective or biased attention, and depressogenic schema, play in the occurrence of depression and suicide among the elderly is rudimentary. Although the relationship of these variables to the occurrence of emotional disorders among adults has received an increasing amount of attention (see Alloy [1988] for reviews), very few well-controlled studies have focused specifically on elderly populations. Findings of depressive attitudes and negative cognitions among depressed elderly persons are not inconsistent with the observations of Durkheim, who in 1897 published a comprehensive sociological examination of the phenomena. He concluded that a common factor in suicides was an increasing sense of alienation between the individual and his or her social group. He argued that anomie—a sense of psychosocial isolation—occurs when the links uniting persons into groups are weakened. One category of self-destructive behavior, the "altruistic" suicide, is of particular interest. Durkheim argued that some individuals may attempt suicide because of an inadequate individuation from their social group—as would be the case of an old person who believes he has become a financial burden to his family and so "sacrifices" his life for their benefit.

Durkheim's model does not specify the "process" or "mechanism" by which sociological factors mediate an individual's behavior. Why, for example, do some elderly individuals who are widowed or single become suicidal, whereas others do not? What factors or processes distinguish one group from the other? These questions can be addressed by integrating the sociological models with cognitive theory. It is, in this approach, the individuals' perception of their "isolation," and their assessment of its significance, that determines their consequent mood. It is their ability to develop, evaluate, and implement alternative solutions that determines their ultimate behavior. General terms, such as "social isolation" and "anomie" explain little and predict less. As such, our clinical goal is to clarify individuals' subjective assessment of the significance of their loss, as it is this assessment that mediates their feelings of loneliness and hopelessness. It is in this sense that the role of anomie—or social isolation—in suicide among the elderly is clearly established.

Our clinical impression is that individuals who become suicidal after the loss of a relationship may be distinguished from those who do not in that the former often report histories of difficulties with separation, intimacy, and dependency in prior relationships. When faced with loss or separations, such persons may respond with feelings of despair and hopelessness, or may engage in a range of behaviors that serve to restore the relationship. Such behaviors range from angry and demanding outbursts to passive solicitousness. Among such individuals, the loss of a spouse or separation from one's friends or children appear to activate assumptions or schemata centering on the importance of relationships in one's life. Such assumptions might include beliefs that "I'm helpless and need other people to care for me," "My value as a person depends on my caring for others," and the like. Although these maladaptive assumptions may have been activated in similar situations in the past, elderly persons may find that their customary ways of responding or adapting are no longer available. As a consequence, they come to feel increasingly hopeless and despondent. For example, women who place a high value on their role as a mother, and on caring for others, may experience heightened feelings of dysphoria as their opportunities for fulfilling these goals become limited. Reactions to the loss of relationships may become severer as patients age. This is reflected in the remarks of a 51-year-old women who became quite depressed and mildly suicidal after her youngest child left for college. As she stated, "I can see I need to find something else to do with my life now . . . but if my husband died, then I'd have to kill myself."

This suggestion that underlying assumptions that people hold about themselves, their relationships, and their world are "activated" in specific situations is supported by the finding that levels of hopelessness among depressed individuals are consistent from one depressive episode to the next. Feelings of hopelessness might be viewed, then, as a "trait" schema, which, when activated, assumes its full value.

In summary, the role of loss in the emergence of depression among the elderly is usually apparent. It may be in the form of the loss of a loved one, of one's physical capacities, of employment, or of one's status in the community. Self-esteem may decline as individuals begin to view themselves as "useless" and "a burden on others." These difficulties are compounded by accompanying feelings of powerlessness, helplessness, and hopelessness. Although none of these processes or factors is unique to the elderly, aging does seem to increase the likelihood of encountering these stressors.

Although we have spoken of "the elderly" as a homogenous group, with the goal of highlighting their unique qualities, experiences, and problems, we do not wish to overgeneralize. Useful distinctions can be made, for example, between elderly persons who are aging, and those who are aged (Neugarten, 1975). The former individuals tend to be active (regardless of age), and are able to participate in a range of meaningful social and personal activities. They are aware, however, of physical changes in their strength, stamina, appearance, and of the emergence of chronic, albeit noncritical, illnesses. Aging persons may be concerned by discrepancies between the goals they have had for their lives, and their actual level of accomplishment. Although there is an increasing awareness of their impending death, this is balanced by their knowledge that time remains to accomplish life's goals. Aging persons are, nonetheless, sensitive to changes and losses in their relationships. They are generative, in the Eriksonian sense, continuing to develop professionally and personally; however, most adopt the role of the elder, passing their experiences, knowledge, and responsibilities on to younger persons. In contrast, the "aged" have become debilitated by serious illness, loss of relationships, grief, and the inability (real or perceived) to pursue activities that had previously given them a sense of pleasure or accomplishment. As a consequence, they become increasingly dependent, hopeless, and despondent. Although both groups may be classified as "elderly," they differ in their concerns, and in their resources and coping capacities. These differences will have important practical implications for treatment. Old age is a period of multiple and diverse losses and stresses. The multiplicative effect of these problems can be extremely distressing and overwhelming. These effects are compounded by a tendency to overestimate age-related losses in functioning, underestimating remaining adaptive capacity, failing to recognize ways in which the elderly can influence important outcomes in their lives, withdrawing from supportive relationships or enjoyable activities, and adopting a pessimistic attitude toward the self, the world, and the future. This is not, in any way, meant to diminish the real-life stresses and losses, but to avoid having the pessimistic views becoming self-fulfilling prophecies.

Individual differences among patients within each age group are quite important. Although we can identify common concerns, issues, problems, and developmental tasks among persons in each age group, psychotherapy must remain an individualized and personal endeavor.

Working with the Elderly

An assessment of the potential for family support is often an important component of psychotherapy with any suicidal patient. The same is true with elderly individuals. When the therapeutic issue is suicidal ideation, the objectives of such an assessment would be the following:

1. *To identify family members who would be able to provide support for the patient*—This serves to ensure the patient's physical safety, assists them in completing therapeutic homework assignments, and reduces their feelings of isolation or loneliness.

2. *To evaluate the quality of the family members' relationship with the elderly patient, and the manner in which this may be contributed to the suicidal thoughts or gestures*—It may, for example, be helpful to explore their feelings toward the patient, and assess whether they had expressed (either subtly or openly) that they felt the elderly parent had become "a burden" or was "in the way."

3. *To identify potential areas of conflict within the family*—These might result from their having been asked to collaborate in the patient's treatment or may stem from other stresses in their lives. For example, children who had lived apart from the elderly patient may resent the commitment of time and energy required of them. The involvement may rekindle old conflicts.

When there has been a suicide attempt, the clinician must work to identify the impact of the patient's suicide attempt on the family. It may, for example, be helpful to discuss their feelings regarding the attempt with them. In addition to feelings of concern, it is not uncommon for loved ones to feel guilt, anger, frustration, or hopelessness. Should these negative feelings emerge, and be apparent to the patient, they could serve as further "proof" that "the family would be better off if I were dead."

As we noted earlier, developmental differences exist in terms of the beliefs and assumptions commonly held by depressed older persons. Elderly individuals may have developed a range of negative beliefs or assumptions about age that become activated, and that render them vulnerable to depression or suicide. These assumptions are established early in life and are supported by our culture. Beliefs that elderly persons cannot make meaningful contributions, or that they are a burden to others, may be particularly upsetting to individuals who have placed an emphasis on achieving career goals, providing for their children, and maintaining an independent life-style. Retirement, then, may be particularly difficult for individuals whose sense of worth was based on achievement or productivity, or who are relatively "autonomous." This is consistent with epidemiological evidence of an increase in the suicide rate for white men who are approximately 65 years of age. The feelings of hopelessness and apathy that accompany the depression may contribute to social withdrawal, and a decrease in the person's participation in enjoyable activities, leading to further feelings of worthlessness, isolation, and depression. A cycle is thus established.

As with any group, the assumptions and schemata developed early in life will continue to govern the individual's behavior. Assumptions that had previously been active may, in old age, be less operative, and other alternative schemata may take precedence. Assumptions that previously has been dormant may be activated by issues of health and loss. An example might be the belief held by a 20-year-old that "I've got a lifetime ahead of me to succeed." At age 60, however, the time remaining to become a success (whatever that means to the individual) is limited. This can lead to other thoughts and feelings of failure, limited time left to "make one's mark," and ruminations about missed opportunities and regretted choices. In doing therapy with the elderly, then, therapeutic success may be limited because of dysfunctional assumptions held by these patients. Explicit attention may need to be given to the assessment and resolution of these assumptions for enduring therapeutic gains to be achieved.

The concept of schema or the resulting negative assumptions is particularly relevant to psychotherapy with the elderly, and relates to the culturally held belief that older persons are weak, inferior, passive, dependent, senile, or sexually inactive. As individuals grow older, they may adopt these beliefs and may integrate them into their views of themselves. These internalized beliefs will color their perceptions of themselves and their relationships with others. Thus, one's perceptions of what it means to age and to be elderly may leave one vulnerable to depression. Cognitive therapy, then, would attempt to identify the negative beliefs that are associated with distorted views of aging.

With the exception of its developmental emphasis, and the focus on age-specific issues, cognitive psychotherapy with the depressed or suicidal elderly person is not substantially different from that with younger adults. Thought records, activity scheduling, guided imagery, and a developmental analysis of underlying assumptions may all be employed with good results. As we have seen, central issues in psychotherapy with the elderly frequently center on coping with deteriorating health; loss of self-esteem, autonomy, or independence; financial difficulties; feelings of abandonment and neglect; concerns with the passage of time; loneliness; and grief. A "life-review" is often useful in assisting aged persons to adjust to their situation (Butler, 1963).

It is worth noting that although elderly persons may present with these common issues, they may, nonetheless, continue to struggle with concerns that they have carried with them throughout their lives. A retired 74-year-old architect remarked, for example, "All my life I've been trying to be tough . . . to earn my dad's approval. . . . It's about time I let go of my dad." Aging, then, need not resolve or cover an individual's preexisting concerns, conflicts, issues, or personality traits.

Busse and Pfeiffer (1969) recommend that, when working with elderly individuals, therapists adopt an "active role in identifying and clarifying patients' current difficulties." Such a therapeutic stance is quite consistent with cognitive therapy techniques. They recommend, for example, that short-term interventions be planned, based on the establishment of specific, attainable goals. An open, active stance is essential in developing a trusting therapeutic collaboration. Patients might be encouraged to identify specific problems, to generate and evaluate alternative solutions, and to express their feelings of pain, sorrow, and hopelessness openly, as well as difficulties adjusting to the changing rules of life. Achte and Karha (1986) have observed that ambivalence regarding the wish to die is frequently apparent among elderly patients. They have recommended, then, that interventions be directed at decreasing this ambivalence.

Often, however, the sharing of information and the evaluation of dysfunctional beliefs is not enough. Some elderly patients may dismiss the data as irrelevant. Schemata about "wisdom coming with age," of "listening to one's elders" (directed at the therapist), and that "experience is the best teacher" may serve to interfere with therapy and limit progress. Standard cognitive techniques can be used, without modification, in addressing these beliefs. Both the patient's and therapist's beliefs about "being too young to understand" and of "being disrespectful of one's elders" can be identified and resolved directly. It is important to be cognizant of therapist's beliefs, which may hamper progress in treatment. These may include assumptions that "old persons are inflexible and can't benefit from therapy," or that "they're just being cantankerous, crotchety, passive, manipulative, or dependent." In essence, we must be careful not to take a pessimistic view mistakenly of the nature and utility of psychotherapy with the elderly. Rigidity and flexibility are not functions of age, but of the individual's personality. It is also important for clinicians to be aware of their own biases regarding the elderly, and to be able to reflect on their own concerns and fears about death, dying, loss, dependency, achievement, and illness that may effect their ability to serve as a compassionate, objective, therapist.

In working with the elderly, it is particularly important to maintain an active role. It is often helpful to "engage them" by discussing their daily activities and by offering practical solutions to daily problems. The use of a collaborative, educational approach may be useful in that it not only encourages the patient to address specific problems actively, but also discourages the development of a passive dependence on therapy, and may reduce the stigmata attached to receiving psychotherapy (in short, do not be passive or withdrawn; rather, be creative and sociable). This active approach to the treatment of the elderly is also seen among more traditional approaches. Franz Alexander (1961), for example, suggested that analytic procedures could be adapted for the elderly, and emphasized support and active participation by the therapist.

In some cases, it will be essential for the therapist to assume an advocacy role for the patient. Within the collaborative model of cognitive therapy, it may be important for the therapist to use the weight of their office, agency, or personal assertiveness to help the elderly patient to move through the bureaucracy of social service agencies.

The goal of the therapeutic interventions is to help dispute the notion that the patient is alone, and is without resources or support.

In sum, cognitive therapy is well suited to the treatment of elderly patients, as depression in this group stems from maladaptive ways of perceiving oneself and one's relationships, and from a loss of previously effective coping strategies for dealing with losses. An emphasis, then, is placed on developing more adaptive ways of viewing oneself, one's life, the future, and one's relationships with others, and in developing a wider range of coping techniques. As noted in chapters 4 and 5, the therapist may assist patients by: (a) assisting them to monitor changes in their affect and concomitant negative thoughts; (b) clarifying with patients the relationship between these thoughts and the shift in their mood; (c) examining evidence for and against these thoughts, beliefs, expectations, and perceptions; (d) developing accurate, adaptive perceptions of themselves, their future, their life, and their relationships; (e) identifying common themes among these beliefs and correcting these dysfunctional assumptions; (f) encouraging their participation in a range of activities that are enjoyable, and provide them with a sense of worth or value; and (g) maintaining or developing their social supports.

The Efficacy of Cognitive Therapy With Elders

Several studies have been published in recent years examining the efficacy of cognitive therapy with elderly depressed patients (Steuer, 1982; Steuer et al., 1984; Steuer & Hammen, 1983; Thompson, Davies, Gallagher, & Krantz, 1986; Gallagher, Thompson, & Thompson, 1992). Few, unfortunately, have included adequate controls, and none has specifically addressed the issue of suicide. Case reports suggest that behavioral interventions, such as contingency contracting and self-reinforcement, may be effective in alleviating grief reactions among elderly individuals (Flannery, 1974; Callahan & Burnette, 1989; Amory, 1981).

Controlled outcome studies of psychotherapy of depression among the elderly have been completed by Gallagher (1981) and Gallagher and Thompson (1982, 1983). In the initial study, a sample of depressed outpatients were randomly assigned to behavioral or supportive psychotherapy groups. Patients in both groups reportedly experienced significant decreases in the level of depression over the course of treatment. These gains were maintained over a 5-week follow-up period.

These findings were replicated and extended by Gallagher and

Thompson (1982, 1983) in a study of 30 elderly outpatients who had received diagnoses of major depression. The patients were randomly assigned to three treatment conditions: cognitive (Beck's model), behavioral (Lewinsohn's model), or insight-oriented (Bellak and Small's model) psychotherapy. Patients received 16 individual counseling sessions over a 12-week period. Sessions were 90 minutes in length, rather than the traditional 50-minute hour, as pilot data revealed that elderly individuals "generally responded to therapeutic interventions more slowly than other clients." The authors reported comparable decreases in depression, as measured by both self-report and clinician ratings, for patients in each of the psychotherapy groups at the completion of treatment. These gains were not maintained to an equal degree, however, during the 12-month follow-up period. Clinician's ratings of depressive symptoms increased for patients in the insight-oriented psychotherapy group during the 6 weeks following treatment, at which point half of the patients in that group were moderately depressed. Moreover, patients who had received insight-oriented psychotherapy reported experiencing significantly more distress during later follow-ups than did patients in the other treatment conditions. Patients who had received cognitive or behavioral psychotherapy tended to maintain their therapeutic gains. When interviewed 12 months after the completion of treatment, one of nine patients in the cognitive and behavioral conditions (11%) were diagnosed as having experienced an episode of major depression, whereas 44% of patients who had received insight-oriented psychotherapy relapsed. Although the generalizability of these findings is limited because of the low suicidal risk of their sample, and their exclusion of patients who experienced concurrent alcohol abuse, their results are encouraging. Their findings support recent suggestions by Mintz, Steuer, and Jarvik (1981); Steuer et al. (1984); and Steuer and Hammen (1983) that short-term psychotherapy can be effective in alleviating depression among the elderly. Moreover, treatment gains were maintained to a greater degree by patients who participated in structured forms of psychotherapy. It is worth noting that patients with active suicidal ideations were excluded from the Steuer study.

Chronically Ill

Living with chronic illness places a great deal of stress on the patient and their family, and can be accompanied by high levels of depression and hopelessness (Greeneberg, 1988; Plumb & Holland, 1977; Rodin & Carvin, 1989; Scharf & Miller, 1989). Adaptation to chronic illness, then, requires well-developed and flexible coping skills. To live with a chronic illness requires more of the individual, however, than simply adapting to the symptoms of the disorder, its treatment, and their side effects. Rather, there are a range of concomitant social and psychological issues that require attention. To view chronic illness as only a medical phenomena, then, is to overlook important family, occupational, financial, social, self-concept, and health issues that require management from patients and their families.

Chronic illness may be defined as any disease or disorder resulting in a permanent impairment that is the result of a nonreversible pathological condition and that results in a continuing, functional disability. This population overlaps with the elderly; 85% of Americans older than the age of 65 suffer from one or more chronic diseases. This is not to say, however, that chronic diseases are uncommon among younger individuals. One of four adults, for example, suffers from cancer or arteriosclerosis, and a growing number of young and middle-aged adults suffer from hypertension. The activities of 1 in 10 adults are limited because of arthritis. Chronic illnesses, then, appear to affect a sizable number of individuals. The importance of understanding the relationship of chronic illness to suicidal risk is underscored by the fact that more than 50% of suicides of persons 30 years of age or older were accompanied by a significant physical illness.

Depression among people hospitalized with medical problems appears to be quite high, with prevalence estimates ranging from as high as 32% (Cavanaugh, 1983). Although most depression among medically ill individuals appears to be mild, and may reflect a common emotional response to the stress of illness and treatment, a sizable minority of patients experience subjectively severe levels of depression. Cavanaugh (1983, 1984), for example, reported that 14% of medically ill patients in a sample of general hospitals were severely depressed. Levels of depression among the medically ill appear to be associated with the severity of their disorder, the limitations placed on their mobility, and level of pain.

Many chronic illnesses are, by nature, progressive. Although they typically are characterized by episodic periods of remission and exacerbation, the ultimate outcome for the chronically ill patient most often is poor in that the illness places increasing demands on the patient for management. Treatment requires continually more of the patient's time, energy, and money. Moreover, these illnesses are accompanied by a range of secondary problems. Such difficulties include decreased mobility, loss of self-care capacities, inability to participate in strenuous or physically taxing activities, and social isolation. Patients' feelings of hopelessness and dysphoria are exacerbated by failures of treatments, particularly when they had attempted to adhere to the treatment protocol.

Unfortunately, the assessment and diagnosis of depression and suicidality among chronically ill persons is complicated by several factors (Robinson & Rabins, 1989). As in the diagnosis of depression among the elderly, the physical illness may itself be accompanied by a range of depressive features. The stress of the illness, and subsequent hospitalizations, may result in an adjustment disorder, or in a grief-like reaction because of the loss of regular contact with family and friends. Moreover, the somatic signs and symptoms that are an integral part of the diagnosis of major depression may also result from the medical illness or its treatment. Cavanaugh, Clark, and Gibbons (1983) reported that more than 50% of medical inpatients report experiencing fatigue, lethargy, psychomotor retardation, loss of appetite and weight, insomnia, and somatic preoccupation. The latter symptom is not surprising. We would expect that hospitalizations and chronic illness would lead individuals to focus attentively on somatic sensations and symptoms.

The stigma that frequently is attached to chronic illnesses can contribute to patients' feelings of depression and despair. The severity of the stigma appears to be related to the visibility of the impairment to others. As a consequence, patients with chronic illnesses may go to great lengths to conceal their difficulties from others. This may include wearing wigs or hats by cancer patients, being fitted with a prosthesis, or the use of makeup and clothing to cover scars. Although these attempts may be useful in reducing the visibility of the impairment, the impact on the patient's body image and sense of physical integrity remains. Feelings of physical vulnerability, and beliefs that one's body is "damaged" or "unacceptable" can become important issues in therapy. As in cognitive therapy with other patients, however, it is important to let the patient's automatic thoughts guide you to the central issue or theme rather than to presume its presence. Once again, sensitive and reflective listening to the patient is essential to identifying the specific beliefs or thoughts that are underlying their distress.

Chronic illness can disrupt individuals' lives in numerous and significant ways. Patients may, for example, become unable to work or to enjoy activities they had found enjoyable, experience losses of their physical or cognitive capacities, become disfigured, lose their physical attractiveness, or become socially isolated. These losses may stem from the illness itself, from the stigma attached to it, or from the time and energy necessary to manage the disease. The therapist needs to keep in mind that their needs to be a distinction made between real and perceived losses. Patients may, for example, tend to catastrophize the impact of their illness on their life and overlook resources and abilities that are unaffected. As we have seen, cognitive errors, such as magnification, minimization, selective abstraction, and the like, can exacerbate patients' feelings of depression and hopelessness. This is particularly true among patients who are facing real and serious losses or limitations because of their illness.

The social world of the chronically ill individual can be altered dramatically as a result of their disorder. They may begin to affiliate with others who share similar difficulties and may come to see old friends on a less frequent basis. These changes may stem from their desire to seek support from others who they believe will be more accepting of their predicament, the social stigma attached to their illness, or the dysphoria and sense of apathy that frequently accompanies chronic illness. Social withdrawal, however, can only serve to exacerbate their feelings of dysphoria and despair.

The family of the patient may also experience changes in their social relationships as a consequence of the illness. This may be related to the time requirements of caring for an ill relative or from other factors. A 24-year-old women, for example, was attending college while living at home to care for her chronically ill mother. She reported that she had "never dated" because of a fear of ultimately having to bring a boyfriend home, where he might see their disheveled home and her mother's condition. We bring this up, as patients' feelings of dysphoria and hopelessness may be heightened by their awareness of the impact of their illness on their family. This can include not only the social isolation of family members, but also the financial hardships they endure, and the time and energy they expend on the patient. Recent research suggests that chronic illness contributes to family instability, and is accompanied by an increased divorce rate, and higher levels of academic and behavioral difficulties among younger children. As a result, the patient may come to feel that "I'm a burden. . . . They'd be better off if I were gone." Clinically, then, it is often quite useful to discuss patients' thoughts and feelings regarding the impact of their illness on their family with them and to incorporate family members in the treatment. It may then be possible both to identify concrete ways of reducing the effects of the illness on family members, and to resolve automatic thoughts or beliefs that contribute to the patient's depression.

The patient's feelings of hopelessness may be exacerbated by the uncertain nature of the illness and its course. The inability to predict exacerbations and remissions makes the planning of day-to-day activities, as well as long-term goals, quite difficult. These feelings of hopelessness are only increased by their belief that they have lost control over their bodies and their social situation. Control is, in essence, given over to the illness and its management. It is this sense of powerlessness and hopelessness that underlies their feelings of depression.

To summarize, patient's reactions to chronic illness may be characterized by the following:

1. Feelings of hopelessness and powerlessness, with consequent depression.
2. Social withdrawal and increasing isolation. This is often accompanied by feelings that they are "unacceptable" to others.
3. Decreased independence and autonomy. There is an increasing need to be assisted or cared for by others.
4. Anxiety regarding uncertainty of outcome. There may be concerns regarding pain, deterioration of their cognitive or physical functioning, and their impending death.
5. Anxiety regarding separations from family and friends. This is particularly common among persons who require long-term convalescent care and elderly persons who are placed in nursing homes.

There should be a single collection point for all of the diverse information regarding the patient's health. We have often been involved in situations in which several different medical professionals were treating the patient without a central organizing agent. In some of these cases, the patient is left with divergent or contradictory views, without the opportunity to fit the divergent pieces into a meaningful whole. The therapist will need to gather the information from the different sources so that the accuracy and reality of the patient's concerns can be assessed. Weissman and Worden (1977) identified a group of cancer patients who experienced high levels of emotional distress and difficulty resolving problems they had been facing. They observed that patients who had difficulty adjusting to their illness had two primary deficits in their coping repertoire. First,

they tended to overuse coping strategies that are less effective in resolving their problems but that provide a brief sense of relief—such
as drinking. Second, they were not able to generate alternative approaches to problem solving. This finding is consistent with our clinical impression that autonomous, achievement-oriented men may be
at risk for depression and suicide when confronted by a serious, progressive illness. Their tendency to adopt a somewhat inflexible belief
system based on the assumption that they must be a "strong pro-
vider" prevents them from accepting a more dependent role and adjusting to their physical limitations. Weissman and Worden (1977)
found, in contrast, that "good copers" were able to try several approaches to problem solving and that they kept going until something was effective in alleviating their distress. Persistence and the
perception that one's efforts will ultimately prove successful plays an
important role in adjustment to chronic problems. Good copers were
also found to be able to evaluate and rank-order their approaches and
implemented them in a systematic manner. Adaptation to chronic illness, then, may be an appropriate goal of psychotherapy. This would
entail assisting individuals to accept an illness as a part of their being
and their life, without a false hope for future cures or a false hopelessness based on the belief that they are unable to influence their
life.

The primary objective with the depressed or suicidal patient is
to instill a wish to live. The same applies here. Only the source of the
hopelessness and desperation differs. In addition to standard cognitive techniques focused on hopelessness, there is a pragmatic focus
on assisting them to restructure their environment so that they can
function more effectively and independently. By collaboratively discussing the patient's primary concerns, they will be better able to
adopt the problem-oriented focus of cognitive therapy. Collaboration
then begets further compliance. The therapist can work on identifying community resources and supports that are available. Activity
scheduling can be used for the development of social interactions,
thereby helping to develop a social support network. An additional
goal would be the alleviation of guilt stemming from the belief that
they may have contributed to the illness (as in cancer of a long-term
smoker).

Sobel and Worden (1980) designed a problem-solving intervention for cancer patients who had been identified as poor copers. This
approach involves a problem-oriented, 4 to 6-week group training
program. This was designed to enhance the patients' sense of control
and responsibility for managing their difficulties. As it was based on

a collaborative model, it avoided the stigma attached to traditional psychotherapy. As Worden (1987) noted, "patients and their families do not want help with their feelings, worries and fears, but rather they want help in getting well physically as well as help in solving immediate problems and planning for future tasks." (pg. 42). It is important in training patients to cope more effectively that they not only be able to generate alternative solutions, but also to recognize the intrapsychic, interpersonal, and environmental consequences of each alternative. That is, they must learn to anticipate what factors may block the implementation of each approach. They can then consider methods of overcoming these obstacles. Overall, the objectives of this approach are to strengthen the patients' internal controls, to reinforce flexibility in problem solving, and to enhance their sense of competence in managing problems resulting from their illness. As a consequence, they may develop hope for the future.

With these goals in mind, the therapist may wish to encourage patients to do the following:

1. Get more information about their illnesses. Be reality based, and do not catastrophize or minimize outcomes.
2. Share feelings with others including family, friends, support group, and therapist.
3. Develop problem-solving capacities.
4. Employ structured techniques such as relaxation, auto-hypnosis, and guided imagery as a means of reducing physical pain.
5. Identify new activities they can pursue that will be enjoyable, meaningful, and satisfying.
6. Adopt an attitude of attacking problems in contrast to experiencing passive resignation.
7. Identify, clarify, and develop coping capacities and personal strengths.
8. Identify new goals for life. That is, things they can look forward to and can work to accomplish.
9. Identify pragmatic approaches to overcoming physical handicaps (e.g., learn braille, get a walker or golf-cart, use a prosthesis to reduce conspicuous feelings when in public).

As with other patients, it is important to identify and resolve therapist automatic thoughts and assumptions that hamper therapeutic progress. Such beliefs might include the stigma attached to illness, the belief that the situation is futile, or a withdrawal from the patient because of a fear of ultimate death of the patient.

Native Americans

The literature with respect to depression and suicide among Native Americans is quite limited. Although few large-scale or systematic studies have been published, epidemiological research indicates that suicide rates of young Native Americans are among the highest of any ethnic group (McIntosh, 1984; McIntosh & Santos, 1981). Studies of individual tribes and regions suggest that important tribal differences exist in the incidence and patterns of suicide (Borunda & Shore, 1978; Shore, Kinzie, & Hampton, 1973; Humphrey & Kupferer, 1982). Further, discrepancies exist between data from various reporting sources, such as the reservations, the Indian Health Service, and the National Center for Health Statistics (Miller, 1979). As a result, it is difficult to make general statements regarding factors contributing to the increased rate of suicide among Native Americans.

In addition to age, other factors associated with an increased risk for suicide among Native Americans include "off-reservation living," incarceration, "cultural disintegration," and "marginality." Marginality refers to individuals' inability to form "dual ethnic identification because of bicultural membership." The specific means by which these factors contribute to suicidal behavior, however, is unclear.

It is not uncommon for Native Americans to distrust professionals who have had little exposure to their culture and experience. This can seriously impede progress in therapy, and should be addressed as quickly as is reasonable. Factors that commonly hinder the development of a therapeutic rapport, and have recommended that therapists avoid "excessive and direct eye contact," as this can be considered rude; tolerate longer periods of silence; and avoid "direct counselling methods" (McIntosh & Santos, 1981).

The role of cultural and religious beliefs about death, and about the appropriateness of seeking professional help for emotional concerns, are poorly understood. Although many Native Americans often use psychiatric services, the reasons vary. With this in mind, it is important to remain both respectful and sensitive to the patient's cultural and tribal values, and to the difficulties frequently experienced when attempting to maintain a dual cultural identity.

Little has been written about problems inherent in doing psychotherapy with Native Americans. In many cases, the Native Americans' negative view of themselves and their world are reinforced by the larger society. Their negative view of the future, and consequent sense of hopelessness, may be accurate given their difficulties in finding employment, academic opportunities, proper housing, and medical care. Many of the beliefs and automatic thoughts contributing to their feelings of hopelessness may, in short, be reasonable. As such, strategic, problem-solving approaches in counseling can be quite helpful. In summary, this is a group that needs to be studied more carefully so that we can understand the processes that need to be altered, thereby allowing the most effective therapeutic interventions.

Summary

There are several groups who are at greater risk for suicide than the general population in that they demonstrate substantially higher rates of self-destructive behavior. These groups include the elderly, chronically ill individuals, and Native Americans.

As a group, elderly persons tend to employ more lethal means in attempting suicide than younger persons. Suicide among the elderly appears, then, to be a clinically important but frequently overlooked phenomena. It reflects, at the least, unnoticed levels of hopelessness and despair among a large segment of our population. The elderly also differ from younger patients in that they seldom seek psychiatric or psychological treatment of their own accord. Although they may feel quite depressed, and may experience suicidal ideations, it is uncommon for them to seek professional help spontaneously for these difficulties. Depression among the elderly may also be iatrogenic, in that a range of medications taken for other illnesses can produce similar symptoms.

The goals of treating the suicidal elderly include assisting them to monitor changes in their affect, and concomitant negative thoughts; clarifying with patients the relationship between these thoughts and the shift in their mood; facilitating examination of evidence for and against these thoughts; developing accurate, adaptive perceptions of themselves, their future, their life, and their relationships; identifying common themes among these beliefs and correcting these dysfunctional assumptions; encouraging their participation in a range of activities that are enjoyable, and provide them with a sense of worth or value; and maintaining or developing their social supports.

The assessment and diagnosis of depression and suicidality among chronically ill persons is complicated by several factors. As in the diagnosis of depression among the elderly, the physical illness may itself be accompanied by a range of depressive features. The stress of the illness, and subsequent hospitalizations, may result in an adjustment disorder, or in a grief-like reaction because of the loss of regular contact with family and friends. Moreover, the somatic and vegetative symptoms that are an integral part of the diagnosis of major depression may also result from the physical illness or its treatment. Patients' feelings of hopelessness may be exacerbated by the uncertain nature of the illness and its course. Patients' reactions to chronic illness may be characterized by feelings of hopelessness and powerlessness, with consequent depression; social withdrawal and increasing isolation often accompanied by feelings that they are "unacceptable" to others; decreased dependence and autonomy; anxiety regarding uncertainty of outcome; and anxiety regarding separations from family and friends. This is particularly common among persons who require long-term convalescent care and elderly persons who are placed in nursing homes. The therapist can work on identifying community resources and supports that are available. Activity scheduling can be used for the development of social interactions, thereby helping to develop a social support network. An additional goal would be the alleviation of guilt stemming from belief that they may have contributed to the illness (as in cancer of a long-term smoker).

Epidemiological research indicates that suicide rates among young Native Americans are the highest of any ethnic group. Many of the beliefs and automatic thoughts contributing to their feelings of hopelessness may be reasonable. As such, strategic, problem-solving approaches in counseling can be quite helpful. In summary, this is a group that needs to be studied more carefully so that we can understand the processes that need to be altered, thereby allowing the most effective therapeutic interventions.

8

Factors Exacerbating
Suicidal Risk

The battle rages loud and long and the stormy winds do blow.

—*Thomas Campbell,* Ye Mariners of England

We have previously identified several vulnerability factors that increase the potential for suicidal behavior. Among groups that are already at high risk, this places them at even greater risk. Principal among these are alcohol and substance abuse. Although the use of alcohol or drugs may be seen as an attempt to manage one's distress by self-medicating, this is rarely successful. From a cognitive perspective, alcoholism and substance abuse potentiate the risk of suicidal behavior by reducing one's ability to inhibit impulsive behavior reducing adaptive problem solving, exacerbating ongoing stressors, and leading potentially supportive persons to withdraw from the individual. It is not surprising, then, that alcohol and substance abuse are common among groups with the highest rates of self-destructive behavior—individuals who have made prior suicide attempts, and Vietnam veterans suffering posttraumatic stress disorder (PTSD). Given the importance of these factors in increasing suicidal risk, it will be helpful to discuss them at some length.

Alcohol and Substance Abuse

The relationship between alcohol abuse, drug addiction, and suicide has been actively studied for more than 50 years. Karl Menninger, in his book *Man Against Himself* (1938), argued that alcohol and drug abuse were conceptually similar to a range of other potentially dangerous behaviors in that they unnecessarily increased the risk of illness, accidents, or death. As such, they might be considered to be unconscious suicide attempts. Similarly, Farberow (1980) characterized alcohol and drug abuse as "indirect suicides," and Shneidman (1985) views them as contributing to "subintentional deaths."

In some respects, however, the relationship between alcohol or substance abuse and suicide is far more direct (Beck, Weissman, & Kovacs, 1976; Berglund, 1984; Hawton, Fagg, & McKeown, 1989). Severe intoxication with alcohol is, in some cases, an intentional attempt to poison oneself. Moreover, alcohol is frequently ingested along with barbiturates or other drugs as a means of potentiating their lethality. Alcohol is consumed along with medications in more than 20% of attempted overdoses (Hawton & Catalan, 1982), and during the hours before overdose attempts in an even larger percentage of individuals (Holding, Buglass, Duffy, & Kreitman, 1977; Morgan, Burns-Cox, Pocock, & Pottle, 1975).

Recent reports suggest that individuals suffering from alcohol or substance abuse are at an increased risk both for attempting, and for successfully completing, a suicidal act. Studies completed in Britain, for example, suggest that between 36% (Morgan et al., 1975) and 48% (Holding et al., 1977) of male suicide attempters have difficulties with alcohol abuse. Similarly, Miles (1977) reviewed the literature to that date regarding factors associated with increased suicide risk and estimated that 15% of individuals suffering from alcohol abuse die by committing suicide. The significance of this finding is highlighted by the fact that less than 1% of persons in the general population die by suicide. Further evidence for a relationship between alcohol abuse and suicide is provided by retrospective studies of individuals who have committed suicide. Recent work by Roy and Linnoila (1986) suggests that between 15% and 26% of suicide completers suffer from alcohol abuse. Given that approximately 5% of the general population suffers from alcohol abuse, these findings strongly suggest that an association exists between alcohol abuse and suicide. The treatment of a suicidal individual who is acutely intoxicated or who has recently taken illicit drugs is quite difficult. An argument can be made that it is impossible to treat persons who, because of alcohol or drug use, is not capable of cogently discussing their concerns. As such, suicidal patients suffering from alcohol or substance abuse should be admitted to an inpatient unit for detoxification. An initial period of drying out, during which withdrawal symptoms are monitored, provides the therapist with the time necessary to conduct a more thorough evaluation of the patient's current situation, to interview family members, and to develop a comprehensive treatment program. Initial interventions are typically directed toward eliminating their drinking or drug use, and toward providing them with more appropriate problem-solving strategies. Patients with a history of alcohol or substance abuse typically have little motivation to participate in therapy. They tend, quite often, to minimize the severity of their difficulties and to overestimate their capacity to resolve their problems. Cognitive distortions, such as these, can be addressed in a direct manner with structured interventions. We have often found it useful, for example, to encourage a patient's spouse and children to express their feelings and concerns openly to the patient during family therapy sessions. Not uncommonly, there has been a conspiracy of silence among family members, in which they have refrained from honestly expressing their concerns because of a fear that this would exacerbate the problems at home. The legitimacy of this fear, however, is also open to exploration through rational responding and other techniques.

Some drug abusers fall into the group we have labeled "histrionic." The repetitive suicide attempts may reflect, in part, attempts to reach the "perfect high." This may involve taking more of the drug than they usually take, experimenting with new and more powerful drugs, or combining drugs, all in the service of achieving the greatest high. Stuart, age 29, described his use of heroin in the following way: "It's better than the best sex. It's better than the best meal. It's the warmest, most best feeling I've ever got. It's like being wrapped in cotton candy . . . each part of me feeling soft and nice. The higher I get, the better I feel. After a while nothin' means nothin'."

The use of the drug lowers whatever self-control the individual has, promoting ever more impulsive and self-destructive behavior.

PTSD

Combat veterans suffering from PTSD constitute a second group that is at increased risk for depression, suicidal thoughts, and self-destructive behavior. Egendorf, Kadushin, Laufer, Rothbart, and Sloan (1981) reported that 16% of all Vietnam era veterans, and 29% of those who participated in combat experienced "significant problems" in readjusting to civilian life. The extent of these difficulties become apparent when it is noted that approximately 800,000 men participated in combat during the Vietnam war (Blank, 1982). These difficulties are severest among veterans suffering from PTSD. Although few disorders have been as carefully described as "combat neuroses" or PTSD, our understanding of the nature and treatment of these disorders remains rudimentary. Reasons appear to include the fact that the specific experiences of veterans has varied from war to war (Blum, Kelly, Meyer Carlson, & Hodson, 1984; Figley, 1978), and that treatments have typically been symptomatic. More recently, however, attempts have been made to identify factors that render individuals susceptible to PTSD, coping strategies or "defenses" that insulate others from the disorder (Hendin & Haas, 1984), and specific interventions that may be helpful in alleviating their difficulties (Balson & Dempster, 1980; Hendin, 1983; Osler, 1985; Sonnenberg, Blank, & Talbott, 1985).

Diagnosis of PTSD

Clinically, it is often difficult to diagnose and treat PTSD. Diagnosis is complicated by the fact that symptoms presented overlap with a range of disorders including schizophrenia, major depression, and generalized anxiety. Moreover, PTSD is frequently accompanied by a range of Axis I and Axis II disorders. Given the resulting potential for misdiagnosis, initial treatments may be inappropriate. Similarly, attempts to treat the disorder symptomatically may not be effective as they do not address underlying beliefs or schemata that maintain the patients difficulties.

A central factor in the onset of PTSD, as in other anxiety disorders, appears to be the development of a sense of vulnerability, in conjunction with a belief that one is unable to cope with threatening situations. These perceived threats may be to an individual's physical well-being (as when hearing a helicopter leads a veteran to belief that an "attack" is imminent) or psychological integrity (as when they fear "losing control" of their emotions).

These notions are consistent with cognitive conceptualizations of anxiety and phobic disorders (Beck, Emery, & Greenberg, 1985), and with recent research into factors that "protected" some veterans from PTSD. Hendin and Haas (1984), for example, found that veterans who did not develop PTSD after combat demonstrated calmness under pressure, intellectual control, acceptance of fear, and lack of excessively violent or guilt-arousing behavior. The authors postulated that these behaviors allowed the veterans to maintain "emotional stability in an unstructured, unstable context." In contrast, veterans who subsequently developed PTSD tended to view their combat experiences in less rational or manageable terms and came to feel "out of control in a meaningless struggle." These observations lend credence to our assumption that individuals' perceptions of an event influence their subsequent emotional reactions. As Hendin and Haas stated, "it is not so much what the individual experiences in Vietnam but how those event and situations were perceived, integrated, and acted on that bears the primary relationship to the postcombat response." Our therapeutic task, then, is to assist patients with PTSD in reconstructing these experiences.

The symptoms of PTSD include depression (insomnia, social withdrawal, dysphoria, built, suicidal ideations, low self-esteem, sexual dysfunction), anxiety (vigilance, tremor, palpitations, sweating), alcohol and drug abuse, and anger. In addition, patients typically experience recurrent and intrusive recollections of traumatic events. It is not surprising, then, that veterans frequently receive multiple psychiatric diagnoses before being characterized as suffering from PTSD (Birkhimer, DeVane, & Muniz, 1985). Given the heterogeneity of the symptom pattern, we might speculate that these individuals also experience a range of automatic thoughts, assumptions, schemata, and cognitive distortions that are characteristic of other disorders. Moreover, the alcohol and drug abuse seen among a large proportion of veterans suffering from PTSD may be seen as an ineffective attempt to relieve their distress through self-medicating. As with other disorders, then, the specific symptoms and automatic thoughts reported by the patient will guide our interventions. Important components of treating the suicidal veteran include the identification of maladaptive beliefs and assumptions, development of social supports, and enhancement of their ability to identify and implement a range of effective solutions for day-to-day difficulties.

Development of Therapeutic Relationship

Several assumptions are made when doing short-term cognitive psychotherapy. Among these are assumptions that the patient will be able to develop a trusting, therapeutic collaboration quickly, and that they will be able to reflect on their emotional experiences. Veterans suffering from PTSD, however, appear to experience difficulty in meeting these prerequisites of short-term psychotherapy. Their sense of distrust and social alienation inhibits the development of a therapeutic rapport, and the intensity of their mood swings frequently leaves them feeling overwhelmed. They tend, as a consequence, to avoid reflecting on automatic thoughts and images, as these engender tremendous amounts of anxiety, guilt, and rage.

With these difficulties in mind, modifications of "standard" cognitive therapy techniques are necessary when working with suicidal combat veterans. Given their feelings of social alienation and distrust, a supportive, nonconfrontational approach is often helpful. Combat veterans' motivation to participate in therapy is frequently hindered by their belief that "only other Vets can understand us." This belief is so common among Vietnam veterans suffering from PTSD, and is so damaging to therapeutic rapport, that it requires immediate exploration and resolution. A careful and empathic examination of the origins of this belief, the evidence supporting it and the serious consequences of maintaining it is often helpful. Given the strength of the belief, however, it is often futile simply to attempt to "dissuade" the veteran with evidence. Rather, their trust must be earned through their experiencing a supportive and accepting relationship with the therapist. We have often found it helpful to acknowledge these difficulties directly. Patients might also be encouraged to conceptualize "understanding" as a continuum, to reflect on the "degree to which they felt understood by the therapist," and to discuss the specific instances in which they felt understood or misunderstood during the session. Similarly, it might be noted that no one, not even another veteran, can "fully" empathize with their personal experiences; however, others, including the therapist, may be able to "empathize enough" to be of assistance. With such patients, it is helpful to inquire regularly as to whether they believe they have expressed their concerns and feeling clearly, and whether they feel they have been adequately "understood."

The development of a collaborative rapport may also be hindered by veterans' identifying the therapist with institutions, such as the Veterans Administration (VA) system. As with other maladaptive thoughts, these beliefs may be addressed in a straightforward manner. Combat veterans frequently are resentful of the VA system and of authority figures. Some of these criticisms may be legitimate, whereas others are not. Nonetheless, it is both possible and beneficial to respect the legitimacy of their feelings toward authority figures and organizations while discussing evidence to the contrary, and noting the negative consequences to them of maintaining these beliefs and attitudes. In developing a collaborative relationship with the veteran we want them to recognize that we are there to work with them and not to serve simply as representatives of the VA. A cognitive approach is particularly useful in this regard. Rather than simply reflecting their feelings of resentment and distrust, and making interpretations of them, we wish to clarify and resolve these issues actively. As Fuentes (1980) suggested, therapy with Vietnam veterans is facilitated by therapists adopting a more active, self-disclosing, and pragmatic approach than is typical of traditional psychodynamic psychotherapy.

The wariness or suspiciousness seen among many combat veterans during the initial stages of psychotherapy is also reflected in their day-to-day life. As Hendin (1984) observed, "one of the common adaptations seen in Vietnam combat veterans with post-traumatic stress disorders could be described as paranoid." This "coping style" is reflected in veterans' "vigilance" in dealing with others, their expectation that others will behave in a malevolent manner, and their belief that it is "best to strike first" when faced with possible aggression. Although such a coping style may have served them well in combat, it is clearly maladaptive in civilian life. This style of adaptation may, nonetheless, serve an adaptive function for the veteran in that it alleviates continuing feelings of fear or anxiety, and may provide the veteran with a "sense of security" by maintaining control over situations. The distrustful stance seen among many combat veterans suffering from PTSD appears to reflect their underlying sense of physical and emotional vulnerability. Our interventions, then, are directed at alleviating their perception that they are vulnerable or "at risk," and at enhancing their sense of competence in handling potentially dangerous situations.

As rapport is established, it may be helpful to identify and reflect the patients' feelings of suspiciousness and anger to them as they occur during session, and have them note the range of situations in which they occur outside of therapy. Traditional cognitive techniques may then be introduced in assisting the patient to evaluate the underlying beliefs. He might be encouraged, for example, to ask:

Are others actually malevolent?

What are the benefits and costs to me of maintaining a vigilant and suspicious approach?

In what ways am I vulnerable? Not vulnerable?

What influence do I have over this specific situation?

Do I actually need "complete" security or control?

Is it necessary to behave "aggressively" or are there alternatives?

Am I really a potential "victim"?

As in cognitive therapy with other patients, our emphasis is on assisting the veteran to identify specific beliefs that maintain his difficulties, and to develop his ability to evaluate these beliefs objectively.

A consensus appears to be developing that Vietnam veterans are particularly vulnerable to PTSD because of the specific nature of their combat experiences (Figley, 1978). They tended to experience a range of traumatic events at central juncture in their development—the point at which they were establishing an adult identity—and were given limited support from others in their attempts to understand these experiences. Few opportunities were provided for them to discuss their experiences, to derive a sense of "meaning" from it, or to resolve the ambiguities of their predicament and their behaviors. An objective of psychotherapy, then, is to reduce the influence of these traumatic experiences by allowing the veteran to reflect on them, to clarify them, and to alleviate consequent dysfunctional beliefs. Catharsis, although important, is not our only objective. Although it is critical that the veteran feel capable of openly discussing his concerns, and of acknowledging the depth and significance of his experiences, this is not sufficient for the alleviation of symptoms. Rather, we wish to encourage the veteran to identify the beliefs, assumptions, and coping strategies that had developed as a consequence of these experiences, and to assist him in developing more adaptive alternatives.

Catherall (1986) identified two important dimensions or realms that are sources of difficulty for combat veterans. He labeled these "mourning of losses" and "examination of the self." Catherall emphasized the importance of a "supportive social network" in facilitating the veteran's ability to mourn losses and adopt an "objective attitude of self-examination." It is in this way, he postulates, that the veteran becomes capable of resolving "identity issues of young adulthood" that underlie PTSD.

Catherall focuses, then, on the importance of veterans feeling "approved of within their social context" as a means of promoting "social healing." We believe, however, that although it is important to alleviate the social isolation that accompanies PTSD, it is not the provision of an acceptant and supportive social environment, per se, that promotes therapeutic improvement. Rather, it is the opportunity these settings provide for confronting traumatic emotions and objectively evaluating one's experiences and beliefs. Moreover, a supportive social environment (whether it is provided by friends, family, the community, an individual therapist, or a veterans group) provides valuable evidence that the veteran is "acceptable," that his experiences are understandable, that others are supportive of him as an individual, and that his behaviors during the war are forgivable.

Catherall's model is also useful in that it suggests a range of specific beliefs and assumptions that may contribute to the symptoms experienced by veterans. These center on the mourning of losses, beliefs that they did not deserve to live, feelings of shame and rage regarding their behavior during the war, attitudes toward civilians and the lack of support from others, as well as a generalized belief that the "world is a dangerous place."

In addition to automatic thoughts and images that engender anxiety, anger, and guilt, veterans also make attributions and express beliefs that serve to reduce the intensity of these emotions. For example, when recalling their behavior in combat, veterans may adopt the attitude that "I was only following orders" or "It was a group mission."

These cognitions serve to reduce the intensity of patients' feelings of guilt or shame by minimizing their sense of responsibility for their actions. In the long run, such coping mechanisms may or may not be adaptive, as the underlying beliefs regarding their experiences remain intact. Therapeutically, it may be helpful to encourage veterans to (a) accept their responsibility for their behavior, and to identify specific criteria for "forgiveness"—that is, "what would be necessary for you to let yourself off the hook", or (b) develop their belief that they "really weren't responsible"—for example, "the situation was ambiguous . . . you couldn't have planned for it . . . you did respond as best you could." In either case, the objective is to alleviate their belief that they had something "morally unpardonable" such that their feelings of guilt are reduced.

The feelings of anger and resentment that accompany PTSD appear to be exacerbated by veterans' tendency to "blame others" (society, the war, the VA, their family) for their current difficulties. Although there may, in fact, be some truth to their belief that others have contributed to their predicament, these beliefs are ultimately maladaptive in that they promote a sense of hopelessness, and inhibit veterans from taking active steps to overcome their difficulties. Moreover, these feelings of anger and resentment are self-perpetuating. By their very nature, they carry a sense of "righteous indignation"—that "I've been wronged, and it's my right to feel this way." Once again, although this may be true, these beliefs serve to prevent veterans from mourning the losses of the war, and from acknowledging and evaluating the effect of the war on their views about themselves, their world, and their relationships with others. Cognitive approaches can be employed in assisting veterans to examine the evidence for and against these beliefs, and the consequences to them of maintaining them.

As in psychotherapy with other patients, then, we believe that assisting the veteran to acknowledge and reflect on strong emotions,

and to develop an understanding of the thoughts and beliefs underlying them, is the first step to alleviating them. In some cases, veterans' combat experiences may have served to "activate" or "consolidate" previously held beliefs. Their reaction to experiences in
Vietnam can be viewed, then, in the context of their prior beliefs and
coping style.

A 32-year-old veteran was seen after have made four suicide attempts. He reported a lengthy history of drug and alcohol abuse, and stated that he frequently "needed the excitement" of dangerous activities—as when he stole a
bulldozer that had been parked in front of a police station. The patient stated
that he "didn't feel he could trust anyone" and that his feelings of depression and hopelessness stemmed from his consequent isolation. He related
these feelings to an experience while on a destroyer off the coast of Vietnam.
as he stated:
    "We just kept pulling people out of the water and off of the boats . . .
they were just floating, hundreds of them. It really showed me how uncaring
people are . . . all those people, they'd been abandoned."
    This experience appeared to activate and reify the patient's memory of
having been abandoned by his father when hew as age 4. As a consequence,
he came to anticipate rejection in relationships and adopted an increasingly
distrustful coping style.

    Group psychotherapy is frequently seen as the treatment of
choice for Vietnam veterans suffering from PTSD. As noted, group
therapy can provide a supportive social environment in which the
veteran can feel accepted and has the opportunity to empathize with
others. As Yalom (1975) has observed, therapy groups also provide
members with practical advice, suggestions, and guidance from other
members; engender a sense of hope through seeing others with similar concerns who have grown through treatment and are now adapting more effectively; provide members with a sense of competence
and personal value through being of help or support to others; and
can provide a forum for modeling of effective coping strategies.
    A frequent concern of Vietnam combat veterans is that they will
"lose control" of their emotions, and that they might inadvertently or
impulsively hurt themselves or others. As cognitive techniques are
designed to provide patients with a sense of control over their emotional experiences, they appear to be particularly well suited to treating PTSD. When flexibly employed, strategic cognitive interventions
can provide patients with a sense of control over these images, emotions, and experiences.
    As Frick and Bogart (1982) observed in their article on transfer-

ence and countertransference in psychotherapy with veterans, the structure of PTSD groups frequently becomes similar to that of a combat patrol. Members come to refer to their therapist in much the same way as they would a "green" officer, and an "intense range of emotions associated with the war experience" are elicited. The veteran's group, then, may be a valuable tool in gaining access to the patients' "hot cognitions," as well as the assumptions and schemata that underlie their difficulties.

Group therapy may not be appropriate, however, for patients who are secretive, suspicious, or uncontrollable aggressive toward other group members. We have, however, found it to be a useful adjunct to individual therapy for veterans with low self-esteem or shame. We recently treated one veteran, for example, who refused a referral to a veterans' group as he believed he hadn't earned the right to go to a VA . . . or even sit in the room with real vets." Individual cognitive therapy, then, was employed in attempting to gain an understanding of the evidence supporting his belief, the origins of it, and the negative consequences of his maintaining it. Although group psychotherapy can be quite helpful in treatment PTSD, it is not always necessary or appropriate. For some combat veterans with PTSD, individual psychotherapy may be the treatment of choice.

Given the strength of the emotions elicited by veterans' automatic thoughts and images, it is essential to maintain a supportive environment during therapy sessions. This is often difficult, however, given the patients' initial distrust, and the intense emotional responses these behaviors may elicit in their therapists (Frick & Bogart, 1982; Williams, 1980). Combat veterans frequently challenge their therapists as "outsiders" or someone who "really doesn't know what it's about." It is necessary to recognize that the rage, suspiciousness, and distrust displayed by these patients is central to their disorder, and reflects their attempts to cope with strong and pervasive feelings of vulnerability. The development of a therapeutic collaboration, then, is central to the treatment itself, and is not simply a prerequisite. The symptoms of PTSD can be exacerbated by its effects on the patients spouse, family, and friends. The high divorce rate among patients suffering from PTSD is well established, as are the negative consequences of the disorder for their families. Marital and family sessions, then, may be a useful adjunct to group or individual psychotherapy sessions. Cognitive approaches to marital and family therapy have been described by Epstein, Schlesinger, and Dryden (1988), Arias and O'Leary (1988), and Bedrosian (1982, 1988).

Veterans' problems are also exacerbated by alcohol and substance abuse. As we have seen, the risk of suicide attempts is markedly increased among patients suffering from alcohol or substance abuse. We have found it quite helpful, then, to require veterans to complete an alcohol or drug detoxification program before initiating outpatient psychotherapy. Cognitive approaches for the treatment of alcohol and substance abuse are described in detail by Emery and Fox (1981), Glantz (1987), and Schlesinger (1988).

In summary, the initial strategies employed in treating the suicidal combat veteran are similar to those employed with other patients. Attempts are made to identify the specific stressors or events that precipitated the suicidal crisis; to identify their resources, supports, and deterrents; to "decastrophize" the immediate situation' and to engender a sense of hope by developing alternative approaches to resolving the difficulties.

Variations from the "standard cognitive approach" are apparent, however, in that a greater emphasis must be placed on developing a trusting therapeutic collaboration, and in addressing the strong tendencies for social withdrawal. As the immediate crisis is resolved, attempts are made to clarify and resolve the specific beliefs, assumptions, and schemata that contribute to their feelings of vulnerability, guilt, resentment, rage, dysphoria, and shame. In treating combat veterans, it is necessary to appreciate the important impact of their combat experiences on their "psychic structures"—that is, their beliefs about themselves, their world, and their relationships with others, as well as their underlying assumptions and schemata. As noted, particular attention must be given to the potential for alcohol and substance abuse that accompanies PTSD, as this places the veteran at an increased risk for further suicidal behaviors.

In summary, specific approaches to the treatment of the PTSD patient would include the following:

1. Cognitive restricting
2. Assertiveness training
3. Group therapy
4. Self-monitoring of stress, anxiety, and panic
5. Relaxation training
6. Stress inoculation training
7. Flooding
8. Systematic desensitization
9. Impulse and anger control
10. Family therapy

Multiple Attempters

A history of prior suicide attempts is one of the strongest predictors of future suicidal behavior (Petrie, Chamberlain, & Clarke, 1988). Although repeat attempters constitute only a small proportion of suicidal individuals, they are among the most challenging and difficult of patients. Retrospective studies of completed suicides reveal that approximately one third of persons who commit suicide have made a prior attempt (Bagley, Jacobson, & Rehin, 1976; Roy, 1985a, 1985b). Moreover, as Maris (1992) observed, "The probability of completing suicide is especially high in the first year or two after the initial nonfatal suicide attempt" (p. 374). This pattern of making repeated suicide attempts is particularly insidious in that it may reflect the establishment of a self-destructive "coping style," and may desensitize the individual to the dangerousness of their behavior such that they make increasingly more lethal attempts. Moreover, it may tend to "desensitize" or alienate those around the patient, contributing to a loss of support and social isolation.

If there is a truism in psychology, it is that the best predictor of future behavior is past behavior. The same applies in predicting suicide. A history of prior suicide attempts has been found to be associated with suicidal ideations, subsequent attempts, and completed suicides (Buglass and McCulloch, 1970; Meyers, 1982; Roy, 1982; Pokorny, 1983).

The results of a 2-year longitudinal study of 690 suicide attempters conducted by Bancroft and Marsack (1977), for example, revealed that 18% made one or more additional attempts, with the large proportion of those attempts coming during the first 3 months after discharge. These findings are consistent with those provided by Buglass and Horton (1974) and Wilkinson and Smeeton (1987), who reported that approximately 16% of their samples of suicidal patients attempted suicide again within 1 year.

These observations are also consistent with those of Morgan, Barton, Pottle, Pocock and Burns-Cox (1976), who followed a group of 279 individuals for 1 to 2 years after an initial suicide attempt. Sixty-seven of these patients (24%) attempted suicide again within 12 months. Repeat attempts were associated with previous psychiatric treatment, a criminal record, and "prior acts of deliberate self-harm." Wang et al. (1985) conducted a 3-year follow-up of 99 patients who had attempted suicide. They found that approximately half of their subjects made a repeat attempt within this period. Most of these attempts came within 1 year after discharge, and 5 of 10 completed suicides occurred within 3 months of discharge. Most attempters were 30- to 40-year-old men who lived alone, whereas most completers were 50- to 60-year-old married women. The authors noted that "around the time of the attempt, many expressed hopelessness, isolation, and suicidal ideations." These observations are consistent with work by Fawcett, Scheftner Clark, Hedeker, Gibbons, and Oryell (1987), and highlight the importance of careful follow-up immediately after an attempt and during the months after discharge from the hospital.

Recent research by Kurz et al. (1987) suggests that subtypes of suicide "repeaters" may exist and that differences in the prognosis for repeat attempters may exist depending on the "seriousness" of their prior attempts. Patients who have made "serious" suicide attempts appear to demonstrate an increased risk of further attempts (Beck, Weissman, Lester, & Trexler, 1976) and completed suicide (Rosen, 1976). Our confidence in these findings is limited, however, as no association was found between the seriousness of the initial suicide attempt and the risk of repeated attempts by Greer and Bagley (1971) or Morgan et al. (1976). Moreover, there is inherent danger in underestimating the risk of subsequent suicide attempts by patients who have made "nonserious" prior attempts. As Hankoff (1982) states, "the individual who has made a feeble suicide attempt, is resistant or antagonistic toward treatment and denies and difficulty or even effort at self-injury is apt to have little or no treatment. . . . The young woman who has taken a few aspirins, has little or no symptomatology, and admits that her act was impulsive, is apt to find a medical counterpart in terms of labelling the problem as an unimportant one. This denial should not be accepted since the individual who toys with suicide may eventually become the individual who becomes a fatal suicide."

It is interesting, as well, that Morgan et al. (1976) did not find the level of patients' suicidal "intent" during their initial attempt to be associated with an increased risk of further suicidal behaviors. Level of suicidal intent has been found in several studies, however, to discriminate suicide attempters from completers, and is strongly associated with the seriousness of the current suicidal attempt (Michel, 1987; Pallis & Sainsbury, 1976). Patients' "knowledge of the danger involved" or "anticipated outcome" of their suicide attempt does appear, however, to be correlated with subsequent risk. Beck, Kovacs, and Weissman (1975) found that although the correlation between suicidal intent and "medical dangerousness" of the attempt was low when suicide attempters were examined as a group; significant correlations emerged, however, when they examined the subgroups of attempters who were able to evaluate the risk inherent in their behavior accurately. Clinically, then, it may be quite helpful to assess patients' understanding of the probable outcome of their act, and whether they anticipated they would be "found in time" or receive help. This is particularly important in evaluating the risk of further suicidal acts by children and adolescents, who may not have a clear understanding of the relative lethality of various means. Several groups of investigators have attempted to develop scales for evaluating the risk of further suicidal behaviors by repeat attempters. A research group in Edinburgh, for example, compared patients who had made one suicide attempt with a sample of patients who had made multiple attempts (Buglass & Horton, 1974). They were able to identify a cluster of factors that discriminated these groups, and presented them as a brief clinical scale. The items included the following:

1. Diagnosis of sociopathy
2. Problems with the use of alcohol
3. Prior inpatient psychiatric treatment
4. Prior self-injury resulting in hospital admission
5. Prior outpatient psychiatric treatment
6. Condition of not living with relatives

They reported that a person scoring 0 on this scale had a 5% probability of attempting suicide again within a year, whereas a person receiving a score of 5 or 6 had a 48% chance of repeating. Given the small number of persons who committed suicide within their sample, however, it is not clear whether their scale predicts successful suicide. Moreover, the utility of their measure may be limited by the characteristics of the sample on which it was validated. The measure was developed with data provided by the Regional Poisoning Treatment Center in Edinburgh. It is possible, then, that this scale may not predict the behavior of persons who attempt suicide by other means.

This scale was cross-validated with a sample of Italian psychiatric inpatients by Garzotto, Siani, Zimmerman-Tansella, and Tansella (1976). The scale was found to discriminate repeaters from nonrepeaters in this sample, and demonstrated similar statistical properties to those found by Buglass and Horton (1974). Garzotto et al. (1976), however, found that a separate set of items also discriminated the repeaters from the nonrepeaters in their Italian sample. Their items included the following:

1. Diagnosis of sociopathy
2. Alcohol taken at the time of the act
3. Previous suicide attempt not admitted to the hospital
4. Patient subjected to physical violence
5. Less than 1 year at present address

As can be seen, the scales share only one item in common—the diagnosis of sociopathy—suggesting that the specific factors that predict repeated suicide attempts may vary from group to group. Moreover, work by Holding, Buglass, Duffy, and Kreitman (1977) indicated that the characteristics of repeat suicide attempters in Edinburgh may vary over time.

Both scales were subsequently cross-validated by Siani, Garzotto, Zimmerman-Tansella and Tansella (1979) with a separate sample of 147 patients admitted after suicide attempts. Although both scales were, once again, found to discriminate repeaters from nonrepeaters, each also demonstrated unacceptably high false-positive and false-negative rates. Even within a population of persons known to be at risk for attempted suicide, then, the statistical problems inherent in predicting a relatively rare behavior for specific individuals are apparent.

The value of these scales remain, however, in that their item content is similar to factors identified by others as related to repeated suicide attempts. Although the specific items may differ, their clinical utility remains in that they appear to reflect more general underlying characteristics that place persons at risk for suicide. Such characteristics include impulsivity, social isolation, relatively severe psychopathology, alcohol or substance abuse, poor occupational adjustment, and limited coping abilities. The risk of repeated suicide attempts appears to be heightened when the "goal" of the initial attempt is not realized, and the precipitating stress remains. As a consequence, these individuals tend to experience one crisis after another and may come to employ suicide attempts as a habitual style of coping with problematic situations.

Although there is an increasing recognition of the importance of identifying and treating chronically suicidal individuals, there is no coherent theory of repeated suicide to guide our clinical practice. The interpersonal, environmental, and intrapsychic or cognitive factors that underlie repeated suicide attempts are poorly understood. Although structured cognitive interventions are effective in reducing immediate suicidal risk, research with these individuals has not, as yet identified specific issues, assumptions, or schemata, which contribute to their recurring attempts. We might speculate that the act of attempting suicide itself may be a momentous event in the individual's life. As such, it may contribute to a schematic shift in patients' perceptions of themselves, their world, and their future. They have crossed the boundary from being persons who "think about suicide" to being persons who are capable of acting on the impulse. The specific meaning of the act for individuals, however, will be idiosyncratic. As with other schemata, these beliefs will guide their subsequent perceptions, memory processes, and thoughts.

Given the chronic history of marginal social and occupational adjustment that characterizes these patients, their long-standing emotional distress and their poorly developed coping strategies, they have good reason to feel hopeless. As one chronically suicidal patient remarked, "I won't let you treat me because you'll just make me feel better." This statement is quite telling. It reflects not only the patient's attempts to control the process of therapy but also the pervasive nature of her hopelessness. When asked to elaborate, she stated that she "knew she could feel better" but that she also "knew no one could give her a guarantee she wouldn't deteriorate again." In essence, she felt hopeless about her ability to maintain her therapeutic gains. Further, her comments reflected her acceptance of suicide as a viable solution or coping strategy. Among such patients, then, it may not be that life has become unbearable because of depression, and that suicide is their only alternative; it is that life is unbearable without suicide as a coping strategy. A history of chronic social and interpersonal difficulties has left the patients without effective alternatives. As Hawton and Catalan (1982) suggest, chronically suicidal patients may employ suicide "to avoid facing up to their problems . . . to deal with intolerable feelings of tension . . . to obtain some sort of excitement from risk taking."

We do not wish to overgeneralize, however, in describing chronically suicidal patients. It is important to recognize that, as individuals, their motives for attempting suicide may vary. The prediction of suicide remains a clinical, rather than a statistical, endeavor. As with other patients, then, it remains important to assess their individual beliefs and cognitions. Automatic thoughts provided by chronically suicidal patients include such beliefs as "I deserved to be punished" and "I always knew I couldn't live past 30." In treating chronically suicidal patients, it is important to maintain regular sessions and to provide them with a "continuity of care," even during periods in which they are not overtly hopeless or suicidal. During these hiatuses, we have found it helpful to aggressively treat the underlying affective (Beck et al., 1979) or personality disorders (Beck & Freeman, 1989; Freeman et al., 1988) as well as alcohol or substance abuse (Glantz, 1987; Greenwood, 1987). Given the severity of the dysphoria, anxiety, and anger experienced by these patients, psychotropic medications are often a useful component of a comprehensive treatment program. Similarly, occupational training and placement may be recommended as a means of stabilizing their work situation, and they might be encouraged to live with friends or family as a means of reducing their sense of isolation. Several authors have recommended outreach programs, such as weekly telephone contacts with their therapists or home visits as a means of maintaining therapeutic contact and alleviating their sense of alienation from others. Although these approaches have been found to reduce patients' feelings of depression, a consequent reduction in suicide rates has not been observed.

A central component of treating the chronically suicidal patient involves preparing them for future crises. A goal is to resolve problems before they become too severe and to provide the patient with a range of coping strategies. As these approaches can be quite pragmatic, they may seem more like counseling or guidance to the patient rather than psychotherapy per se. Nonetheless, we believe that they are highly valuable and should not be dismissed. Specifically, it is often helpful to identify situations that are likely to precipitate suicidal feelings and then identify the specific automatic thoughts, images, and emotions that are elicited. Gestalt techniques may be employed to heighten their sense of "realism" and allow them to envision how they would typically respond. We then prepare them to meet these challenges by reviewing alternative techniques for gaining control over their affect and resolving the situation. Problem-solving approaches can be employed during sessions, then, to prevent difficult situations from developing into crises, and to assist the patient in developing more effective coping skills. Specifically, we endeavor to help the patient recognize that

1. Suicide attempts are a coping strategy.
2. There are more effective alternatives available.
3. It is not adaptive to behave impulsively in problematic situations. Rather, they should attempt to identify the "cues" that more effective coping may be necessary.

A combat veteran with a history of four serious suicide attempts recognized that he "gets a warm feeling . . . a tension . . . like I have to jump out of my skin . . . then, I have to do something" prior to his self-destructive behaviors. He was then trained to use this "warm feeling" as a cue that something was upsetting him, that he should reflect on what it was, and that he should list several ways of dealing with it. If these were unsuccessful, he could call his therapist or the crisis line before acting on the impulse.

4. Present the patient with possible crises-practice alternative approaches to coping. Have the patient imagine the most effective strategy, how he'd feel when it worked, and write it down for ready reference.

In sum, chronically suicidal patients appear to require more extended and intensive treatment. Medications and supportive, problem-oriented techniques are used in conjunction with cognitive interventions designed to clarify and resolve underlying beliefs and assumptions.

In addition to the time and energy often expended in treating chronically suicidal patients, they can be difficult in that their behavior frequently antagonizes both their therapist and the medical treatment staff. The apparent "manipulativeness" of their suicidal behaviors, their difficulty in actively engaging in psychotherapy and in completing homework assignments, and the generally slow rate of improvement readily contribute to feelings of helplessness, hopelessness, and resentment on the part of the staff. These feelings, however, can cloud one's clinical judgment and contribute to a loss of empathy for the patient. They lead to increasingly strenuous efforts on the part of the staff to "control" the patient's behavior. These attempts, however, ultimately are futile. They reinforce the patient's feelings of powerlessness, reduce their sense of responsibility for their own actions, and undermine their legitimate or adaptive attempts to influence their environment. Moreover, these feelings disrupt the development of the collaborative rapport that is central to cognitive therapy. The therapist and patient are no longer working together toward a common goal but are attempting to "protect themselves" from the narcissistic injuries inflicted by the other. When this occurs, it is often helpful for the therapist to "disengage" from the emotions of the moment and to reflect on their personal automatic thoughts. In what ways, for example, is the patient behaving in a "manipulative" manner? Might their behavior, alternatively, be seen as highly maladaptive—the only way the patient sees for resolving his or her predicament? What are the consequences for you, as a therapist and a person, if the patient actually completed his or her threat?

A few outcome studies have been completed with chronically suicidal patients. Greer and Bagley (1971) reported the results of an 18-month retrospective follow-up study of 204 patients who had attempted suicide. They found that patients who had received no psychiatric care before discharge from the hospital were more likely to attempt suicide again during the follow-up period (39%) than were patients who had received either brief (26%) or intensive (20%) psychiatric care. These findings remained when variables known to correlate with repetition (history of prior suicide attempts, antisocial personality, drug or alcohol dependence, male sex, and refusal of psychiatric help) were controlled. Moreover, their results suggested that patients who had received only brief psychiatric treatment immediately after their initial attempt benefitted from additional treatment at a later time.

Montgomery et al. (1979) reported the results of a double-blind placebo-controlled trial of Flupenthixol with patients who had made recurrent suicide attempts. They found the medication was effective in reducing the number of subsequent attempts over a several-month follow-up period. Liberman and Eckman (1981) found that both behavioral and insight-oriented psychotherapy were associated with decreases in the number of repeat attempts in a sample of chronically suicidal patients. Moreover, the behavioral approaches were more effective in reducing patients' levels of depression and anxiety and in improving their assertiveness skills, than was insight-oriented psychotherapy. Our confidence in their finding that psychotherapy may be effective in reducing the risk of repeated attempts is lessened, however, by the lack of a no-treatment control group. We are not aware of any well-controlled studies; however, we are examining the value of cognitive approaches in reducing the risk of repeat attempts among chronically suicidal patients. Our clinical impression is that when cognitive techniques are employed in ongoing therapy, they can be effective in reducing the risk of relapse.

Summary

If there is one common theme relating the factors we have discussed in this chapter, it is that impulsivity and poor problem solving place individuals at greater risk for suicidal behavior, particularly when they are placed in subjectively stressful situations. Alcoholism and drug abuse, for example, may be seen as ineffective coping strategies that inadvertently exacerbate problematic situations. Similarly, PTSD among Vietnam veterans is often associated with a withdrawal from available supports or resources, and is compounded by difficulties with substance abuse. Chronic suicide reflects the acceptance of suicide as an effective coping strategy. Although the origins of behavioral impulsivity and poor problem-solving capacities are varied, and most likely have multiple determinants, their role in increasing the suicidal potential of individuals is clear. Moreover, the identification of impulsivity and poor problem solving as contributors to suicidal risk has important therapeutic implications. Interventions directed specifically toward reducing impulsivity, and at enhancing patients' ability to develop, evaluate, and implement alternative solutions would be expected to promote a realistic sense of hope and to thereby reduce suicidal potential.

Nonetheless, the prediction of suicidal acts by persons with a history of alcohol or substance abuse, or of prior self-destructive behavior, and the treatment of factors contributing to this style of adaptation, continue to be important problems. Despite the fact that we have a reasonably good understanding of factors associated with an increased risk of suicide, we have not been able to use these items, either individually or in combination, to predict the behavior of specific individuals at specific points in time. Moreover, they have not contributed to our understanding of the intrapsychic processes of chronically suicidal individuals.

The reasons for these difficulties are both statistical and conceptual in nature. Bayesian statistical theory precludes us from predicting low base-rate behaviors, such as completed suicides. Our attempts to increase the base rate by examining high-risk groups, such as persons with a history of prior suicide attempts, are ultimately unsatisfactory as they lead us to overlook increasing numbers of potentially suicidal individuals. The generalizability of our findings are reduced as we limit the nature of our samples. Moreover, there is a presumption that "suicidal risk" is a characteristic of the individual and that it is "there to be found" if only we had the right assessment techniques (Burk, Kurz, & Moller, 1985). We would suggest, however, that this assumption is incorrect. Suicidal risk or intent is not a "static" entity, but varies from moment to moment and setting to setting (Keith-Spiegel & Spiegel, 1967). It reflects the ongoing and variable contributions of a range of cognitive, interpersonal, physiological, and environmental factors. Cognitive assessment instruments, such as the HS, appear to be strong predictors of an individual's behavior because they are state-dependent measures of the individual's perceptions. Consistent with cognitive theory, it is these perceptions that mediate the individual's behavior on a moment-by-moment basis.

With this in mind, future efforts might be directed more usefully at examining the interface between cognitive, interpersonal, physiological, and environmental factors during the hours and days immediately surrounding a suicidal crisis. What exactly are the cognitive, affective, perceptual, and physiological changes and processes that occur in the individual at the time they choose to act? Further, we may wish to examine the underlying assumptions and schemata of the chronically suicidal patient, and the manner in which their views of themselves, others, their world, and their future are affected by their having acted on their suicidal impulses. We are, in essence, advocating an idiographic and "microanalytic" approach to predicting the behavior of individuals. Although our clinical interventions are currently effective in reducing immediate suicide danger, an alternative approach may be useful in guiding the development of techniques to reduce the long-term risk for individuals with the greatest potential for dying at their own hand.

Epilogue

I sought where cutting winds are at their worst?
I learned to dwell
Where no one lives, in bleakest polar hell,
Unlearned mankind and god, prayer and curse?
Became a ghost that wanders over glaciers . . .

Your hope stayed strong:
Don't shut your gates, new friends may come along.
Let old ones go. Don't be a memory monger!
Once you were young—now you are even younger.

—Friedrich Nietzsche, *From High Mountains—Aftersong*

Beck et al. (1990) identified five stages in the development of a book. As the idea for the book matures, some ideas seem to grow and take precedence, whereas other ideas, seemingly bright stars at first, recede into the background. This book grew out of the shared clinical experience of the authors in their work at the Center for Cognitive Therapy at the University of Pennsylvania under Aaron T. Beck.

The second stage is the development of the manuscript. It was during this stage that the project became bogged down. Wanting to write the perfect text that would cover everything that everyone would ever want to know about suicidal ideation and suicidal behavior on the part of suicidal patients and their families was overly ambitious. Our perception was that, unlike more general texts on cognitive therapy, the consequences of leaving something out of this one was more weighty. It was only through the work of our editors that we were able to hone the manuscript down to a publishable size. We were always receiving new material, seeing new patients, and reading new studies that we thought ought to be included.

The third stage comes when the manuscript is in the hands of the publisher who asks all sorts of impossible questions regarding form, format, references, and grammar. Once these are answered, the final editing and typing of the manuscript occurs.

Finally, the book is published and in the hands of you, the reader.

Readers may well question why we have not answered their questions about a suicidal patient that they are going to see this very day. The reader may ask, "why have you not discussed the treatment of a suicidal, obese, transsexual, borderline personality disordered, geriatric patient?" Our answer can only be that we had to stop somewhere.

The treatment of the suicidal patient will continue to vex therapists because of the life and death consequences of the act. For the chronically suicidal patient, the therapeutic problem will be how to control the impulsive behavior. For therapists treating suicidal patients, the need will be to deal with their own dysfunctional thoughts that feed the therapist's heightened stress and anxiety, or increased depression and hopelessness.

The short-term, active, directive, focused, problem-oriented, structured, collaborative, and psychoeducational nature of cognitive therapy will continue to be empirically tested by clinical researchers around the world. Following the lead of Beck and others, the empirical and clinical testing of cognitive therapy will undoubtedly bring about alterations and modifications to the basic model for the treatment of suicidal behavior, recognizing that often times, the therapist may be the only person between the patient's life and death. We offer to the reader our clinical experience, case examples, good wishes, empathy, and respect for being willing to stand on the side of life.

References

References

Abrahms, J. L. (1983). Cognitive-behavioral strategies to induce and enhance a collaborative set in distressed couples. In A. Freeman, (Ed.), *Cognitive therapy with couples and groups* (pp. 125–156). New York: Plenum.

Abramson, L., & Alloy, L. (1981). Depression, nondepression, and cognitive illusions: Reply to Schwartz. *Journal of Experimental Psychology: General, 110,* 436–447.

Abramson, L., Alloy, L., & Metalsky, G. (1988). The cognitive diathesis-stress theories of depression: Toward an adequate evaluation of the theories' validities. In L. Alloy (Ed.), *Cognitive processes in depression.* New York: Guilford.

Abramson, L., Metalsky, G., & Alloy, L. (1989). Hopelessness depression: A theory-based subtype of depression. *Psychological Review, 96,* 358–372.

Abramson, L., Seligman, M., & Teasdale, (1978). Learned helplessness in humans: Critique and reformulation. *Journal of Abnormal Psychology, 87,* 49–74.

Achte, K., & Karha, E. (1986). Some psychodynamic aspects of the para-suicide syndrome with special reference to older persons. *Crisis, 7,* 24–32.

Ackerly, W. (1967). Latency-age children who threaten or attempt to kill themselves. *Journal of the American Academy of Child Psychiatry, 6,* 242–261.

Adam, K. (1986). Early family influences on suicidal behavior. In J. Mann & M. Stanley (Eds.), *Psychobiology of suicidal behavior.* New York: New York Academy of Sciences.

Adam, K., Bouckoms, A., & Scarr, G. (1980). Attempted suicide in Christ-church: A controlled study. *Australia and New Zealand Journal of Psychiatry, 14,* 305–314.

Adam, K., Bouckoms, A., & Streiner, D. (1982). Parental loss and family stability in attempted suicide. *Archives of General Psychiatry, 39*, 1081–1085.

Adam, K., Lohrenz, J., Harper, D., & Streiner, D. (1982). Early parental loss and suicidal ideation in university students. *Canadian Journal of Psychiatry, 27*, 275–281.

Akiskal, H., & McKinney, W. (1975). Overview of recent research in depression. *Archives of General Psychiatry, 32*, 285–305.

Alexander, F. (1961). *The scope of psychoanalysis, 1921–1961: Selected papers of Franz Alexander.* New York: Basic Books.

Alloy, L. (Ed.). (1988). *Cognitive processes in depression.* New York: Guilford.

Alloy, L., & Abramson, L. (1979). Judgement of contingency in depressed and nondepressed students: Sadder but wiser? *Journal of Experimental Psychology: General*, 441–485.

Alloy, L., & Abramson, L. (1988). Depressive realism: Four theoretical perspectives. In L. Alloy (Ed.), *Cognitive processes in depression.* New York: Guilford.

Alloy, L., Abramson, L., Metalsky, G., & Hartlage, S. (1988). The hopelessness theory of depression: Attributional aspects. *British Journal of Clinical Psychology, 27*, 5–21.

Arias, I., & O'Leary, K. (1988). Cognitive-behavioral treatment of physical aggression in marriage. In N. Epstein, S. Schlesinger, & W. Dryden (Eds.), *Cognitive-Behavioral therapy with families.* New York: Bruner-Mazel.

Asberg, M., Nordstrom, P., & Traskman-Bendz, L. (1986). Biological factors in suicide. In A. Roy (Ed.), *Suicide.* Baltimore, MD: Williams and Wilkins.

Asberg, M., Schalling, D., Rydin, E., & Traskman-Benz, L. (1981). Suicide and depression. In J. Soubrier & J. Vedrinne (Eds.), *Depression et Suicide.* New York: Pergamon Press.

Asberg, M., Traskman, K., & Thoren, P. (1976). 5-HIAA in the cerebrospinal fluid: A biochemical suicide predictor. *Archives of General Psychiatry, 33*, 1193–1197.

Bagley, C., Jacobson, S., & Rehin, A. (1976). Completed suicide: A taxonomic analysis of clinical and social data. *Psychological Medicine, 6*, 429–438.

Bagley, C., & Ramsey, R. (1985). Psychosocial correlates of suicidal behaviors in an urban population. *Crisis, 6*, 63–77.

Balson, P., & Dempster, C. (1980). Treatment of war neuroses from Vietnam. *Comprehensive Psychiatry, 21*, 167–175.

Bancroft, J., & Marsack, P. (1977). The repetitiveness of self-poisoning and self-injury. *British Journal of Psychiatry, 131*, 394–399.

Bandura, A. (1977). Self-efficacy: Toward a unifying theory of behavioral change. *Psychological Review, 84*, 191–215.

Barraclough, B. (1971). Suicide in the elderly. In D. Kay & A. Walk (Eds.), *Recent developments in psychogeriatrics*. Ashford, Kent: Headley Brothers.

Barraclough, B. (1973). Differences between national suicide rates. *British Journal of Psychiatry, 122*, 247–256.

Barraclough, B., Bunch, J., Nelson, B., & Sainsbury. (1974). A hundred cases of suicide: Clinical aspects. *British Journal of Psychiatry, 125*, 355–373.

Barter, J., Swaback, D., & Todd, D. (1968). Adolescent suicide attempts: A follow-up study of hospitalized patients. *Archives of General Psychiatry, 19*, 523–527.

Baucom, D., & Epstein, N. (1990). *Cognitive-Behavioral Marital Therapy*. New York: Bruner-Mazel.

Baucom, D., & Epstein, N. (1991). Will the real cognitive-behavioral marital therapy please stand up? *Journal of Family Psychology, 4*(4), 394–401.

Beck, A. (1967). *Depression: Clinical, Experimental, and Theoretical Aspects*. New York: Hoeber.

Beck, A. (1973). *The diagnosis and management of depression*. Philadelphia: University of Pennsylvania Press.

Beck, A. (1976). *Cognitive therapy and the emotional disorders*. New York: International Universities Press.

Beck, A. (1985). *Cognitive therapy of depression*. (unpublished manuscript)

Beck, A., & Beamesderfer, A. (1974). Assessment of depression: The Depression Inventory. In P. Pichot (Ed.), *Psychological measurements in psychopharmacology: Vol. 7 Modern Problems in Pharmacopsychiatry*. Basel: Karger.

Beck, A., Brown, G., & Steer, R. (1989). Prediction of eventual suicide in psychiatric inpatients by clinical ratings of hopelessness. *Journal of Consulting and Clinical Psychology, 57*, 309–310.

Beck, A., & Emery, G. (1985). *Anxiety disorders and phobias: A cognitive perspective*. New York: Basic Books.

Beck, A., & Freeman, A. (1989). *Cognitive therapy of personality disorders*. New York: Guilford.

Beck, A., & Greenberg, R. (1978). *Coping with depression*. (Unpublished manuscript, Center for Cognitive Therapy, Department of Psychiatry, University of Pennsylvania, Philadelphia.

Beck, A. T., Emery, G., & Greenberg, R. L. (1985). *Anxiety disorders and phobias*. New York: Basic Books.

Beck, A., Freeman, A., & Associates. (1990). *Cognitive therapy of personality disorders*. New York: Guilford.

Beck, A., Hollon, S., Young, J., Bedrosian, R., & Budenz, D. (1985). Treatment of depression with cognitive therapy and amitriptyline. *Archives of General Psychiatry, 42,* 142–148.

Beck, A., Kovacs, M., & Weissman, A. (1975). Hopelessness and suicidal behavior: An overview. *Journal of the American Medical Association, 234,* 1146–1149.

Beck, A., Kovacs, M., & Weissman, A. (1979). Assessment of suicidal intention: The Scale for Suicidal Ideation. *Journal of Consulting and Clinical Psychology, 47,* 343–352.

Beck, A., & Lester, D. (1973). Components of depression in attempted suicide. *Journal of Psychology, 85,* 257–260.

Beck, A. T., Resnick, H. L. P., & Lettieri, D. J. (Eds.). (1974). *The prediction of suicide.* Bowie, MD: Charles Press.

Beck, A. T., Rush, A. J., Shaw, B. F., & Emery, G. (1979). *Cognitive therapy of depression.* New York: Guilford.

Beck, A., Schuyler, D., & Herman, I. (1974). Development of suicidal intent scales. In A. Beck, H. Resnik, & D. Lettieri (Eds.), *The prediction of suicide.* Philadelphia: Charles Press.

Beck, A., Steer, R., & Garbin, M. (1988). Psychometric properties of the Beck Depression Inventory: Twenty-five years of evaluation. *Clinical Psychology Review, 8,* 77–100.

Beck, A., Steer, R., Kovacs, M., & Garrison, B. (1985). Hopelessness and eventual suicide: A 10-year prospective study of patients hospitalized with suicide ideation. *American Journal of Psychiatry, 142,* 559–563.

Beck, A., Ward, C., Mendelson, M., Mock, J., & Erbaugh, J. (1961). An inventory for measuring depression. *Archives of General Psychiatry, 4,* 561–571.

Beck, A., Weissman, A., Lester, D., & Trexler, L. (1974). The measurement of pessmisism: The Hopelessness Scale. *Journal of Consulting and Clinical Psychology, 42,* 861–865.

Beck, A., Weissman, A., Lester, D., & Trexler, L. (1976). Classification of suicidal behaviors: II. Dimensions of suicidal intent. *Archives of General Psychiatry, 33,* 835–837.

Beck, A., Weissman, A., & Kovacs, M. (1976). Alcoholism, hopelessness, and suicidal behavior. *Journal of Studies Alcohol, 37,* 66–76.

Beck, R., Morris, J., & Lester, D. (1974). Suicide notes and risk of future suicide. *Journal of the American Medical Association, 228,* 495–496.

Bedrosian, R. (1981). Ecological factors in cognitive therapy: The use of significant others. In G. Emery, S. Hollon, & R. Bedrosian (Eds.), *New directions in cognitive therapy.* New York: Guilford.

Bedrosian, R. (1982). Using cognitive and systems intervention in the treatment of marital violence. In J. Hansen & L. Barnhill (Eds.), *Clinical approaches to family violence*. Rockville, MD: Aspen Systems Corporation.

Bedrosian, R. (1986). Cognitive and family interventions for suicidal patients. *Journal of Psychotherapy and the Family, 2,* 129–152.

Bedrosian, R. (1988). Treating depression and suicidal wishes within the family context. In N. Epstein, S. Schlesinger, & W. Dryden (Eds.), *Cognitive-behavioral therapy with families*. New York: Bruner-Mazel.

Bedrosian, R., & Beck, A. (1979). Cognitive aspects of suicidal behavior. *Suicide and Life Threatening Behavior, 9,* 87–96.

Bedrosian, R., & Epstein, N. (1984). Cognitive therapy of depressed and suicidal adolescents. In H. Sudak, A. Ford, & N. Rushforth (Eds.), *Suicide in the young*. Littleton, MA: John Wright.

Bellack, A., & Hersen, M. (1987). *Dictionary of behavior therapy techniques*. New York: Pergamon.

Benedict, R. (1934). *Patterns of culture*. Boston: Houghton Mifflin.

Berglund, M. (1984). Suicide in alcoholism: A prospective study of 88 suicides: I. The multidimensional diagnosis at first admission. *Archives of General Psychiatry, 41,* 888–891.

Bergstrand, C., & Otto, U. (1962). Suicidal attempts in adolescence childhood. *Acta Paediatrica, 51,* 17–26.

Berman, A., & Jobes, D. (1991). *Adolescent suicide: Assessment and intervention*. Washington, DC: American Psychological Association.

Binder, R. (1978). Dealing with patients' suicide. *American Journal of Psychiatry, 135*(9), 1113.

Birkhimer, L., DeVane, C., & Muniz, C. (1985). Post-traumatic stress disorder: Characteristics and pharmacological response in the veteran population. *Comprehensive Psychiatry, 26,* 304–310.

Birtchnell, J. (1981). Some familial and clinical characteristics of female suicidal psychiatric patients. *British Journal of Psychiatry, 138,* 381–390.

Black, D., Winokur, G., & Nasrallah, A. (1987). Suicide in subtypes of major affective disorder: A comparison with general population suicide mortality. *Archives of General Psychiatry, 44,* 878–880.

Blaney, P., Behar, V., & Head, R. (1980). Two measures of depressive cognitions: Their association with depression and with each other. *Journal of Abnormal Psychology, 89,* 678–682.

Blank, A. (1982). Apocolypse terminable and interminable: Operation outreach for Vietnam Veterans. *Hospital and Community Psychiatry, 33,* 913–918.

Bleuler, M. (1978). *The schizophrenic disorders: Long-term and family studies*. New Haven, CT: Yale University.

Blum, M., Kelly, E., Meyer, M., Carlson, C., & Hodson, (1984). An assessment of the treatment of the needs of Vietnam-era veterans. *Hospital and Community Psychiatry, 35,* 691–696.

Blumenthal, S. (1984). "An overview of suicide risk factor research." Paper presented at the Annual Meeting of the American Psychiatric Association. Los Angeles, CA.

Blumenthal, S., & Kupfer, D. (1986). Generalizable treatment strategies for suicidal behavior. In J. Mann & M. Stanley (Eds.), *Psychobiology of suicidal behavior.* New York: New York Academy of Sciences.

Bongar, B. (1991). *The suicidal patient: clinical and legal standards of care.* Washington, DC: American Psychological Association.

Borunda, P., & Shore, J. (1978). Neglected minority: Urban Indians and mental health. *International Journal of Social Psychiatry, 24,* 220–224.

Bowers, W. (1989). Cognitive therapy with inpatients. In A. Freeman, K. Simon, L. Beutler, & H. Arkowitz (Eds.), *Comprehensive handbook of cognitive therapy.* New York: Plenum.

Bowlby, J. (1980). *Attachment and loss: Vol. 3. Loss: Sadness and depression.* New York: Basic Books.

Brandt, R. B. (1975). The morality and rationality of suicide. In S. Perlin (Ed.), *A handbook for the study of suicide.* London: Oxford University Press.

Breier, A., & Astrachan, B. (1984). Characterization of schizophrenic patients who commit suicide. *American Journal of Psychiatry, 141,* 206–209.

Brent, S. (1977). Puns, metaphors, and misunderstanding in a 2–year-old's conception of death. *Omega, 8,* 285–295.

Brown, H. N. (1987). The impact of suicide on psychiatrists in training. *Comprehensive Psychiatry, 28,* 101–112.

Brown, T., & Sheran, T. (1972). Suicide prediction: A review. *Life Threatening Behavior, 2,* 67–98.

Brownell, K., Marlatt, G., Lichtenstein, E., & Wilson, G. (1986). Understanding and preventing relapse. *American Psychologist, 41(7),* 765–782.

Brozan, (1986). Life after a son's suicide: One family's struggle. *New York Times,* January 13, 1986, p. B-5.

Bruhn, J. (1962). Broken homes among attempted suicides and psychiatric out-patients: A comparative study. *Journal of Mental Science, 108,* 772–779.

Buglass, D., & Horton, J. (1974). A scale for predicting subsequent suicidal behaviour. *British Journal of Psychiatry, 124,* 573–578.

Buglass, D., & McCulloch, J. (1970). Further suicidal behaviour: The development and validation of predictive scales. *British Journal of Psychiatry, 116,* 483–491.

Bumberry, W., Oliver, J., & McClure, J. (1978). Validation of the Beck Depression Inventory in a university population using psychiatric estimate as the criterion. *Journal of Consulting and Clinical Psychology, 46,* 150–155.

Bunch, J., Barraclough, B., Nelson, B., & Sainsbury, P. (1971). Early parental bereavement and suicide. *Social Psychiatry, 6,* 200–202.

Burk, F., Kurz, A., & Moller, H. (1985). Suicide risk scales: Do they help to predict suicidal behaviour? *European Archives of Psychiatry and Neurological Sciences, 235,* 153–157.

Burns, D. (1980). *Feeling good: The new mood therapy.* New York: William Morrow.

Burrows, G. D. (Ed.). (1977). *Handbook of studies on depression.* Amsterdam: Exerpta Medica.

Busse, E., & Pfeiffer, E. (1969). *Behavior and Adaptation in Late Life.* Boston: Little-Brown.

Butler, R. (1963). The life review: An interpretation of reminiscence in the aged. *Psychiatry, 26,* 65–76.

Callahan, E., & Burnette, M. (1989). Intervention for pathological grieving. *Behavior Therapist, 12*(7), 153–157.

Carver, C., Ganellen, R., & Behar-Mitrani, V. (1985). Depression and cognitive style: Comparisons between measures. *Journal of Personality and Social Psychology, 49*(3), 722–728.

Carver, C., & Scheier, M. (1982). Control theory: A useful conceptual framework for personality—social, clinical, and health psychology. *Psychological Bulletin, 92*(1): 111–135.

Carver, C., & Ganellen, R. (1983). Depression and components of self-punitiveness: High standards, self-criticalness, and overgeneralization. *Journal of Abnormal Psychology, 92,* 330–337.

Catherall, D. (1986). The support system and amelioration of PTSD in Vietnam veterans. *Psychotherapy, 23*(3), 472–482.

Cavanaugh, S. (1983). The prevalence of emotional and cognitive dysfunction in a general medical population: Using the MMSE, GHQ, and BDI. *General Hospital Psychiatry, 5,* 15–24.

Cavanaugh, S. (1984). Diagnosing depression in the hospitalized patient with chronic medical illness. *Journal of Clinical Psychiatry-Monograph, 2*(4), 17–22.

Cavanaugh, S., Clark, D., & Gibbons, R. (1983). Diagnosing depression in the hospitalized medically ill. *Psychosomatics, 24,* 809–815.

Coccaro, E., Siever, L., Klar, H., Maurer, G., Cochrane, K., Cooper, T., Mohs, R., & Davis, K. (1989). Serotonergic studies in patients with affective and personality disorders: Correlates with suicidal and impulsive aggressive behavior. *Archives of General Psychiatry, 46,* 587–599.

Cohen, E., Motto, J., & Seiden, R. (1966). An instrument for evaluating suicide potential: A preliminary study. *American Journal of Psychiatry, 122*: 886–891.

Cohen-Sandler, R., & Berman, A. (1982). Teaching suicidal children how to problem-solve in non-suicidal ways. Paper presented at the annual meeting of the American Association of Suicidology, Dallas, TX.

Cohen-Sandler, R., Berman, A., & King, R. (1982a). A follow-up study of hospitalized suicidal children. *Journal of the American Academy of Child Psychiatry, 21*, 398–403.

Cohen-Sandler, R., Berman, A., & King, R. (1982b). Life stress and symptomatology: Determinants of suicidal behavior in children. *Journal of the American Academy of Child Psychiatry, 21*, 178–186.

Coyne, J. (1976). Depression and the response of others. *Journal of Abnormal Psychology, 85*, 186–193.

Coyne, J., & Gotlib, I. (1983). The role of cognition in depression: A critical appraisal. *Psychological Bulletin, 94*, 472–505.

Coyne, J., Kessler, R., Tal, M., Turnbull, J., Wortman, C., & Greden, J. (1987). Living with a depressed person. *Journal of Consulting and Clinical Psychology, 55*, 347–352.

Crook, T., & Raskin, A. (1975). Association of childhood parental loss with attempted suicide and depression. *Journal of Consulting and Clinical Psychology, 43*, 277.

Crowne, D., & Marlowe, D. (1960). A new scale of social desirability independent of psychopathology. *Journal of Consulting Psychology, 24*, 349–354.

Crumly, F. (1979). Adolescent suicide attempts. *Journal of the American Medical Association, 241*, 2404–2407.

Davidson, L. (1989). Suicide clusters and youth. In C. Pfeffer (Ed.), *Suicide among youth: Perspectives on risk and prevention*. Washington, DC: American Psychiatric Press.

Davidson, L., Rosenberg, M., Mercy, J., Franklin, J., & Simmons, J. (1989). An epidemiological study of risk factors in two teenage suicide clusters. *Journal of the American Medical Association, 262*(19), 2687–2692.

Davis, M., & Schrodt, G. (1992). Inpatient treatment. In A. Freeman & F. Dattilio (Eds.), *Comprehensive Casebook of Cognitive Therapy*. New York: Plenum.

Depue, R., & Spoont, M. (1986). Conceptualizing a serotonin trait: A behavioral dimension of constraint. In J. Mann & M. Stanley (Eds.), *Psychobiology of Suicidal Behavior*. New York: New York Academy of Sciences.

Devries, A. (1966). A potential suicide personality inventory. *Psychology Reports, 18*, 731–738.

Diekstra, R., & Hawton, K. (Ed.). (1987). *Suicide in adolescence*. Dordrecht: Martinus Nijhoff.

Diekstra, R. (1974). A social learning theory approach to the prevention of suicidal behavior. *Proceedings of the 7th International Congress for Suicide Prevention* (pp. 55–66). Amsterdam: Swets & Zeitlinger.

DiGiuseppe, R. (1989). Cognitive therapy with children. In A. Freeman, K. Simon, L. Beutler, & H. Arkowitz (Eds.), *Comprehensive handbook of cognitive therapy*. New York: Plenum.

Dobson, K. (1988). The present and future of the cognitive-behavioral therapies. In K. Dobson (Ed.), *Handbook of cognitive-behavioral therapies*. New York: Guilford.

Dobson, K., & Breiter, H. (1983). Cognitive assessment of depression: Reliability and validity of three measures. *Journal of Abnormal Psychology, 92*, 107–109.

Dobson, K., & Shaw, B. (1986). Cognitive assessment with major depressive disorders. *Cognitive Therapy and Research, 10*, 13–29.

Dorpat, T. (1973). Suicide loss, and mourning. *Life-Threatening Behavior, 3*, 213–224.

Drake, R., Gates, C., Whitaker, A., & Cotton, P. (1985). Suicide among schizophrenics. *Comprehensive Psychiatry, 26*, 90–100.

Dublin, L. I. (1963). *Suicide*. New York: Ronald Press.

Dunne, E. J., McIntosh, J. L., & Dunne-Maxim, K. (Eds.). (1987). *Suicide and its aftermath*. New York: Norton.

Durkheim, E. (1951). *Suicide*. Glencoe, IL: Free Press. (Original work published 1897.)

Dyer, J., & Kreitman, N. (1984). Hopelessness, depression and suicidal intent in parasuicide. *British Journal of Psychiatry, 144*, 127–133.

Eaves, G., & Rush, A. (1984). Cognitive patterns in symptomatic and remitted unipolar major depression. *Journal of Abnormal Psychology, 93*, 31–40.

Egeland, J., & Hostetter, A. (1983). Amish study: I. Affective disorders among the Amish, 1976–1980. *American Journal of Psychiatry, 1983, 140*, 56–61.

Egeland, J., & Sussex, J. (1985). Suicide and family loading for affective disorders. *Journal of the American Medical Association, 254*, 915–918.

Egendorf, A., Kadushin, C., Laufer, R., Rothbart, G., & Sloan, L. (1981). *Legacies of Vietnam: Comparative adjustment of veterans and their peers*. New York: Center for Policy Research.

Ellis, A. (1958). Rational psychotherapy. *Journal of General Psychology, 59*, 35–49.

Ellis, A. (1962). *Reason and emotion in psychotherapy*. New York: Stuart.

Ellis, A. (1979). The theory of rational-emotive therapy. In A. Ellis & J. Whiteley (Eds.), *Theoretical and Empirical Foundations of Rational-Emotive Therapy*. Monterey, CA: Brooks-Cole.

Ellis, A. (1984). *Rational-Emotive Therapy and Cognitive Behavior Therapy*. New York: Springer Publishing Co.

Ellis, A. (1985). Expanding the ABC's of Rational-Emotive Therapy. In M. Mahoney & A. Freeman (Eds.), *Cognition and Psychotherapy*. New York: Plenum.

Ellis, A., & Harper, R. (1975). *A new guide to rational living*. North Hollywood, CA: Wilshire Books.

Ellis, T. (1985). The Hopelessness Scale and social desirability: More data and a contribution from the Irrational Beliefs Test. *Journal of Clinical Psychology, 41*, 634–639.

Emery, G. (1981). Cognitive therapy with the elderly. In G. Emery, S. Hollon, & R. Bedrosian (Eds.), (1981). *New directions in cognitive therapy*. New York: Guilford.

Emery, G. (1988). *Getting undepressed: How a woman can change her life through cognitive therapy*. New York: Simon & Schuster.

Emery, G., & Fox, A. (1981). Cognitive therapy of alcohol dependency. In G. Emery, S. Hollon, & R. Bedrosian (Eds.), *New directions in cognitive therapy*. New York: Guilford.

Endicott, J., & Spitzer, R. (1978). A diagnostic interview: The Schedule for Affective Disorders and Schizophrenia. *Archives of General Psychiatry, 35*, 837–844.

Epstein, N. (1982). Cognitive therapy with couples. *American Journal of Family Therapy, 10*, 5–16.

Epstein, N. (1985). Depression and marital dysfunction: Cognitive and behavioral linkages. *International Journal of Mental Health, 13*, 86–104.

Epstein, N. (1986). Cognitive marital therapy: Multi-level assessment and intervention. *Journal of Rational-Emotive Therapy, 4*, 86–104.

Epstein, N., & Schlesinger, S. (1993). "Cognitive-behavioral treatment of marital and family problems" (unpublished manuscript).

Epstein, N., Schlesinger, S., & Dryden W. (1988). Concepts and methods of cognitive-behavioral family treatment. In N. Epstein, S. Schlesinger, & W. Dryden (Eds.), *Cognitive-behavioral therapy with families*. New York: Bruner-Mazel.

Erikson, E. (1968). *Identity: Youth and crisis*. New York: Norton.

Ettigi, P., & Brown, G. (1977). Psychoneuroendocrinology of affective disorders: An overview. *American Journal of Psychiatry, 134*, 493–501.

Evenson, R., Wood, J., Nuttall, E., & Cho, D. (1982). Suicide rates among public mental health patients. *Acta Psychiatrica Scandanavica, 66*, 254–264.

Farberow, N. (1950). Personality patterns of suicidal mental hospital patients. *Genetic Psychology Monographs, 42*, 3–79.

Farberow, N. (Ed.). (1980). *The many faces of suicide*. New York: McGraw-Hill.

Farberow, N. (1981). Assessment of suicide. In P. McReynolds (Ed.), *Advances in Psychological Assessment*. San Francisco: Jossey-Bass.

Fawcett, J. (1988). Predictors of early suicide: Identification and appropriate intervention. *Journal of Clinical Psychiatry, 49* (suppl.), 7–8.

Fawcett, J., Scheftner, W., Clark, D., Hedeker, D., Gibbons, R., & Corywell, W. (1987). Clinical predictors of suicide in patients with major affective disorders: A controlled prospective study. *American Journal of Psychiatry, 144*, 35–40.

Feifel, H. (Ed.). (1954). *The meaning of death*. New York: McGraw-Hill.

Fenichel, O. (1945). *The psychoanalytic theory of neurosis*. New York: Norton.

Figley, C. (Ed.). (1978). *Stress disorders among Vietnam veterans: Theory, research, and treatment*. New York: Bruner-Mazel.

Flannery, R. (1974). Behavior modification of geriatric grief: A transactional perspective. *International Journal of Aging and Human Development, 5*, 197–203.

Flavell, J. (1963). *The developmental psychology of Jean Piaget*. New York: Van Nostrand.

Foelker, G., Shewchuk, R., & Niederehe, G. (1987). Confirmatory factor analysis of the short form Beck Depression Inventory in elderly community samples. *Journal of Clinical Psychology, 43*, 111–118.

Frances, A., Fyer, M., & Clarkin, J. (1986). Personality and suicide. In J. Mann & M. Stanley (Eds.), *Psychobiology of Suicidal Behavior*. New York: New York Academy of Sciences.

Frances, A., & Pfeffer, C. (1987). Reducing environmental stress for a suicidal ten-year-old. *Hospital and Community Psychiatry, 38*(1), 22–24.

Frances, R., Franklin, J., & Flavin, D. (1987). Suicide and alcoholism. *American Journal of Drug and Alcohol Abuse, 13*, 327–341.

Franks, J. (1974). Toward understanding understanding. In W. Weimer & D. Palermo (Eds.), *Cognition and the symbolic processes*. Hillsdale, NJ: Erlbaum.

Frederick, C. (1981). Suicide prevention and crisis intervention in mental health emergencies. In C. Walker (Ed.), *Clinical practice of psychology*. New York: Pergamon.

Freeman, A. (1981). Dreams and images in cognitive therapy. In G. Emery, S. Hollon, & R. Bedrosian (Eds.), *New directions in cognitive therapy*. New York: Guilford.

Freeman, A. (1987). Understanding personal, cultural, and religious schema in psychotherapy. In A. Freeman, N. Epstein, & K. Simon (Eds.), *Depression in the family*. New York: Haworth.

Freeman, A. (1988). Cognitive therapy of personality disorders. In C. Perris, H. Perris, & I. Blackburn (Eds.), *The theory and practice of cognitive therapy*. Heidelberg: Springer Verlag.

Freeman, A., & Boyll, S. (1992). The use of dreams in cognitive therapy. In *Psychotherapy in clinical practice*. New York: Haworth.

Freeman, A., & DeWolf, R. (1989). *Woulda, coulda, shoulda*. New York: William Morrow.

Freeman, A., & DeWolf, R. (1989). *The 10 Dumbest Mistakes that Smart People Make and How to Avoid Them: Simple and Sure Techniques for Gaining Greater Control of Your Life*. New York: Harper Collins.

Freeman, A., & Leaf, R. (1989). Cognitive therapy applied to personality disorders. In A. Freeman, K. Simon, L. Beutler, & H. Arkowitz (Eds.), *Comprehensive handbook of cognitive therapy*. New York: Plenum.

Freeman, A., & Greenwood, V. (1987). *Cognitive therapy: Applications in psychiatric and medical settings*. New York: Human Sciences Press.

Freeman, A., Pretzer, J., Fleming, B., & Simon, K. (1990). *Clinical applications of cognitive therapy*. New York: Plenum.

Freeman, A., Simon, K., Beutler, L., & Arkowitz, H. (Eds.), (1989). *Comprehensive Handbook of Cognitive Therapy*. New York: Plenum.

Freeman, A., & White, D. (1989). Cognitive therapy of suicide. In A. Freeman, K. Simon, H. Arkowitz, & L. Beutler (Eds.), *Comprehensive handbook of cognitive therapy*. New York: Plenum.

Freud, S. (1978a). *Mourning and melancholia*. In J.Strachey (Trans./Eds.), *The standard edition of the complete psychological works* (Vol. 14). New York: Norton. (Original work published 1917)

Freud, S. (1978b). Analysis of a phobia in a five year-old boy. In J. Strachey (Trans./Ed.), *The standard edition of the complete psychological works* (Vol. 10). New York: Norton. (Original work published 1909)

Frick, R., & Bogart, L. (1982). Transference and countertransference in group therapy with Vietnam veterans. *Bulletin of the Menninger Clinic, 46*, 429–444.

Friedman, R., Aronoff, M., Clarkin, J., Corn, R., & Hurt, S. (1983). History of suicidal behavior in depressed borderline inpatients. *American Journal of Psychiatry, 140*, 1023–1026.

Friedman, R., Corn, R., Hurt, S., Fibel, B., Schulick, J., & Swirsky, S. (1984). Family history of illness in the seriously suicidal adolescent: A life-cycle approach. *American Journal of Orthopsychiatry, 54*, 390–397.

Fromm-Reichmann, F. (1959). *Principles of Intensive Psychotherapy*. Stuttgart: Hippokrates-Verlag.

Frommer, E., & O'Shea, G. (1973). The importance of childhood experience in relation to problems of marriage and family-building. *British Journal of Psychiatry, 123,* 157–160.

Frost, R., & MacInnis, D. (1983). The Cognitive Bias Questionnaire: Further evidence. *Journal of Personality Assessment, 47,* 173–177.

Fuentes, R. (1980). Therapist transparency. In T. Williams (Ed.), *Post-traumatic stress disorders of the Vietnam veteran: Observations and recommendations for the psychosocial treatment of the veteran and his family.* Cincinnati: Disabled American Veterans.

Gabbard, G. (1990). *Psychodynamic psychiatry in clinical practice* (pp. 1–9). Washington, DC: American Psychiatric Press.

Gallagher, D. (1981). Behavioral group therapy with elderly depressives: An experimental study. In D. Upper & S. Ross (Eds.), *Behavioral group therapy.* Champaign, IL: Research Press.

Gallagher, D., & Thompson, L. (1982). Treatment of major depressive disorder in older adult outpatients with brief psychotherapies. *Psychotherapy: Theory, research, and practice, 19,* 482–490.

Gallagher, D., & Thompson, L. (1983). Effectiveness of psychotherapy for both endogenous and nonendogenous depression in older adult outpatients. *Journal of Gerontology, 38,* 707–712.

Gallagher-Thompson, D., & Thompson, L. (1992). The older adult. In A. Freeman & F. Dattilio (Eds.), *Comprehensive Casebook of Cognitive Therapy.* New York: Plenum Press.

Gardner, R. (1972). *The mutual storytelling technique.* New York: Science House.

Gardner, D., & Cowdry, (1985). Suicidal and parasuicidal behavior in borderline personality disorder. *Psychiatric Clinics of North America, 8,* 389–403.

Garfinkel, B., Foese, A., & Hood, J. (1982). Suicide attempts in children and adolescents. *American Journal of Psychiatry, 139,* 1257–1261.

Garzotto, N., Siani, R., Zimmerman-Tansella, C., & Tansella, M. (1976). Cross-validation of a predictive scale for subsequent suicidal behaviour in an Italian sample. *British Journal of Psychiatry, 128,* 137–140.

Girgus, J., Nolen-Hoeksema, S., Seligman, M., Paul, G., & Spears, H. (1991). *Why do girls become more depressed than boys during early adolescence?* Symposium conducted at the Ninety-Ninth Annual Meeting of the American Psychological Association, San Francisco.

Glantz, M. (1987). Day hospital treatment of alcoholics. In A. Freeman & V. Greenwood (Eds.), *Cognitive therapy: Applications in medical and psychiatric settings.* New York: Human Sciences Press.

Glassman, R., & Salzman, C. (1987). Interactions between psychotropic and other drugs: An update. *Hospital and Community Psychiatry, 38,* 236–242.

Goldfried, M. (Ed.). (1982). *Converging themes in psychotherapy*. New York: Springer.

Goldney, R. (1981). Parental loss and reported childhood stress in young women who attempt suicide. *Acta Psychiatrica Scandanavica, 64*, 34–59.

Goldstein, L. S., & Buongiorno, P. A. (1984). Psychotherapists as suicide survivors. *American Journal of Psychotherapy, 38*, 392–398.

Goss, M., & Reed, J. (1971). Suicide and religion. *Life Threatening Behavior, 1*, 163–177.

Gove, W., & Herb, T. (1974). Stress and mental illness among the young: A comparison of the sexes. *Social Forces, 53*, 256–265.

Greenberg, D. B. (1989). Depression and cancer. In R. G. Robinson & P. V. Rabins, (Eds.), *Depression and coexisting disease*. New York: Igaku-Shoin.

Greene, S. (1981). Levels of measured hopelessness in the general population. *British Journal of Social and Clinical Psychology, 20*, 11–14.

Greene, S., O'Mahony, P., & Rungasamy, P. (1982). Levels of measured hopelessness in physically ill patients. *Journal of Psychosomatic Research, 26*, 591–593.

Greenberg, M., Vasquez, C., & Alloy, L. (1988). Depression versus anxiety: Differences in self and other schemata. In L. Alloy (Ed.), *Cognitive processes in depression*. New York: Guilford.

Greenhill, L., Shopsin, B., & Temple, H. (1980). Psychiatric morbidity in the offspring of patients with affective disorders: A preliminary report. *Neuropsychobiology, 6*, 159–169.

Greenwood, V. (1987). Cognitive therapy with the chronic young adult patient. In A. Freeman & V. Greenwood (Eds.), *Cognitive therapy: Applications in psychiatric and medical settings*. New York: Human Science Press.

Greenwood, V. (1983). Cognitive therapy with the chronic young adult patient. In A. Freeman (Ed.), *Cognitive Therapy with Couples and Groups*. New York: Plenum.

Greer, S., & Bagley, C. (1971). Effect of psychiatric intervention in attempted suicide: A controlled study. *British Medical Journal, 1*, 310–312.

Grollman, E. A. (1971). *Suicide: Prevention, intervention, postvention*. Boston: Beacon.

Guidano, V., (1987). *Complexity of the self: A developmental approach to psychopathology and therapy*. New York: Guilford.

Guidano, V., & Liotti, G. (1983). *Cognitive processes and emotional disorders*. New York: Guilford.

Haas, A., & Hendon, H. (1983). Suicide among older people: Projections for the future. *Suicide and life-threatening behavior, 13*, 147–154.

Hafen, B. Q., & Frandsen, K. J. (1986). *Youth suicide*. Provo, UT: Behavioral Health Associates.

Hagnell, O., & Rorsman, B. (1978). Suicide and endogenous depression with somatic symptoms in the Lundby study. *Neuropsychobiology, 4,* 180–187.

Hagnell, O., Lanke, J., & Rorsman, B. (1981). Suicide rates in the Lundby study: Mental illness as a risk factor for suicide. *Neuropsychobiology, 7,* 248–253.

Haider, I. (1968). Suicidal attempts in children and adolescents. *British Journal of Psychiatry, 114,* 1113–1134.

Hamilton, E., & Abramson, L. (1983). Cognitive patterns and major depressive disorders: A longitudinal study in a hospital setting. *Journal of Abnormal Psychology, 92,* 173–184.

Hammen, C., & Krantz, S. (1976). Effects of success and failure on depressive cognitions. *Journal of Abnormal Psychology, 85,* 577–586.

Hammen, C., & Krantz, S. (1985). Measures of psychological processes in depression. In E. Beckham & W. Leber (Eds.), *Handbook of depression.* Homewood, IL: Dorsey Press.

Hankoff, L. (1982). Suicide and attempted suicide. In F. Paykel (Ed.), *Handbook of affective disorders.* New York: Guilford.

Harrell, T., & Ryon, N. (1983). Cognitive-behavioral assessment of depression: Clinical validation of the Automatic Thoughts Questionnaire. *Journal of Consulting and Clinical Psychology, 51,* 721–725.

Hawton, K. (1986). *Suicide and attempted suicide among children and adolescents.* Beverly Hills: Sage.

Hawton, K. (1987). Assessment of suicide risk. *British Journal of Psychiatry, 150,* 145–153.

Hawton, K., & Catalan, J. (1982). *Attempted suicide: A practical guide to its nature and management.* Oxford: Oxford University Press.

Hawton, K., Fagg, J., & McKeown, S. (1989). Alcoholism, alcohol, and attempted suicide. *Alcohol and Alcoholism, 24,* 3–9.

Hawton, K., Osburn, M., O'Grady, J., & Cole, D. (1982). Classification of adolescents who take overdoses. *British Journal of Psychiatry, 140,* 124–131.

Hendin, H. (1983). Psychotherapy for Vietnam veterans with posttraumatic stress disorders. *American Journal of Psychiatry, 37,* 86–99.

Hendin, H. (1984). Combat never ends: The paranoid adaptation to posttraumatic stress. *American Journal of Psychotherapy, 38,* 121–131.

Hendin, H. (1987). Youth suicide: A psychosocial perspective. *Suicide and Life Threatening Behavior, 17*(2), 151–165.

Hendin, H. (1991). Psychodynamics of suicide, with particular reference to the young. *American Journal of Psychiatry, 148*(9), 1150–1158.

Hendin, H., & Haas, A. (1984). Combat adaptations of Vietnam veterans without posttraumatic stress disorders. *American Journal of Psychiatry, 141,* 956–960.

Henn, R. F. (1978). Patient suicide as part of psychiatric residency. *American Journal of Psychiatry, 135*, 745–746.

Henry, A. F., & Short, J. F. (1954). *Suicide and homicide*. New York: Free Press.

Hirsch, S., Walsh, C., & Draper, R. (1982). Parasuicide: A review of treatment intervention. *Journal of Affective Disorders, 4*, 299–311.

Holden, R., & Mendonca, J. (1984). Hopelessness, social desirability, and suicidal behavior: A need for conceptual and empirical disentanglement. *Journal of Clinical Psychology, 40*, 1342–1345.

Holden, R., Mendonca, J., & Mazmanian, D. (1985). Relationship of response set to observed suicide intent. *Canadian Journal of Behavioural Science, 17*(4), 359–368.

Holden, R., Mendonca, J., & Serin, R. (1989). Suicide, hopelessness, and social desirability: A test of an interactive model. *Journal of Consulting and Clinical Psychology, 57*, 500–504.

Holding, T., Buglass, D., Duffy, J., & Kreitman, N. (1977). Parasuicide in Edinburgh—a seven year review 1968–1974. *British Journal of Psychiatry, 130*, 534–543.

Hollon, S., & Kendall, P. (1980). Cognitive self-statements in depression: Development of an automatic thoughts questionnaire. *Cognitive Therapy and Research, 4*, 383–395.

Hollon, S., Kendall, P., & Lumry, A. (1986). Specificity of depressotypical cognitions in clinical depression. *Journal of Abnormal Psychology, 95*, 52–59.

Humphrey, J., & Kupferer, H. (1982). Homicide and suicide among the Cherokee and Lumbee Indians of North Carolina. *International Journal of Social Psychiatry, 28*, 121–128.

Humphry, D. (1991). *Final Exit*. Eugene, OR: Hemlock Society.

Husain, S., & Vandiver, T. (1984). *Suicide in children and adolescents*. New York: SP Medical & Scientific Books.

Jacobs, D. (1982). Evaluation and care of suicidal behavior in emergency settings. *International Journal of Psychiatry in Medicine, 12*, 295–310.

Jacobson, N., & Moore, D. (1981). Spouses as observers of the events in their relationship. *Journal of Consulting and Clinical Psychology, 49*, 269–277.

James, J. W., & Cherry, F. (1988). *The grief recovery handbook*. New York: Harper & Row.

Jamison, K. (1986). Suicide and bipolar disorders. In J. Mann & M. Stanley (Eds.), *Psychobiology of Suicidal Behavior*. New York: New York Academy of Sciences.

Janoff-Bulman, R. (1979). Characterological versus behavioral self-blame: Inquiries into depression and rape. *Journal of Personality and Social Psychology, 37*, 1798–1809.

Janoff-Bulman, R., Madden, M., & Timko, C. (1983). Victims' reactions to aid: The role of perceived vulnerability. In A. Nadler, J. Fisher, & B. De-Paulo (Eds.), *New directions in helping*. New York: Academic Press.

Janoff-Bulman, R., & Hecker, B. (1988). Depression, vulnerability, and world assumptions. In L. Alloy (Ed.), *Cognitive processes in depression*. New York: Guilford.

Joan, P. (1986). *Preventing teenager suicide*. New York: Human Sciences Press.

Johns, C., Stanley, M., & Stanley, B. (1986). Suicide in schizophrenia. In J. Mann & M. Stanley (Eds.), *Psychobiology of Suicidal Behavior*. New York: New York Academy of Sciences.

Jones, R. (1969). A factored measure of Ellis' irrational belief system, with personality and maladjustment correlates. *Dissertation Abstracts International*, *29*, 11–13.

Juel-Nielsen, N., & Videbech, T. (1970). A twin study of suicide. *Acta Geneticae Medicae et Gemmellologiae*, *19*, 307–310.

Kane, B. (1979). Children's conception of death. *Journal of Genetic Psychology*, *134*, 141–153.

Kaplan, A. (1986). The self-in-relation: Implications for depression in women. *Psychotherapy*, *23*, 234–242.

Kastenbaum, R. (Ed.). (1979). *Between life and death*. New York: Springer.

Keith-Spiegel, P., & Spiegel, D. E. (1967). Affective states of patients immediately preceding suicide. *Journal of Psychiatric Research*, *5*, 89–93.

Kelly, G. (1955). *The psychology of personal constructs*. New York: Norton.

Kendall, P., Hollon, S., Beck, A., Hammen, C., & Ingram, R. (1987). Issues and recommendations regarding use of the Beck Depression Inventory. *Cognitive Therapy and Research*, *11*, 289–299.

Kety, S. (1986). Genetic factors in suicide. In A. Roy (Ed.), *Suicide*. Baltimore: Williams & Wilkin.

Kofkin, M. (1979). Suicide. In M. Josephson & R. Porter (Eds.), *Clinician's Handbook of Childhood Psychopathology*. New York: Aronson.

Kovacs, M., & Beck, A. (1977). An empirical-clinical approach toward a definition of childhood depression. In J. Schulterbrandt & A. Raskin (Eds.), *Depression in childhood: Diagnosis, treatment and conceptual models*. New York: Raven.

Kovacs, M., Beck, A., & Weissman, A. (1975). Hopelessness: An indicator of suicidal risk. *Suicide*, *5*, 98–103.

Kovacs, M., Beck, A., & Weissman, A. (1975). The use of suicidal motives in the psychotherapy of attempted suicides. *American Journal of Psychotherapy*, *29*, 363–368.

Kovacs, M., Beck, A., & Weissman, A. (1976). The communication of suicidal intent. *Archives of General Psychiatry*, *33*, 198–201.

Kovacs, M., & Paulauskas, S. L. (1984). Development stage and the expression of depressive disorders in children: An empirical analysis. In D. Cicchetti & K. Schneider-Rosen (Eds.), *Childhood depression*. San Francisco: Jossey-Bass.

Kramer, M., Pollack, E. Redick, R., & Locke, B. (1972). *Mental disorders/suicide*. Cambridge, Harvard University Press.

Krantz, S., & Hammen, C. (1979). Assessment of cognitive bias in depression. *Journal of Abnormal Psychology, 88*, 611–619.

Kurz, A., Moller, H., Baindl, G., Burk, F., Torhorst, A. Wachtler, C., & Lauter, H. (1987). Classification of parasuicide by cluster analysis: Types of suicidal behaviour, therapeutic and prognostic implications. *British Journal of Psychiatry, 150*, 520–525.

Lang, M., & Tisher, M. (1978). *Children's Depression Scale*. Victoria, Australia: Australian Council for Educational Research.

LaPointe, K., & Crandell, C. (1980). Relationships of irrational beliefs to self-reported depression. *Cognitive Therapy Research, 4*, 247–250.

Lazarus, R. (1966). *Psychological stress and the coping process*. New York: McGraw-Hill.

Lazarus, R. (1982). Thoughts on the relations between emotion and cognition. *American Psychologist, 37*, 1019–1024.

Lazarus, R. (1984). On the primacy of cognition. *American Psychologist, 39*, 124–129.

Lazarus, R., & Folkman, S. (1984b). *Stress, Appraisal, and Coping*. New York: Springer Publishing Co.

Lesse, S. (Ed.). (1988). *What we know about suicidal behavior and how to treat it*. Northvale, NJ: Aronson.

Lester, D. (1970). Attempts to predict suicide risk using psychological tests. *Psychological Bulletin, 74*, 1–17.

Lester, D. (1974). Demographic versus clinical prediction of suicidal behaviors: A look at some issues. In A. Beck, H. Resnik, & D. Lettieri (Eds.), *The prediction of suicide*. Philadelphia: Charles Press.

Lester, D. (1983). *Why people kill themselves*. Springfield, IL: Charles C. Thomas.

Lester, D., & Beck, A. (1975a). Suicidal intent, medical lethality of the suicide attempt, and components of depression. *Journal of Clinical Psychology, 31*, 11–12.

Lester, D., & Beck, A. (1975b). Attempted suicide: Correlates of increasing medical lethality. *Psychological Reports, 37*, 1236–1238.

Lester, D., & Beck, A. (1975c). Suicide in the spring. *Psychology Report, 35*, 893–894.

Lester, D., Beck, A., & Bruno, S. (1976). Correlates of choice of method for suicide. *Psychology, 13*, 70–73.

Lester, G., & Lester, D. (1971). *Suicide: The game with death*. Englewood Cliffs, NJ: Prentice-Hall.

Lettieri, D. (1974). Suicidal death prediction scales. In A. Beck, H. Resnik, & D. Lettieri (Eds.), *The prediction of suicide*. Philadelphia: Charles Press.

Lewinsohn, P., Mischel, W., Chaplin, W., & Barton, R. (1980). Social competence and depression: The role of illusory self-perceptions. *Journal of Abnormal Psychology, 89*, 203–212.

Liberman, R., & Eckman, T. (1981). Behavior therapy vs. insight-oriented therapy for repeated suicide attempters. *Archives of General Psychiatry, 38*, 1126–1130.

Linehan, M., & Nielsen, S. (1981). Assessment of suicide ideation and parasuicide: Hopelessness and social desirability. *Journal of Consulting and Clinical Psychology, 49*, 773–775.

Linehan, M., & Nielsen, S. (1983). Social desirability: Its relevance to the measurement of hopelessness in suicidal behavior. *Journal of Consulting and Clinical Psychology, 51*, 141–143.

Linehan, M., Goodstein, J., Neisen, S., & Chiles, J. (1983). Reasons for staying alive when you are thinking of killing yourself: The reasons for Living Inventory. *Journal of Consulting and Clinical Psychology, 51*, 276–286.

Linzer, N. (Ed.). (1984). *Suicide: The will to live vs. the will to die*. New York: Human Sciences Press.

Litman, R. E. (1965). When patients commit suicide. *American Journal of Psychotherapy, 19*, 570–576.

Litman, R. E., & Tabachnick, N. D. (1968). Psychoanalytic theories of suicide. In H. L. P. Resnik (Ed.), *Suicidal behaviors*. Boston: Little, Brown.

Lonetto, R. (1980). *Children's conceptions of death*. New York: Springer.

Lonsdorf, R. G. (1968). Legal aspects of suicide. In H. L. P. Resnik (Ed.), *Suicidal behaviors*. Boston: Little, Brown.

Louhivuori, K., & Hakama, M. (1979). Risk of suicide among cancer patients. *American Journal of Epidemiology, 109*, 59–65.

Louks, J., Hayne, C., & Smith, J. (1989). Replicated factor structure of the Beck Depression Inventory. *Journal of Nervous and Mental Disease, 177*, 473–479.

Ludgate, J., Reinecke, M., & Beck, A. (1987). *Cognitive vulnerability for depression: The DAS as a predictor of relapse after psychotherapy*. Paper presented at the meeting of the Association for the Advancement of Behavior Therapy, Boston.

Luka, C., & Seiden, H. M. (1987). *Silent Grief*. New York: Scribners.

Lukianowicz, N. (1968). Attempted suicide in children. *Acta Psychiatrica Scandinavica, 44*, 415–435.

Lyons, M. (1984). Suicide in later life: Some putative causes with implications for prevention. *Journal of Community Psychology, 12*, 379–388.

Mac Lean, G. (1990). *Suicide in children and adolescents.* Lewiston, NY: Hogrefe & Huber.

Maris, R. (1975). Sociology. In S. Perlin (Ed.), *A handbook for the study of suicide.* New York: Oxford University Press.

Maris, R. (1981). *Pathways to suicide: A survey of self-destructive behavior.* Baltimore: Johns Hopkins University Press.

Maris, R. (1992). The relationship of nonfatal suicide attempts to completed suicides. In R. Maris, A. Berman, J. Maltsberger, & R. Yufit (Eds.), *Assessment and Prediction of Suicide.* New York: Guilford.

Marlatt, G. (1979). A cognitive-behavioral model of the relapse process. *NIDA - Research Monograph, 25*, 191–200.

Marlatt, G., Baer, J., Donovan, D., & Kivlahan, D . (1988). Addictive behaviors: Etiology and treatment. *Annual Review of Psychology, 39*, 223–252.

Marlatt, G., & George, W. (1984). Relapse prevention: Introduction and overview of the model. *British Journal of Addiction, 79*(3), 261–273.

Martin, R., Cloninger, C., Guze, S., & Clayton, P. (1985). Mortality in a follow-up of 500 psychiatric outpatients: II. Cause-specific mortality. *Archives of General Psychiatry, 42*, 58–66.

Menninger, K. (1933). Psychoanalytic aspects of suicide. *International Journal of Psychoanalysis, 14*: 376–390.

McIntire M., & Angle, C. (1981). The taxonomy of suicide and self-poisoning: A pediatric perspective. In C. Wells & I. Stuart (Eds.), *Self-destructive behavior in children and adolescents.* New York: Van Nostrand Reinhold.

McIntosh, J. (1984). Suicide among Native Americans: Further tribal data and considerations. *Omega Journal of Death and Dying, 14*, 215–229.

McIntosh, J., & Santos, J. (1981). Suicide among Native Americans: A compilation of findings. *Omega Journal of Death and Dying, 11*, 303–316.

McMullin, R., & Casey, W. (1975). *Talk sense to yourself: A guide to cognitive restructuring therapy.* Lakewood, CO: Counseling Research Institute.

Meichenbaum, D. (1977). *Cognitive behavior modification.* New York: Plenum.

Meehan, P., Saltzman, L., & Sattin, R. (1991). Suicides among older United States residents: Epidemiologic characteristics and trends. *American Journal of Public Health, 81*, 1198–1205.

Meichenbaum, D. (1977). *Cognitive-behavior modification: An integrative approach.* New York: Plenum.

Mendonca, J., Holden, R., Mazmanian, D., & Dolan, J. (1983). The influence of response style on the Beck Hopelessness Scale. *Canadian Journal of Behavioral Science, 15,* 237–247.

Menninger, K. (1938). *Man against himself.* New York: Harcourt, Brace, Jovanovich.

Meyers, E. (1982). Subsequent deliberate self-harm in patients referred to a psychiatrist: A prospective study. *British Journal of Psychiatry, 140,* 132–137.

Michel, K. (1987). Suicide risk factors: A comparison of suicide attempters with suicide completers. *British Journal of Psychiatry, 150,* 78–82.

Miles, C. (1977). Conditions predisposing to suicide: A review. *Journal of Nervous and Mental Disease, 164,* 231–246.

Miller, D., & Moretti, M. (1988). The causal attributions of depressives: Self-serving or selfdisserving? In L. Alloy (Ed.), *Cognitive processes in depression.* New York: Guilford.

Miller, I., & Norman, W. (1986). Persistence of depressive cognitions within a subgroup of depressed inpatients. *Cognitive Therapy and Research, 10,* 211–224.

Miller, M. (1979). Suicides on a southwestern American Indian reservation. *White Cloud Journal, 1,* 14–18.

Minkoff, K., Bergman, E., Beck, A., & Beck, R. (1973). Hopelessness, depression, and attempted suicide. *American Journal of Psychiatry, 130,* 455–459.

Mintz, J., Steuer, J., & Jarvik, L. (1981). Psychotherapy with depressed elderly patients: Research considerations. *Journal of Consulting and Clinical Psychology, 49,* 542–548.

Miranda, J., & Persons, J. (1988). Dysfunctional attitudes are mood-state dependent. *Journal of Abnormal Psychology, 97,* 76–79.

Miranda, J., Persons, J., & Byers, C. (1990). Endorsement of dysfunctional beliefs depends on current mood state. *Journal of Abnormal Psychology, 99*(3), 237–241.

Missel, P., & Sommer, G. (1983). Depression and self-verbalization. *Cognitive Therapy and Research, 7,* 141–148.

Montgomery, S., Montgomery, D., Rani, S., Roy, D., Shaw, P., & McAvley, R. (1979). Maintenance therapy in repeated suicidal behavior: A placebo controlled trial. In *Proceedings Communication: 10th International Congress for Suicide Prevention and Crisis Intervention.* Ottowa.

Morgan, H., Burns-Cox, C., Pocock, H., & Pottle, S. (1975). Deliberate self-harm: Clinical and socioeconomic characteristics of 368 patients. *British Journal of Psychiatry, 126,* 564–574.

Morgan, H., Barton, J., Pottle, S., Pocock, H., & Burns-Cox, C. (1976). Deliberate self-harm: A follow-up study of 279 patients. *British Journal of Psychiatry, 128,* 361–368.

Morrison, J. (1982). Suicide in a psychiatric practice population. *Journal of Clinical Psychiatry, 43*, 348–352.

Motto, J., Heilbron, D., & Juster, R. (1985). Development of a clinical instrument to estimate suicidal risk. *American Journal of Psychiatry, 142*, 680–686.

Murphy, G., Simons, A., Wetzel, R., & Lustman, P. (1984). Cognitive therapy and pharmacotherapy. *Archives of General Psychiatry, 41*, 33–41.

Murphy, G. (1979). The physician's responsibility for suicide. *Annals of Internal Medicine, 82*, 301–309.

Nagy, M. (1948). The child's view of death. *Journal of Genetic Psychology, 73*, 3–27.

Nathan, R., & Rousch, A. (1984). Which patients commit suicide? *American Journal of Psychiatry, 141*, 1017.

Neisser, U. (1967). *Cognitive Psychology.* New York: Appleton-Century-Crofts.

Nekanda-Trepka, C., Bishop, S., & Blackburn, I. (1983). Hopelessness and depression. *British Journal of Clinical Psychology, 22*, 49–60.

Nelson, R. (1977). Irrational beliefs in depression. *Journal of Consulting and Clinical Psychology, 45*, 1190–1191.

Neugarten, B. (1975). The future and the young old. *The Gerontologist, 15*(2), 4–9.

Neuringer, C. (Ed.). (1974a). *Psychological assessment of suicidal risk.* Springfield, IL: Charles C. Thomas.

Neuringer, C. (1974b). Suicide and Rorschach: A rueful postscript. *Journal of Personality Assessment, 38*, 535–539.

Neuringer, C., & Lettieri, D. J. (1982). *Suicidal women.* New York: Gardner Press.

Nevid, J. (1983). Hopelessness, social desirability, and construct validity. *Journal of Consulting and Clinical Psychology, 51*, 139–140.

Nordstrom, P., & Asberg, M. (1992). Suicide risk and serotonin. *Int. Clin. Psychopharmacology, 6* (suppl.), 12–21.

Norman, W., Miller, I., & Klee, S. (1980). Assessment of cognitive distortion in a clinically depressed population. *Cognitive Therapy and Research, 7*, 133–140.

Oliver, J., & Simmons, M. (1984). Depression as measured by DSM–III and the Beck Depression Inventory in an unselected adult sample. *Journal of Consulting and Clinical Psychology, 52*, 892–898.

Olser, J. (1985). *Vietnam Veterans: The Road to Recovery.* New York: Plenum.

Orbach, I. (1988). *Children who don't want to live: Understanding and treating the suicidal child.* San Francisco: Jossey-Bass.

Orbach, I., Gross, Y., Glaubman, H., & Berman, D. (1985). Children's perception of death in humans and animals as a function of age, anxiety, and cognitive level. *Journal of Child Psychology and Psychiatry, 26,* 453–463.

Pallis, D., & Birtchnell, J. (1977). Seriousness of suicide attempts in relation to personality. *British Journal of Psychiatry, 130,* 253–259.

Pallis, D., & Sainsbury, P. (1976). The value of assessing intent in attempted suicide. *Psychological Medicine, 6,* 487–492.

Parker, G., & Hadzi-Pavlovic, D. (1984). Modification of levels of depression in mother-bereaved women by parental and marital relationships. *Psychological Medicine, 14,* 125–135.

Patros, P. G., & Shamoo, T. K. (1989). *Depression and suicide in children and adolescents: Prevention, intervention, and postvention.* Boston: Allyn & Bacon.

Paykel, E., & Dienelt, M. (1971). Suicide attempts following acute depression. *Journal of Nervous and Mental Disease, 153,* 234–243.

Paykel, E., Weissman, M., & Prusoff, B. (1978). Social maladjustment and severity of depression. *Comprehensive Psychiatry, 19,* 121–128.

Peck, M. (1978). *The Road Less Travelled.* New York: Simon and Schuster.

Peck, M., Farberow, N., & Litman, R. (Eds.). (1985). *Youth suicide.* New York: Springer Publishing Co.

Perlin, S. (Ed.). (1975). *A handbook for the study of suicide.* London: Oxford University Press.

Perloff, L. (1983). Perceptions of vulnerability to victimization. *Journal of Social Issues, 39,* 41–61.

Perlmutter, R., & Jones, J. (1985a). Problem-solving with families in psychiatric emergencies. *Psychiatric Quarterly, 57,* 23–32.

Perlmutter, R., & Jones, J. (1985b). Assessment of families in psychiatric emergencies. *American Journal of Orthopsychiatry, 55,* 130–139.

Perugi, G. Musetti, L., Pezzica, P., & Piagentini, F. (1988). Suicide attempts in primary major depressive subtypes. *Psychiatrica Fennica, 19,* 95–102.

Peterson, C., Schwartz, S., & Seligman, M. (1981). Self-blame and depressive symptoms. *Journal of Personality and Social Psychology, 41,* 253–259.

Petrie, K., & Chamberlain, K. (1983). Hopelessness and social desirability as moderator variables in predicting suicidal behavior. *Journal of Consulting and Clinical Psychology, 51,* 485–487.

Petrie, K., Chamberlain, K., & Clarke, D. (1988). Psychological predictors of future suicidal behaviours in hospitalized suicide attempters. *British Journal of Clinical Psychology, 27,* 247–257.

Pfeffer, C. (1981a). Suicidal behavior of children: A review with implications for research and practice. *American Journal of Psychiatry, 138*(2), 154–159.

Pfeffer, C. (1981b). The family system of suicidal children. *American Journal of Psychotherapy, 35*(3), 330–341.

Pfeffer, C. (1982). Interventions for suicidal children and their parents. *Suicide and Life Threatening Behavior, 12*(4), 240–248.

Pfeffer, C. (1984). Clinical assessment of suicidal behavior in children. In H. Sudak, A. Ford, & N. Rushforth (Eds.), *Suicide in the young.* Boston: John Wright-PSG.

Pfeffer, C. (1985). Elements of treatment for suicidal preadolescents. *American Journal of Psychotherapy, 41*(2), 172–184.

Pfeffer, C. (1986). *The suicidal child.* New York: Guilford.

Pfeffer, C. (1989). Life stress and family risk factors for youth fatal and nonfatal suicidal behavior. In C. Pfeffer (Ed.), *Suicide among youth: Perspectives on risk and prevention.* Washington, DC: American Psychiatric Press.

Pfeffer, C. (Ed.). (1989). *Suicide among youth: Perspectives on risk and prevention.* Washington, DC: American Psychiatric Press.

Pfeffer, C., Adams, D. Weiner, A., & Rosenberg, J. (1988). Life event stresses on parents of suicidal children. *International Journal of Family Psychiatry, 9*, 341–350.

Pfeffer, C., Conte, H., Plutchik, R., & Jerritt, I. (1979). Suicidal behavior in latency age children. *Journal of the American Academy of Child Psychiatry, 18*, 679–696.

Pfeffer, C., & Trad, P. (1988). Sadness and suicidal tendencies in preschool children. *Journal of Developmental and Behavioral Pediatrics,9*(2), 86–88.

Piaget, J. (1970). Piaget's theory. In P. Mussen (Ed.), *Carmichael's Manual of Child Psychology* (Vol. 1). New York: John Wiley.

Platt, J., Spivak, G., & Bloom, W. (1975). *Manual for the means-ends problem-solving procedure (MEPS): A measure of interpersonal problem-solving skill.* Philadelphia: Hahnemann Medical College.

Plumb, M. & Holland, J. (1977). Comparative studies of psychological function in patients with advanced cancer: I. Self-reported depressive symptoms. *Psychosomatic Medicine, 39*, 264–276.

Pokorny, A. (1960). Characteristics of forty-four patients who subsequently committed suicide. *Archives of General Psychiatry, 2*, 314.

Pokorny, A. (1968). Myths about suicide. In H. L. P. Resnik (Ed.), *Suicidal behaviors.* Boston: Little, Brown.

Pokorny, A. (1983). Prediction of suicide in psychiatric patients. *Archives of General Psychiatry, 40*, 249–257.

Polanyi, M. (1966). *The tacit dimension.* Garden City, NY: Doubleday.

Polyani, M. (1969). *Knowing and being.* Chicago, IL: University of Chicago Press.

Poznanski, E., Cook, S., & Carroll, B. (1979). A depression rating scale for children. *Pediatrics, 64,* 442–450.

Pretzer, J. (1983). Borderline personality disorder: Too complex for cognitive-behavioral approaches? (ERIC Document Reproduction Service No. ED 243 007) Paper presented at the annual meeting of the American Psychological Association, Anaheim, CA.

Progoff, I. (1956). *The death and rebirth of psychology.* New York: Julian.

Puig-Antich, J., & Chambers, W. (1978). *Schedule for affective disorders and schizophrenia for school-age children (6–16 years)-Kiddie-SADS.* Unpublished manuscript, New York State Psychiatric Institute, New York.

Ranieri, W., Steer, R., Lawrence T., Rissmiller, D., Piper, G., & Beck, A. (1987). Relationships of depression, hopelessness, and dysfunctional attitudes to suicide ideation in psychiatric patients. *Psychological Reports, 61,* 967–975.

Reda, M. Carpiniello, B., Secchiaroli, L., & Blanco, S. (1985). Thinking, depression, and antidepressants: Modified and unmodified depressive beliefs during treatment with amitriptyline. *Cognitive Therapy and Research, 9,* 135–143.

Rehm, L. (1977). A self-control model of depression. *Behavior Therapy, 8,* 787–804.

Reinecke, M. (1987). *Advances in cognitive therapy of emotional disorders.* Paper presented at the Sixth National Congress of Clinical Psychology, Santiago, Chile.

Reinecke, M. (1992). Childhood depression. In A. Freeman & F. Dattilio (Eds.), *Comprehensive Casebook of Cognitive Therapy.* New York: Plenum.

Rihmer, Z., Barsi, J., Arato, M., & Demeter, E. (1990). Suicide in subtypes of primary major depression. *Journal of Affective Disorders, 18,* 221–225.

Riskind, J., Beck, A., Berchick, R., Brown, G., & Steer, R. (1987). Reliability of DSM–III diagnoses for major depression and generalized anxiety disorder using the structured clinical interview for DSM–III. *Archives of General Psychiatry, 44,* 817–820.

Robins, E., Gassner, S., Kayes, J., Wilkinson, R. H., & Kayes, J. (1959). Some clinical considerations in the prevention of suicide based on a study of 134 successful suicides. *American Journal of Public Health, 49,* 888.

Robins, L., Helzer, J., Croughan, J., & Ratcliff, K. (1981). National Institute of Mental Health diagnostic interview schedule: Its history, characteristics, and validity. *Archives of General Psychiatry, 38,* 381–389.

Rodin, G., & Carven, J. (1989). Depression and endstage renal disease. In R. G. Robinson & P. V. Rabins (Eds.), *Depression and coexisting disease.* New York: Igaku-Shoin.

Rogers, S., & Luenes, A. (1979). A psychometric and behavioral comparison of delinquents who were abused as children with their nonabused peers. *Journal of Clinical Psychology, 35,* 470–472.

Rogers, Sheldon, Barwick, Letofsky, & Lancee. (1982). Help for families of suicide: Survivors support program. *Canadian Journal of Psychiatry, 27*(6), 444–449.

Rosen, D. (1976). The serious suicide attempt: 5 year follow-up of 886 patients. *Journal of the American Medical Association, 235,* 2105–2109.

Rosen, G. (1975). History. In S. Perlin (Ed.), *A handbook for the study of suicide.* London: Oxford University Press.

Robinson, R. G., & Rabins, P. V. (Eds.). (1989). Depression and coexisting disease. New York: Igaku-Shoin.

Rosen, H. (1985). *Piagetian dimensions of clinical relevance.* New York: Columbia University Press.

Rosen, H. (1989). Piagetian theory and cognitive therapy. In A. Freeman, K. Simon, L. Beutller, & H. Arkowitz (Eds.), *Comprehensive handbook of cognitive therapy.* New York: Plenum.

Rounsaville, B., Weissman, M., Prusoff, B., & Herceg-Baron, R. (1979). Marital disputes and treatment outcome in depressed women. *Comprehensive Psychiatry, 20,* 483–490.

Roy, A. (1982a). Risk factors for suicide in psychiatric patients. *Archives of General Psychiatry, 39,* 1089–1095.

Roy, A. (1982b). Suicide in chronic schizophrenia. *British Journal of Psychiatry, 141,* 171–177.

Roy, A. (1985a). Suicide and psychiatric patients. *Psychiatric Clinics of North America, 8,* 227–241.

Roy, A. (1985b). Suicide: A multidetermined act. *Psychiatric Clinics of North America, 8,* 243–250.

Roy, A. (1986). Genetics of suicide. In J. Mann & M. Stanley (Eds.), *Psychobiology of suicidal behavior.* New York: New York Academy of Sciences.

Roy, A. (Ed.). (1986). *Suicide.* Baltimore: Williams & Wilkins.

Roy, A. (1992). Genetics, biology, and suicide in the family. In R. Maris, A. Berman, J. Maltsberger, & R. Yufit (Eds.), *Assessment and Prediction of Suicide.* New York: Guilford.

Roy, A., Agren, H., Pickar, D., Linnoila, M., Doran, A, Cutler, N., & Paul, S. (1986). Reduced cerebrospinal fluid homovanillic acid and lower ratio of homovanillic acid to 5–hydroxyindolacetic acid in depressed patients: Relationship to suicidal behavior and dexamethasone nonsuppression. *American Journal of Psychiatry, 143,* 1539–1545.

Roy, A., & Linnoila, M. (1986). Alcoholism and suicide. *Suicide and life-threatening behavior, 16,* 244–273.

Roy, A., & Linnoila, M. (1988). Suicidal behavior, impulsiveness, and serotonin. *Acta Psychiatrica Scandinavica, 78,* 529–535.

Roy, A., Mazonson, A., & Pickar, D. (1984). Attempted suicide in chronic schizophrenia. *British Journal of Psychiatry, 144,* 303–306.

Russianoff, P. (1981). *Women in crisis.* New York: Human Sciences Press.

Rutter, M. (1981). *Maternal deprivation reassessed* (2nd ed.). Harmondsworth, England: Penguin.

Rutter, M., Izard, C., & Read, P. (1986). *Depression in young people.* New York: Guilford.

Salzman, C. (1982). A primer on geriatric psychopharmacology. *American Journal of Psychiatry, 139,* 67–74.

Sandler, J., & Jofee, W. (1965). Notes of childhood depression. *International Journal of Psychoanalysis, 46,* 88–96.

Sartorius, N. (1974). Description and classification of depressive disorders: Contributions for the definition of the therapy-resistance and of therapy resistant depressions. *Pharmakopsychiatry-Neuropsychopharmacology, 7*(2), 76–79.

Sawyer, J., Adams, K., Conway, W., Reeves, J., & Kvale, P. (1983). Suicide in cases of chronic pulmonary disease. *Journal of Psychiatric Treatment and Evaluation, 5*(2/3), 281–283.

Schaerf, F. W., & Miller, R. R. (1989). Depression and human immunodeficiency virus (HIV) infection. In R. G. Robinson & P. V. Rabins (Eds.), *Depression and coexisting disease.* New York: Igaku-Shoin.

Shafii, M., Carrigan, S., Whittinghill, J., & Derrick, A. (1985). Psychological autopsy of completed suicide in children and adolescents. *American Journal of Psychiatry, 142,* 1061–1064.

Schotte, D. & Clum, G. (1987). Problem-solving skills in suicidal psychiatric patients. *Journal of Consulting and Clinical Psychology, 55,* 49–54.

Schlesinger, S. (1988). Cognitive-behavioral approaches to family treatment of addictions. In N. Epstein, S. Schlesinger, & W. Dryden (Eds.), *Cognitive-behavioral therapy with families.* New York: Bruner-Mazel.

Seager, C. (1986). Suicide in neurosis and personality disorder. In A. Roy (Ed.), *Suicide.* Baltimore: Williams & Wilkins.

Seligman, M., Abramson, L., Semmel, A., & von Baeyer, C. (1979). Depressive attributional style. *Journal of Abnormal Psychology, 88,* 242–248.

Sendbuehler, J., & Goldstein, S. (1977). Attempted suicide among the aged. *Journal of the American Geriatric Society, 25,* 245–248.

Shaffer, D. (1974). Suicide in childhood and early adolescence. *Journal of Child Psychology and Psychiatry, 15,* 275–291.

Shaffer, J. Perlin, S., Schmidt, C., & Stephens, J. (1974). The prediction of suicide in schizophrenia. *Journal of Nervous and Mental Disease, 159,* 349–355.

Shneidman, E. (1968). Suicidal phenomena: Their definition and classification. In *International Encyclopedia of the Social Sciences.* New York: Macmillan.

Shneidman, E. (1979). A bibliography of suicide notes: 1856–1979. *Suicide and Life Threatening Behavior, 9,* 57–59.

Shneidman, E. (1985). *Definition of Suicide.* New York: Wiley-Interscience.

Shneidman, E., Farberow, N., & Litman, R. (Eds.). (1970). *The psychology of suicide.* New York: Science House.

Shore, J., Kinzie, J., & Hamptson, J. (1973). Psychiatric epidemiology of an Indian Village. *Psychiatry, 36,* 70–81.

Siani, R., Garzotto, N., Zimmerman-Tansella, C., & Tansella, M. (1979). Predictive scales for parasuicide repetition: Further results. *Acta Psychiatrica Scandinavica, 59,* 17–23.

Silver, M., Bohnert, M., Beck, A., & Marcus, D. (1971). Relation of attempted suicide and seriousness of intent. *Archives of General Psychiatry, 25*(6), 573–576.

Simmons, R., & Blyth, D. (1987). *Moving into adolescence: The impact of pubertal change and school context.* New York: Aldine DeGruyter.

Slaiku, K. A. (1990). *Crisis intervention* (2nd ed.). Boston: Allyn & Bacon.

Sobel, H., & Worden, J. (1980). *Helping cancer patients cope: A problem-solving intervention program for health care professionals.* New York: Guilford.

Sonnenberg, S., Blank, A., & Talbott, J. (Eds.), (1985). *The Trauma of War: Stress and Recovery in Vietnam Veterans.* Washington, DC: American Psychiatric Press.

Soubrier, J. P., & Vedrinne, J. (Eds.). (1983). *Depression and suicide.* New York: Pergamon.

Speec, M., & Brent, S. (1984). Children's understanding of death: A review of three components of the death concept. *Child Development, 55,* 1671–1686.

Spirito, A., Brown, L., Overholser, J., & Fritz, G. (1989). Attempted suicide in adolescence: A review and critique of the literature. *Clinical Psychology Review, 9,* 335–363.

Spitzer, R., & Williams, J. (1983). *Instruction manual for the structured clinical interview for DSM–III (SCID).* Biometrics Research Department, New York State Psychiatric Institute, New York.

Steer, R., Beck, A., & Garrison, B. (1986). Applications of the Beck Depression Inventory. In N. Sartorius & T. Ban (Eds.), *Assessment of depression.* New York: Springer-Verlag.

Stein, M., Levy, M., & Glasberg, M. (1974). Separations in black and white suicide attempters. *Archives of General Psychiatry, 31,* 815–821.

Stengel, E. (1964) *Suicide and attempted suicide.* New York: Penguin.

Steuer, J. (1982a). Psychotherapy with depressed elders. In D. Blazer (Ed.), *Depression in late life.* St. Louis: Mosby.

Steuer, J. (1982b). Psychotherapy with the elderly. *Psychiatric Clinics of North America, 5,* 199–214.

Steuer, J., & Hammen, C. (1983). Cognitive-behavioral group therapy for the depressed elderly: Issues and adaptations. *Cognitive Therapy and Research, 7,* 285–296.

Steuer, J., Mintz, J., Hammen, C., Hill, M., Jarvik, L., McCarley, T., Motoike, P., & Rosen, R. (1984). Cognitive-behavioral and psychodynamic group psychotherapy in treatment of geriatric depression. *Journal of Consulting and Clinical Psychology, 52,* 180–189.

Strosahl, K., Linehan, M., & Chiles, J. (1984). Will the real social desirability please stand up? Hopelessness, depression, social desirability, and the prediction of suicidal behavior. *Journal of Consulting and Clinical Psychology, 52,* 449–457.

Sudak, H., Ford, A., & Rushforth, N. (1984). *Suicide in the young.* Boston: John Wright-PSG.

Tarasoff v. Regents of the University of California. (1976). 551 P.2d 334, 131 Cal. Rptr. 14, California Sup. Ct.

Teichman, Y. (1984). Cognitive family therapy. *British Journal of Cognitive Psychotherapy, 2,* 1–10.

Teichman, Y. (1986). Family therapy of depression. *Journal of Psychotherapy and the Family, 2,* 9–39.

Teichman, Y., & Teichman, M. (1990). Interpersonal view of depression: Review and integration. *Journal of Family Psychology, 3,* 349–367.

Thompson, L., Davies, R., Gallagher, D., & Krantz,. (1986). Cognitive therapy with older adults. *Clinical Gerontologist, 5,* 245–279.

Tiger, L. (1979). *Optimism: The biology of hope.* New York: Simon & Schuster.

Toolan, J. (1975). Suicide in children and adolescents. *American Journal of Psychotherapy, 29,* 339–344.

Trad, P. V. (1987). *Infant and childhood depression: Developmental factors.* New York: Wiley Interscience.

Traskman-Bendz, L. (1983). CSF 5-HIAA and family history of psychiatric disorder. *American Journal of Psychiatry, 140,* 1257.

Tsuang, M. (1977). Genetic factors in suicide. *Diseases of the Nervous System, 38,* 498–501.

Tsuang, M. (1978). Suicide in schizophrenics, manic depressives, and surgical controls. *Archives of General Psychiatry, 35,* 153–155.

Tuckman, J., Kleiner, R., & Lavell, M. (1959). Emotional content of suicide notes. *American Journal of Psychiatry, 116,* 59–63.

Turvey, M. (1974). Constructive theory, perceptual systems and tacit knowledge. In W. Weimar & D. Palermo (Eds.), *Cognition and the symbolic processes.* Hillsdale, NJ: Erlbaum.

Urwin, P., & Gibbons, J. (1979). Psychiatric diagnosis in self-poisoning patients. *Psychological Medicine, 9,* 501–507.

Vaillant, G. (1966). Twelve-year follow-up of New York narcotic addicts. *American Journal of Psychiatry, 122:* 727–737.

Van Praag, H. (1977). Significance of biochemical parameters in the diagnosis, treatment, and prevention of depressive disorders. *Biological Psychiatry, 12:* 101–131.

Van Praag, H. (1982). Depression, suicide, and the metabolism of serotonin in the brain. *Journal of Affective Disorders, 4,* 275–290.

Vezina, J., & Bourque, P. (1984). The relationship between cognitive structure and symptoms of depression in the elderly. *Cognitive Therapy and Research, 8,* 29–36.

Wang, A., Nielsen, B., Bille-Brahe, U., Hansen, W., & Kolmos, L. (1985). Attempted suicide in Denmark: III. Assessment of repeated suicide behaviour. *Acta Psychiatrica Scandinavica, 72,* 389–394.

Waters, B., Sendbuehler, J., Kincel, R., Boodoosingh, L., & Marchenko, I. (1982). The use of the MMPI for the differentiation of suicidal and non-suicidal depressions. *Canadian Journal of Psychiatry, 27,* 663–667.

Weckowicz, T., Muir, W., & Cropley, A. (1967). A factor analysis of the Beck Inventory of Depression. *Journal of Consulting Psychology, 31,* 23–28.

Weinstein, N. (1980). Unrealistic optimism about future life events. *Journal of Personality and Social Psychology, 39,* 806–820.

Weissman, A., & Beck, A. (1978). Development and validation of the Dysfunctional Attitudes Scale (DAS): A preliminary investigation. Paper presented at the meeting of the American Educational Research Association, Toronto, Canada.

Weissman, A., & Worden, J. (1977). *Coping and vulnerability in cancer patients: A research report.* Boston: Massachusetts General Hospital.

Weissman, M., & Meyers, J. (1979). Depression in the elderly: Research directions in psychopathology, epidemiology, and treatment. *Journal of Geriatric Psychiatry, 12,* 187–201.

Weissmann, M. (1974). The epidemiology of suicide attempts. *Archives of General Psychiatry, 30,* 737–746.

Wells, C. F., & Stuart, I. R. (Eds.). (1981). *Self-destructive behavior in children and adolescents.* New York: Van Nostrand Reinhold.

Wetzel, R. (1976). Hopelessness, depression, and suicide intent. *Archives of General Psychiatry, 33*, 1069–1073.

Wetzel, R., Margulies, T., Davis, R., & Karam, E. (1980). Hopelessness, depression, and suicide intent. *Journal of Clinical Psychiatry, 41*, 159–160.

Whitters, A., Cadoret, R., & Widmer, R. (1985). Factors associated with suicide attempts in alcohol abusers. *Journal of Affective Disorders, 9*(1), 19–23.

Wilkinson, D. (1982). The suicide rate in schizophrenia. *British Journal of Psychiatry, 140*, 138–141.

Wilkinson, G., & Smeeton, N. (1987). The repetition of parasuicide in Edinburgh 1980–1981. *Social Psychiatry, 22*, 14–19.

Williams, G. (1957). *The sanctity of life and the criminal law.* New York: Knopf.

Williams, T. (1980). *Post-traumatic stress disorders of the Vietnam veteran: Observations and recommendations for the psychological treatment of the veteran and his family.* Cincinnati: Disabled American Veterans.

Wills, T., Weiss, R., & Patterson, G. (1974). A behavioral analysis of the determinants of marital satisfaction. *Journal of Consulting and Clinical Psychology, 42*, 802–811.

Wilson, M. (1981). Suicidal behavior: Toward an explanation of differences in female and male rates. *Suicide and Life Threatening Behavior, 11*, 131–140.

Worden, J. (1987). Cognitive therapy with cancer patients. In A. Freeman & V. Greenwood (Eds.), *Cognitive therapy: Applications in psychiatric and medical settings.* New York: Human Sciences Press.

Wright, J., & Schrodt, G. (1989). Combined cognitive therapy and pharmacotherapy. In A. Freeman, K. Simon, L. Beutler, & H. Arkowitz (Eds.), *Comprehensive handbook of cognitive therapy.* New York: Plenum.

Wright, J., Thase, M., Beck, A., & Ludgate, J. (1993). *Cognitive therapy with inpatients: Developing a cognitive milieu.* New York: Guilford.

Yalom, I. (1975). *The theory and practice of group psychotherapy* (2nd ed.). New York: Basic Books.

Yarden, P. (1974). Observations on suicide in chronic schizophrenics. *Comprehensive Psychiatry, 15*, 325–333.

Young, J., & Swift, W. (1988). Schema-focused cognitive therapy for personality disorders: I. *International cognitive Therapy Newsletter, 4*, 13–14.

Zetzel, E. (1965). Metapsychology of aging. In M. Berezin & S. Cath (Eds.), *Geriatric psychiatry.* New York: International Universities Press.

Zung, W. (1974). Index of potential suicide. In A. Beck, H. Resnik, & D. Lettieri (Eds.), *The prediction of suicide.* Philadelphia: Charles Press.

Index

𝕊 *Springer Publishing Company*

PREVENTING ELDERLY SUICIDE
Overcoming Personal Despair, Professional Neglect, and Social Bias

Joseph Richman, PhD

The elderly have the highest suicide rate of any population group. Richman tackles the problem of suicide in the final stages of life, offering reasons to help explain the phenomenon, as well as responses to various issues. Throughout the book, he advocates therapies most suited to particular cases, rather than a specific kind of therapy.

Richman speaks from experience. For 45 years, he has helped elderly people combat depression, and in that length of time, he has seen thousands of people regain a thirst for life after being down. The mental health professional says he has learned one simple fact: "by and large, depressed, old people get better."

Partial Contents:
I. Demography and the Theoretical Foundations of Elderly Suicide • Danger Signs and Recovery Factors • Family Risk Factors
II. Assessment and Early Intervention • Recognition of the Problem • Assessment and Testing
III. Crisis Intervention • An Outline of Crisis Intervention • The Effect of Past Crises • The Many Faces of Psychiatric Crises
IV. Therapy: The Healing Relationship
V. Family Tensions and Suicide
VI. Group Psychotherapy with Suicidal Patients • The Healing Power of Groups
VII. Individual Psychotherapy • Homage to the Individual

0-8261-7480-9 hardcover

536 Broadway, New York, NY 10012-3955 • (212) 431-4370 • Fax (212) 941-7842